IMAGES
of America

MILFORD TO THE MINISINK VALLEY

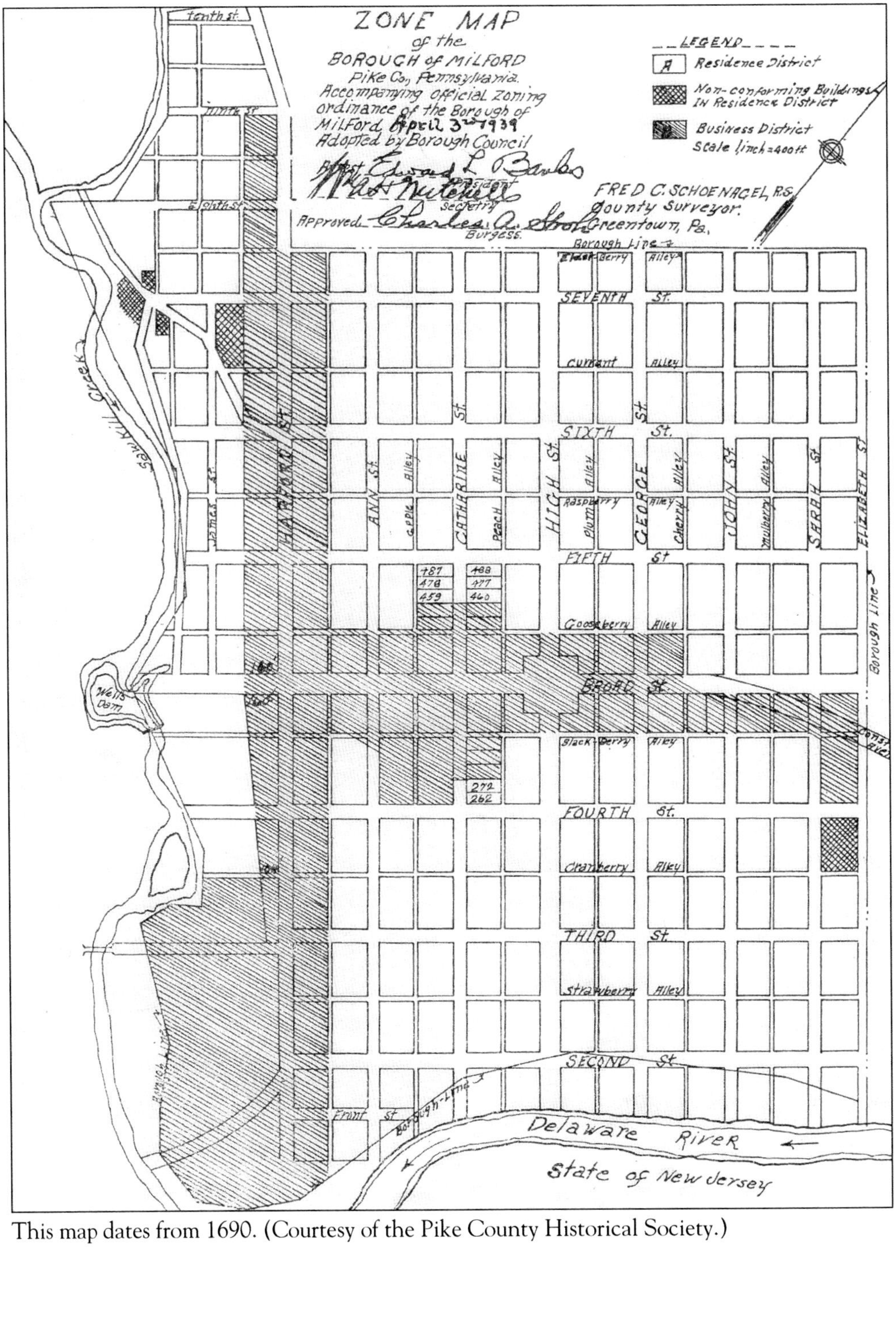

This map dates from 1690. (Courtesy of the Pike County Historical Society.)

IMAGES
of America

MILFORD TO THE MINISINK VALLEY

Susan Titus Mickley

ARCADIA
PUBLISHING

ISBN 978-0-7385-3718-4

Published by Arcadia Publishing
Charleston, South Carolina

Printed in the United States of America

Library of Congress Catalog Card Number: 2004112890

For all general information, contact Arcadia Publishing:
Telephone 843-853-2070
Fax 843-853-0044
E-mail sales@arcadiapublishing.com
For customer service and orders:
Toll-free 1-888-313-2665

Visit us on the Internet at www.arcadiapublishing.com

Contents

Acknowledgments

A book of this nature could not be written without the full support an author's family. My family gave me their support and cheered me on, and I want to thank them for that, especially my husband, Lou, and my children, Andrew and Jennifer.

Many others supported me and made this endeavor possible through their generous contributions of precious family archives. These special people were among the countless lovers of history who had the foresight to preserve their family's history and photographs. Their ability to see the value in those "boxes of stuff" that most people throw away when a loved one dies has improved our lives by allowing us to learn from previous generations. I thank the keepers of the past who helped me, and I honor them. They are Diane Banach, who preserved hundreds of photographs and postcards that she found in the attic of her old house; Criss Crosby Stone of Texas, who responded wholeheartedly to my query for photographs; Criss Stone's sister Frances Hotalen, who has lived most of her life in Milford; Carol Ramagosa, who is descended from some of the early pioneer families and who sent letters full of photographs from North Carolina; Matthew M. Osterberg, who provided great advice on authoring the book; Carl Mulhauser, who was one of the first to share some of his collection of postcards with me; Mary Jane Oxford, a Jervis Gordon descendant whom I contacted through her daughter, Sharon Gothard, the Easton Area Public Library historian; Barbara (Mrs. Harry) Buchanan, who cheered me on and shared several terrific photographs of the people of Milford in the 1950s and 1960s; and the Titus-Heery family, especially my grand-aunt Til, who even though she left this world 10 years ago at the age of 98, lives on through the many stories she told and the precious photographs she left to me.

A special thank-you goes to those historians who left the wonderful gift of their research in the following books and documents: *A History of Pike County* (1989), by Norman B. Lehde; *History of Wayne County* (1880), by P. G. Goodrich; *History of the Lackawanna Valley* (1857), by H. Hollister, M.D.; *Biographical Record of Northeastern Pennsylvania* (1900), by J. H. Beers and Company; *The Mills of Milford* (1968), by William F. Henn; *The Homes of Our Ancestors* (1925), by R. T. H. Halsey and Elizabeth Tower; *Indians in Pennsylvania* (1991), by Paul A. W. Wallace; *The Lenape: Archaeology, History, and Ethnography* (1986), by Herbert C. Kraft; and *The Minisink: A Chronicle of One of America's First and Last Frontiers* (1975), by Donald Bertland, Patricia M. Valence, and Russell J. Woodling.

Lastly, but most importantly, I cannot express strongly enough my gratitude to the staff and many contributors and supporters of the Pike County Historical Society, especially the historian, Lori Strelecki. Without their dedication to preserving the county's history, no book like this would be possible.

Introduction

Milford to the Minisink Valley is a humble endeavor to capture the spirit and history of a beautiful area loved and enjoyed by many since its founding in the 1700s. Communities and their citizens are molded by their founding fathers, and Milford and the Minisink Valley are no exceptions. The decisions made by the early ancestors strongly influenced where towns were located, how those towns were laid out, and what religions, businesses, schools, and farms prospered.

This book shows how major developments influenced the path that Milford's progress took and how Milford interacted with the outside world. The first such development was the decision to locate the railroad in Port Jervis and not on the Pennsylvania side of the Delaware. This decision resulted in the preservation of Milford's character and Victorian charm, as well as the tranquility of the Minisink Valley south of Milford. The trains benefited the Milford businesses that catered to the thousands of visitors to Milford who came through stations that were just a short carriage or stage ride away.

Milford and the surrounding area flourished until the second significant development occurred—the development of the automobile, which allowed tourists to travel farther on their own. Places like Niagara Falls and points farther west and south flourished, while many of the boardinghouses in eastern Pennsylvania had to close and revert back to farming or other pursuits. When the Great Depression came, only the strong business establishments survived. The larger boardinghouses, inns, and hotels were at the greatest risk of completely disappearing during this time because of abandonment, fires, conversion, and demolition. The book contains photographs of many of these long lost treasure houses.

The third event that greatly influenced the Minisink Valley was the federal government's takeover of the valley between Milford and Bushkill for the Tocks Island Dam project. With the exception of the turning out of the original natives, no other event has sacrificed so much history in this area. Towns were completely eliminated, houses torn down, farms and businesses dismantled. The footprints of all the citizens who inhabited the area for over 200 years were virtually erased forever. This book includes a chapter showing the Minisink before Tocks Island. However, the subject deserves its own book, and Matthew M. Osterberg intends to do just that.

Since the 1960s, Milford has been rediscovered. The automobile became Milford's friend when owning a second home in the country became popular. Developments such as Gold Key Lake, Sunrise Lakes, and Hemlock Farms brought many weekenders to the area, and business life flourished again. The influx of people has revived the hotel and tourist industry, and the surviving buildings have found new lives as inns, hotels, resorts, restaurants, second homes, boutiques, and bed-and-breakfasts.

This book portrays the spirit of Milford and the Minisink and those who have lived and loved within its bounds. It could not possibly portray every soul, every building, every organization, every scenic site, every founder, or every business, but the hope is that a good representation has been achieved. The reader will begin by going back in time to the days of log cabins, dirt paths, and skirmishes with the natives. Each chapter brings the reader from the past to the near present for each topic and shows how the area grew into a modern community with a full-fledged school system, beautiful churches, thriving businesses, and sophisticated roads and byways. The reader will hopefully enjoy the historic facts and profiles contained throughout the book and walk away learning something new about their history.

—Susan Titus Mickley

One

NATIVES AND PIONEERS

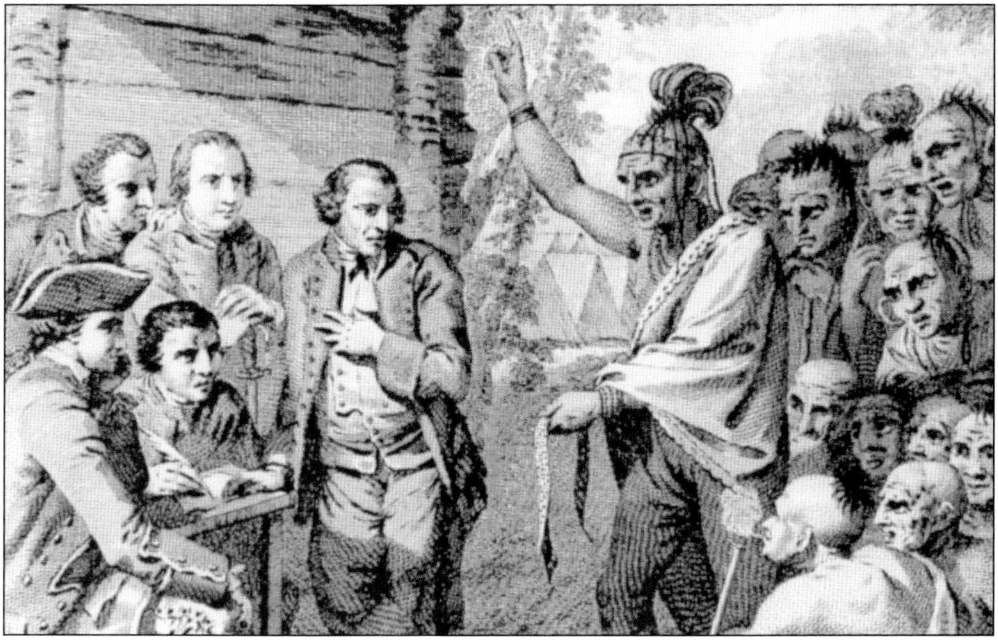

Negotiations and treaties prevailed in the early relations between natives and pioneers. The Society of Friends experienced years of peace with their native neighbors because of William Penn's respectful philosophy. His two sons, however, did not share his beliefs, and relations fell apart. The treaty called the Walking Purchase (executed by William Penn's sons in 1737) resulted in the loss of 1,200 square miles of land and the extraction of the natives from their ancestral homelands. The natives' bitterness was flamed by the French, and many lives were lost during the French and Indian War through 1763. During the Revolution, the British took the same advantage of the natives' anger. In 1779, George Washington commissioned Sullivan's March, which left Easton and proceeded through the Wyoming Valley to where the great Six Nations and the British and Tories made their last stand near Elmira. The battle settled the dispute on the frontier in favor of the new nation and brought peace to the Minisink Valley at great expense to the natives. (Courtesy of the Library of Congress.)

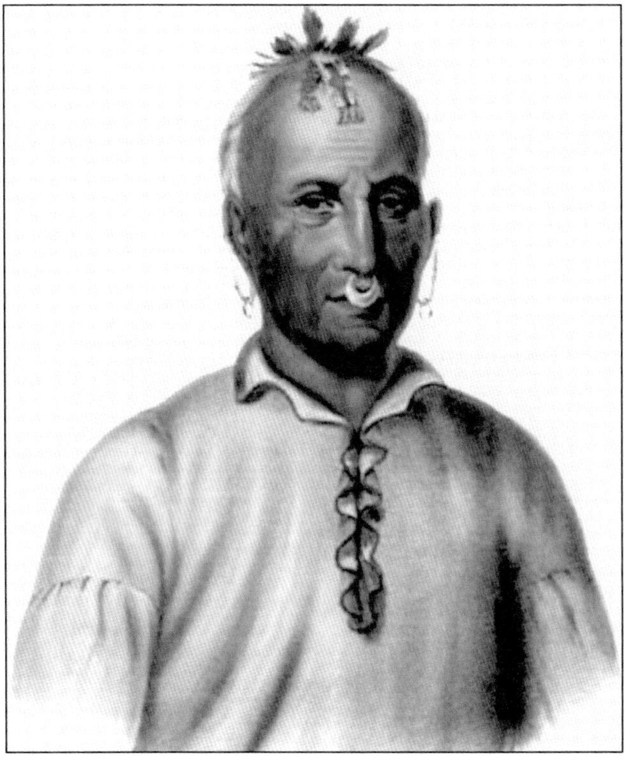

This early-1700s portrait of Kishkalwa shows the hair style, ear cutting, and tattooing practiced by the Minisink. The clothing is in the Colonial style. The Minisink, or Munsee, occupied the area along the Delaware River from Milford to Bushkill. They fished, hunted, and farmed from the planting season to the harvest. Every winter, the tribes would migrate to the Wyoming Valley, where they would join with many other tribes. (Courtesy of the Library of Congress.)

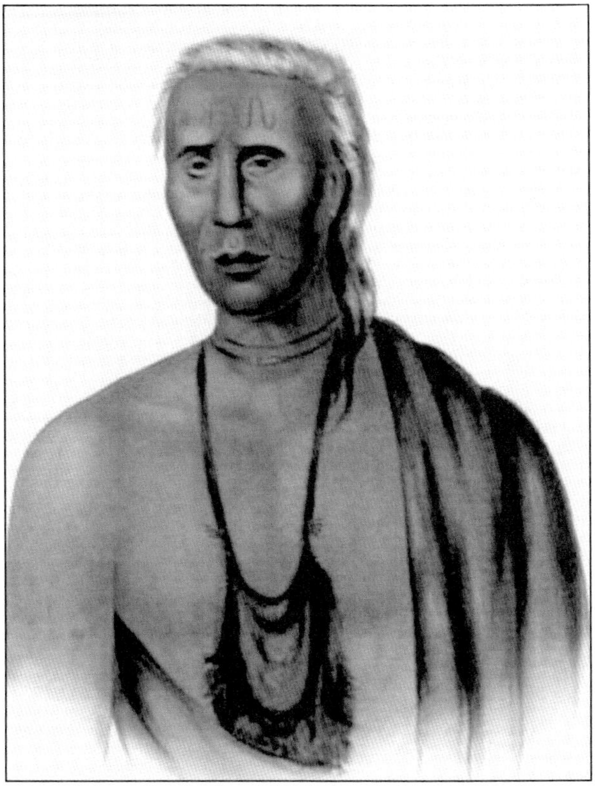

Lappawinsoe (right) was one of the Lenni Lenape Indians who signed the 1737 treaty commonly called the Walking Purchase. He was furious when he realized how they had been cheated when the line was drawn to include 1,200 square miles including all of the Minisink Valley on the Pennsylvania side. He said, "The Walkers should have walkt for a few miles and then have sat down and smoakt a Pipe, and now and then have shot a squirrel, and not have kept upon the run, run, all day." This portrait can be found at the Historical Society of Pennsylvania.

Thundercloud, a Blackfoot from Canada, came to live in Milford in the early 1900s. He posed for many an artist against local backdrops but was not a true portrayal of the local natives with his attire and hair fashion. Some historians have speculated that the Minisink wintered in the Wyoming Valley near Scranton because it provided abundant coal for their fires. (Courtesy of the Pike County Historical Society.)

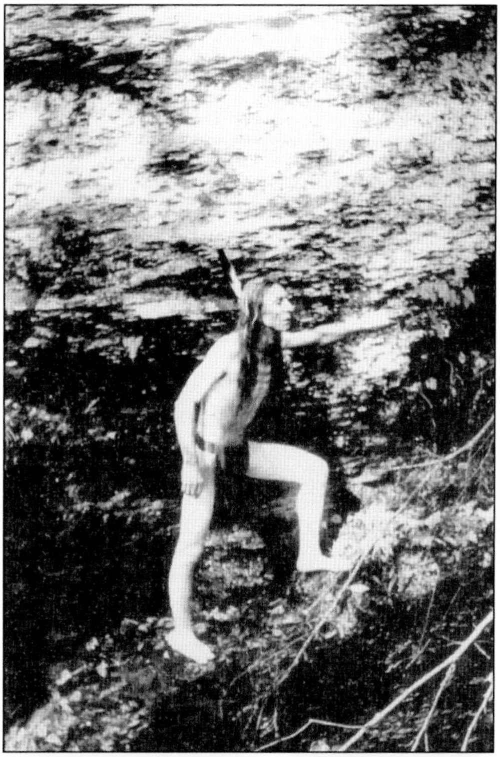

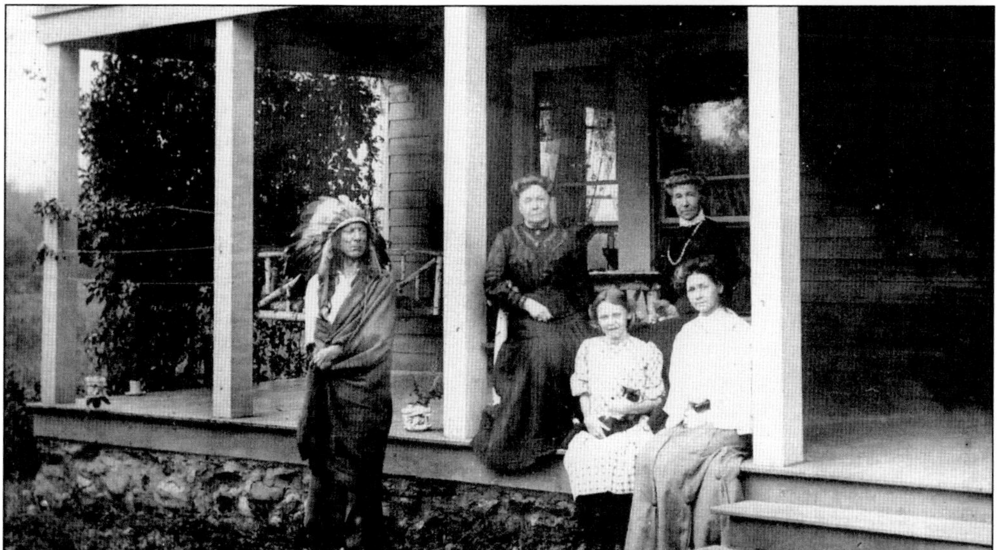

Thundercloud married a white woman. He is seen here in front of his home with his family. Minisink women bundled their babies in packs. When a woman worked in the field, she would hang her child on a nearby tree, out of harm's way. Discipline was handled mostly without hitting; the Minisink believed a child who was hit would become an adult who hit. Instead, they kept the children in line with stories about forest beasts who would steal wayward children. Sometimes, parents would dip children in the cold waters of the Delaware for punishment. (Courtesy of the Pike County Historical Society.)

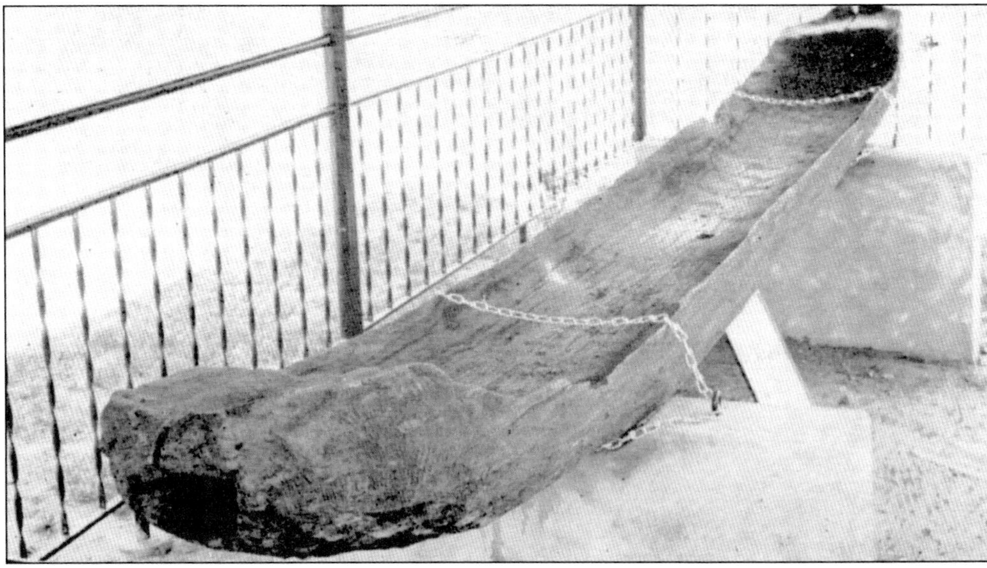

This 18-foot canoe, hewn from a chestnut tree, was discovered in the area of the Wallenpaupack River, where Lake Wallenpaupack is now. It is estimated to have been made in the late 1600s. A portion of it is on display at the Pike County Historical Society. The natives rarely felled living trees, except for shelter. The tree used to make this canoe may have fallen naturally. Trees were also used to make hunting bows; the shape of the bow was carved into the tree, and the bow was dug out without killing the tree. Early pioneers found many bow-shaped scars on the trees in the area. (Courtesy of the Pike County Historical Society.)

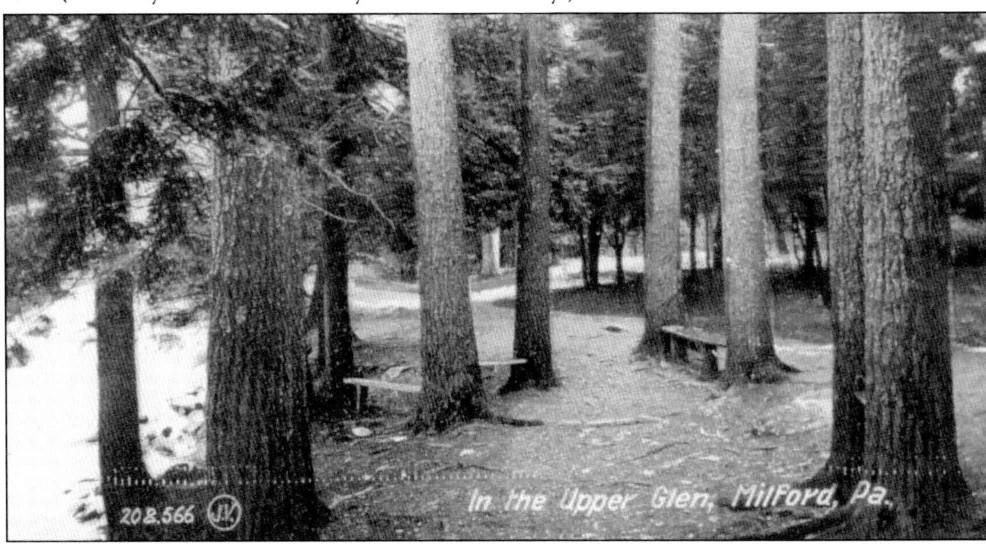

The Glen, in Milford, is a favorite destination for hikers. Pennsylvania's greatest resource is its trees, but many species are threatened or lost. Dutch elm disease destroyed that species about 40 years ago. Chestnut trees have all but disappeared from the landscape of Pennsylvania because of a disease that kills most trees by their 18th year of growth. A few hearty specimens have survived and are being used to cross with a Chinese variety to produce disease-resistant stock. When chestnuts were prevalent, it was said their blossoms were so white that it looked like snow had covered the woods. Hemlocks, ash, and oaks are species that are currently under assault by diseases or parasites. (Courtesy of the Pike County Historical Society.)

Early pioneer life was harsh. One of the first settlers, Tom Quick, witnessed his father's death during an attack by natives. He spent the rest of his life exacting revenge and is purported to have killed 99 natives before his death. Controversy still revolves around whether this monument is appropriate to display in Milford. (Courtesy of the Pike County Historical Society.)

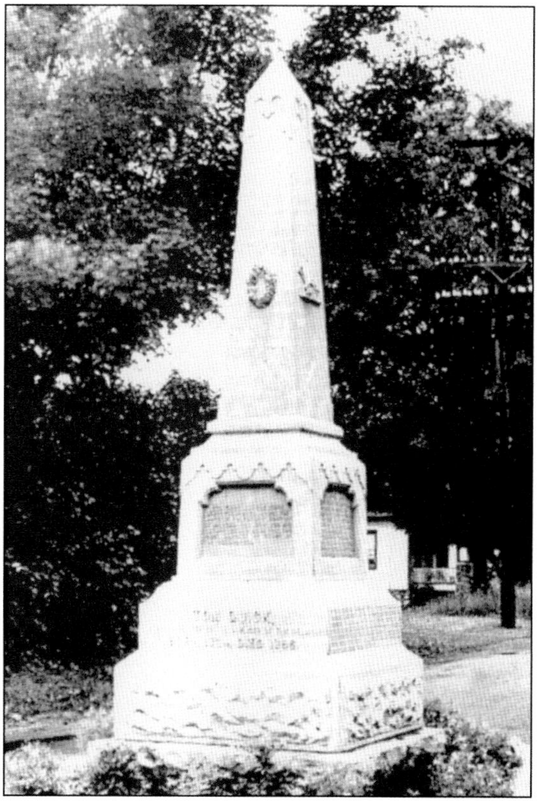

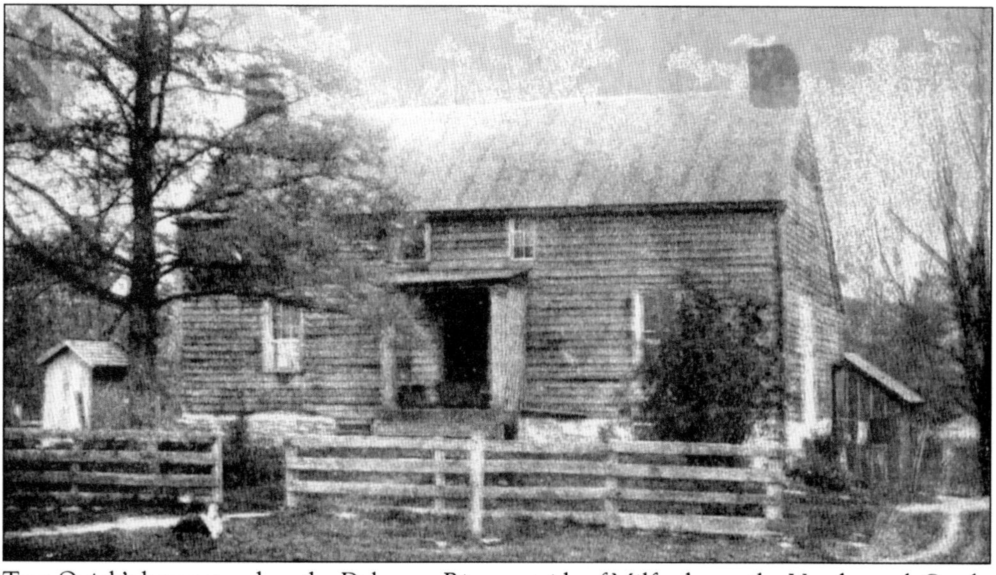

Tom Quick's home stood on the Delaware River outside of Milford near the Vandermark Creek. (Courtesy of Diane Banach.)

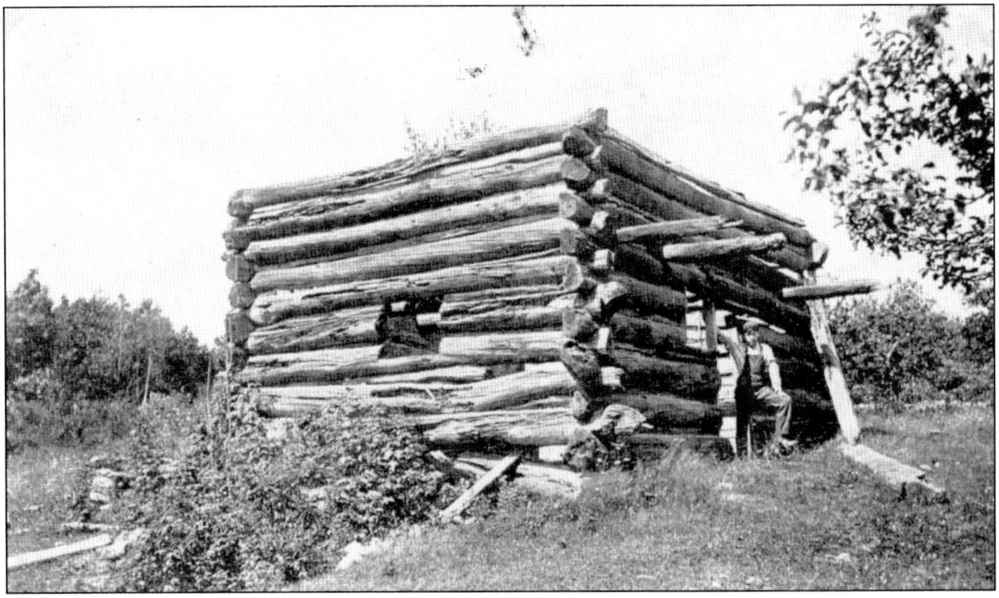

Log houses were the norm in the early pioneer days. The settlers often enlisted the help of the natives to build these homes. Very few examples of these early log homes remain today. These remains were of an old log cabin near Shohola just north of Milford. The cabin, occupied by a sister of Gen. Robert Lee, was often the destination of the general. This photograph was taken c. 1908. Businesses were often made of logs. Below is a logging camp in Shohola Farms. (Courtesy of Diane Banach.)

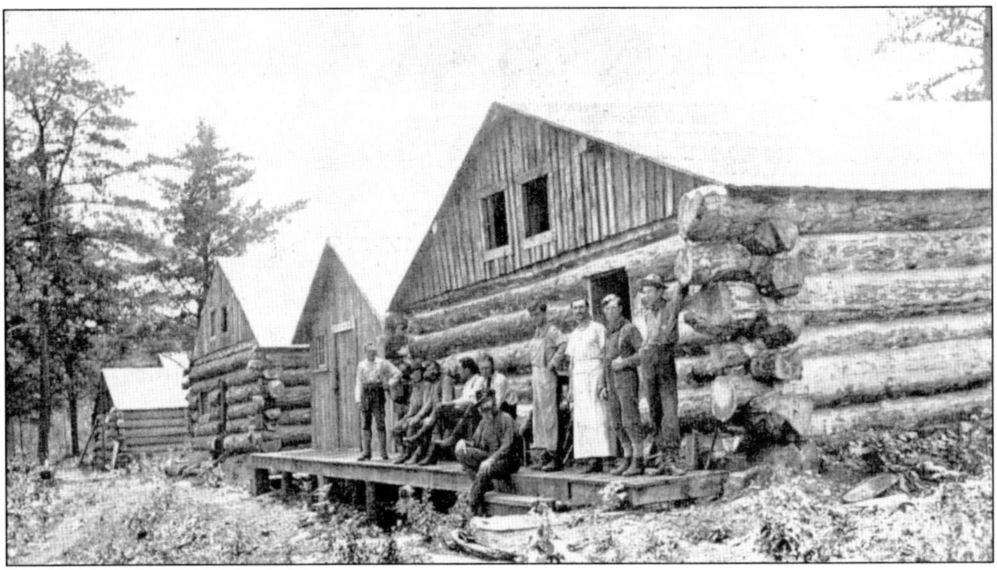

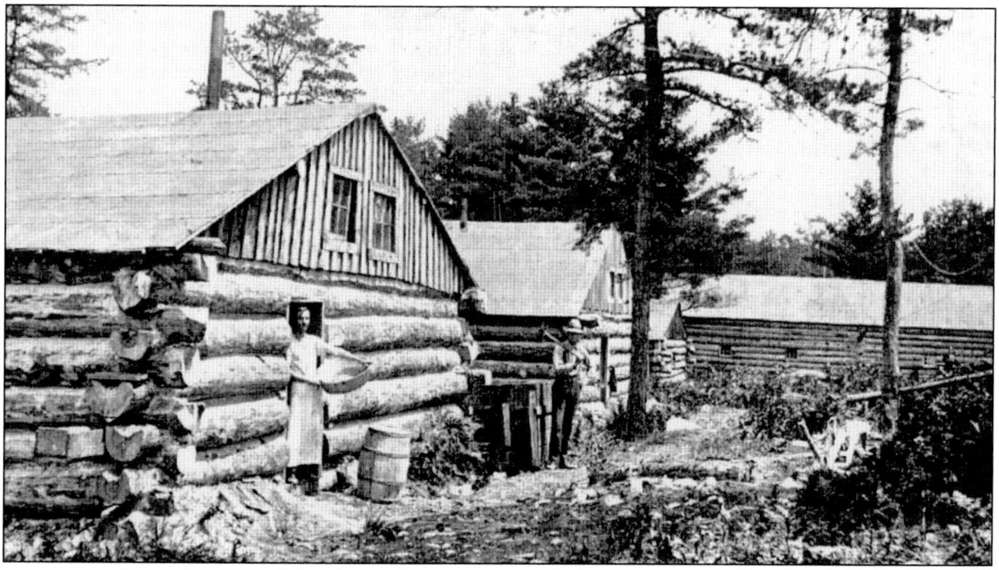

Living in a log cabin was difficult, and amenities were few. Water had to be totted from a river or stream. Debris was discarded outside or in pits dug in the ground. The floor was dirt unless the inhabitants were fortunate enough to have slate slabs loosely fitted together to create a floor that could be swept and covered by rag rugs. One fireplace heated the cabin and provided a place for all the cooking. Privacy was usually nonexistent, and drafty breezes filtered through the fragile poured-glass windows and cracks in the chinking between the logs. Anything was used to repair the chinking. Old clothes, used bottles, sticks, animal hair, and straw were stuffed in the cracks and covered with mud or mortar. When the pioneer realized some success in the wilderness, he could afford a stone house or could cover over his logs with lathe and plaster on the inside and clapboard on the outside. Below is an example of an early stone house in Matamoras. The local community used many of the early stone houses, built by more affluent citizens, as forts for protection. (Courtesy of Diane Banach.)

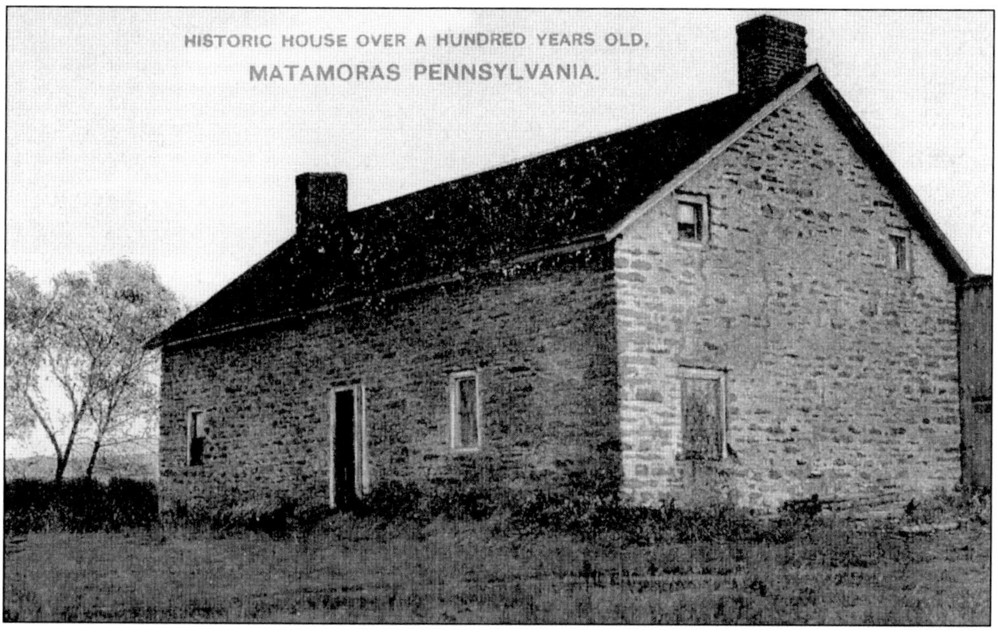

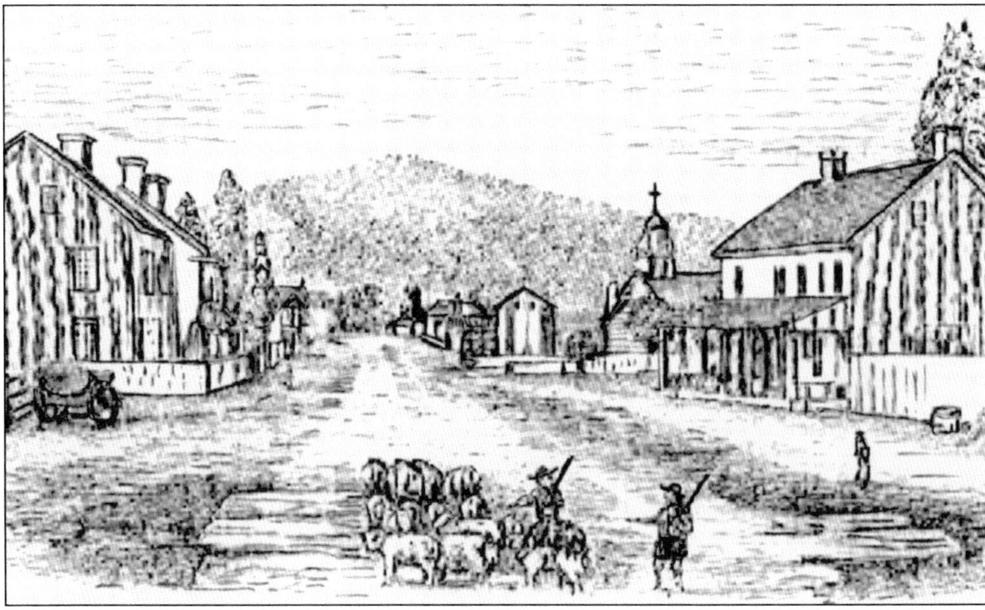

This early engraving depicts how Milford looked in the early days. John Biddis laid out the village in 1796. His father, William Biddis, came from Milford Haven, in Wales. The first settlers were primarily from Connecticut and New York. Several early family names are still found in Milford today, including DePue, Quick, Buchanan, Quinn, Van Tassell, Greening, Foster, Myer, Stroyan, Mulhausser, Helms, Cron, Orben, Gregory, Nearing, and Drake.

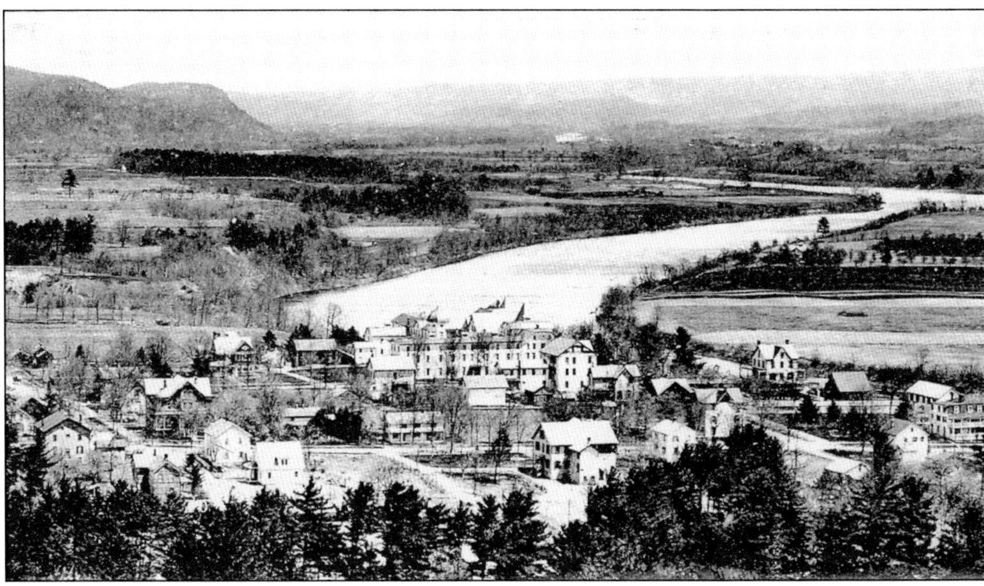

By the early 1900s, Milford had grown into a well-planned, Victorian-style hamlet nestled between the Delaware River and the Pocono Mountains. John Biddis laid out the streets using the Philadelphia model and named the unnumbered streets after relatives and friends. Here is a view of Milford from the knob. (Courtesy of Carl Muhlhauser.)

Two

Tilling the Soil

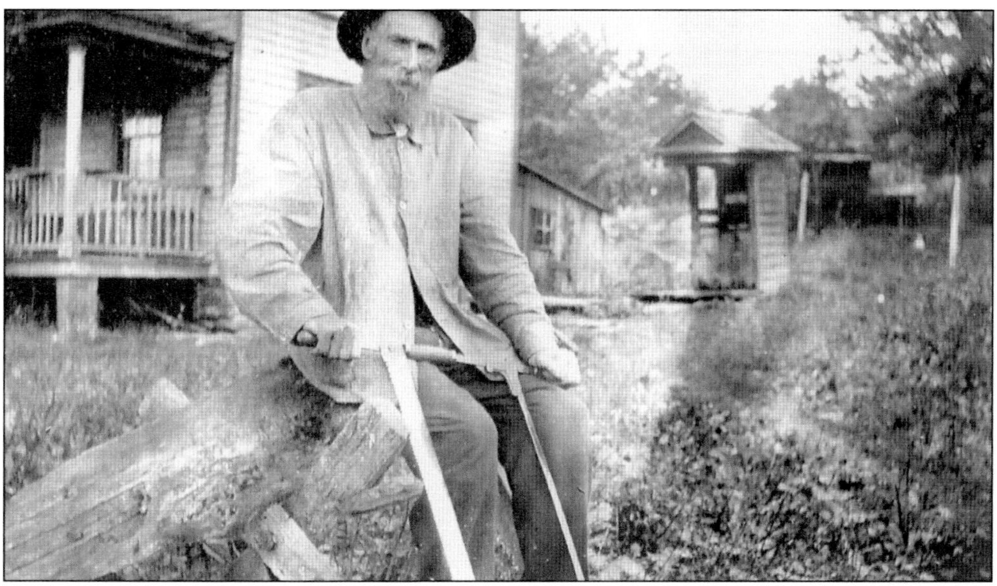

The hearty Minisink farmers tilled fields of crops, made beautiful stone walls from rocks removed from the land, raised top-grade livestock, and kept quaint, sturdy homes. Life was hard, but it was rewarding to work the land, raise a family, and tend to the needs of the living things under one's care. After a marriage of many years between the land and the farmer, the tired souls would repose to watch progress take or leave their farms. Today, the farms have been replaced by developments, resorts, businesses, and highways. (Courtesy of Diane Banach.)

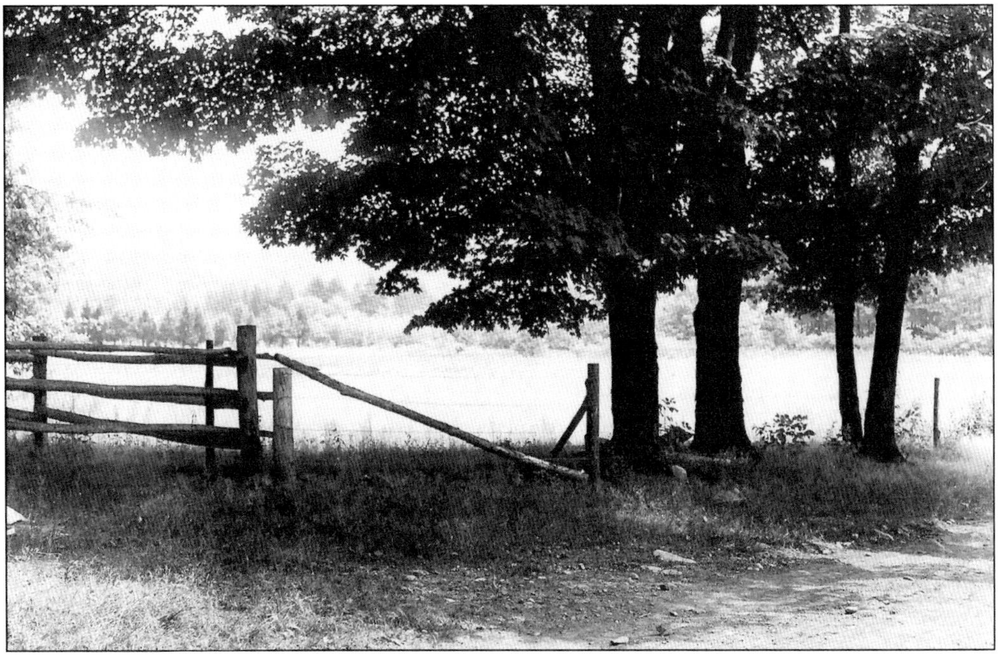

Farm life in the country meant the eye was constantly filled with pastoral scenes and quiet walks through the cool woods. Many courting moments were shared over a neighbor's fence or on a woodland trail. (Courtesy of Diane Banach.)

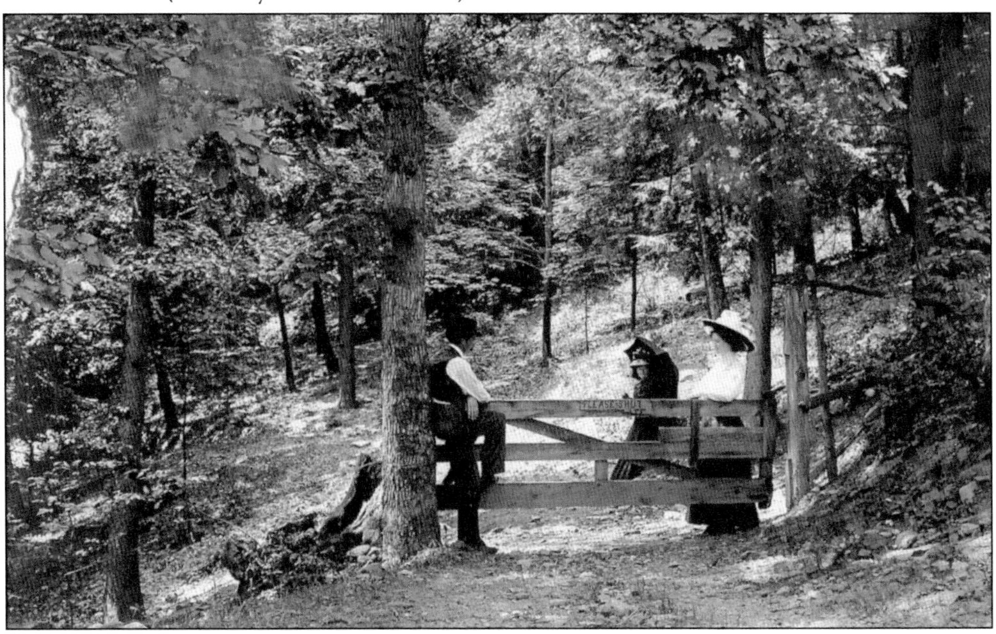

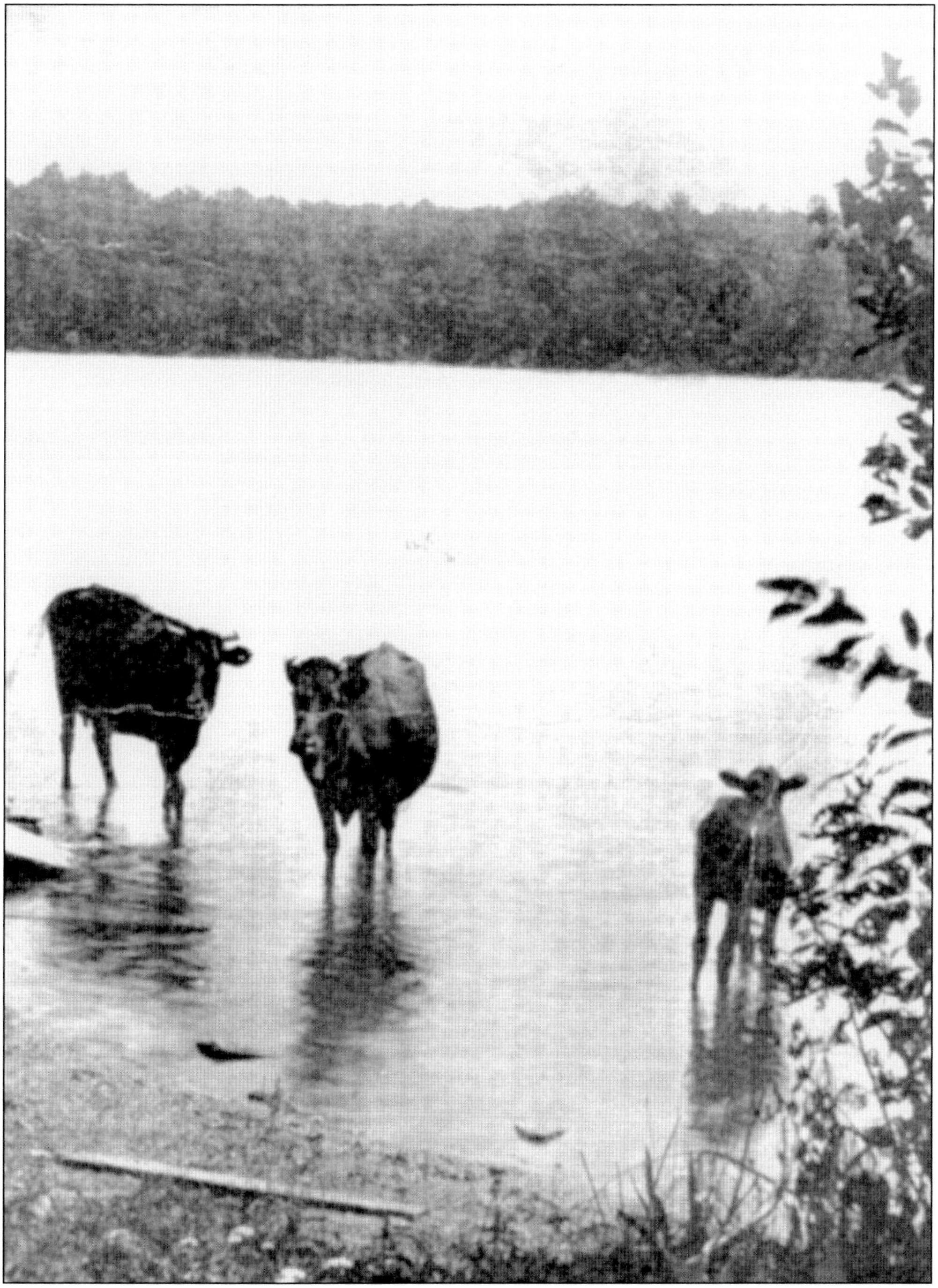

Mountain land was less forgiving than the rich land by the river, and it favored livestock and poultry. Those lucky enough to possess bottom land along the Delaware were successful cash crop growers with crops such as corn, wheat, beans, pumpkins, and squash. The bounty was usually good unless it was destroyed by floods. In the early days, fencing was not a priority compared to clearing fields and putting up stores of food for winter. Many communities had to pass laws to force the citizens to contain their livestock. (Courtesy of Diane Banach.)

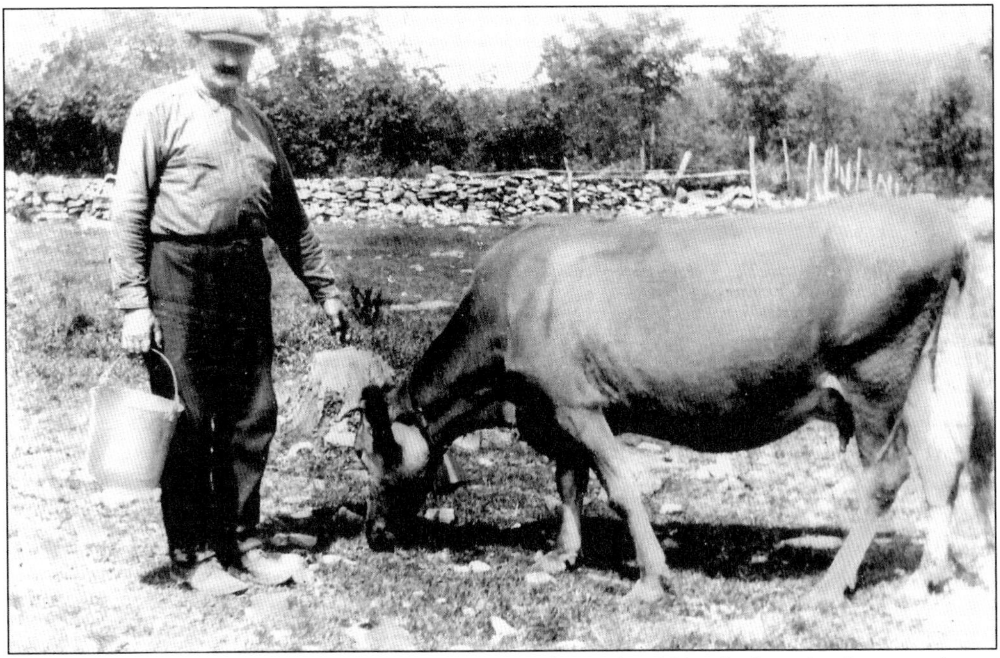

Carl Tumm is shown with his favorite cow, Bess. In the early 1900s, the boardinghouse industry was hit hard by the advent of the automobile, which gave vacationers more freedom and made places like Niagara Falls a feasible vacation spot. Many proprietors went back to farming and raising poultry and livestock for the New York City restaurant market. The name Minisink derives from a Native American word meaning "where the stones are gathered together," and these farm fields show why. Below, Ottilie, Carl's wife, feeds the chickens.

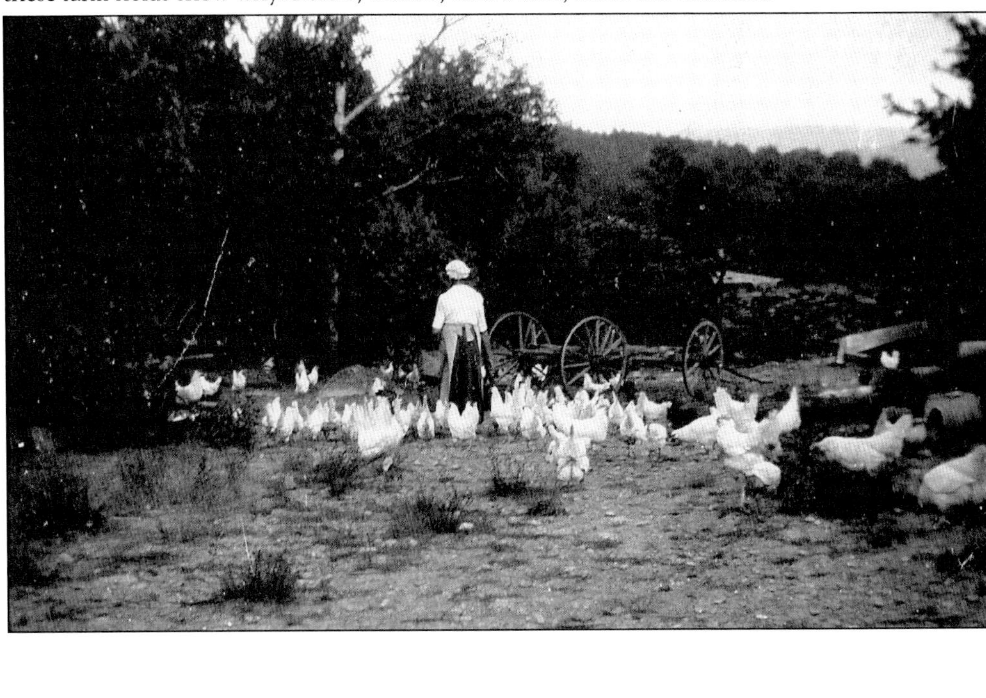

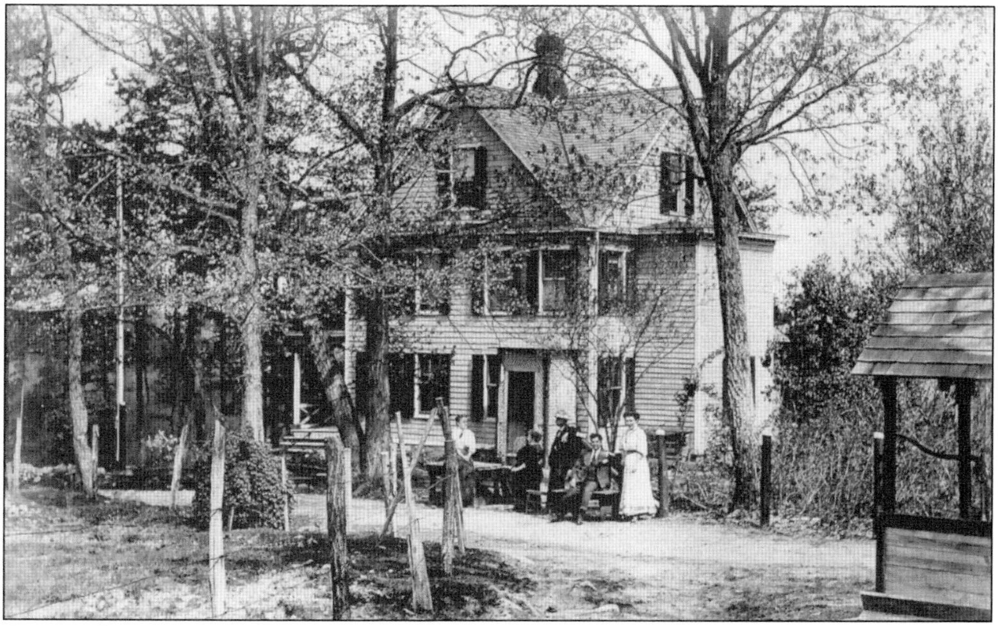

Country living was full of necessities and some luxuries. Inside plumbing was a goal of most homeowners, and the side addition on the house above probably contained a bathroom and laundry. The hearth was an important family gathering spot, and many chores were accomplished next to the warm fire. (Courtesy of Diane Banach.)

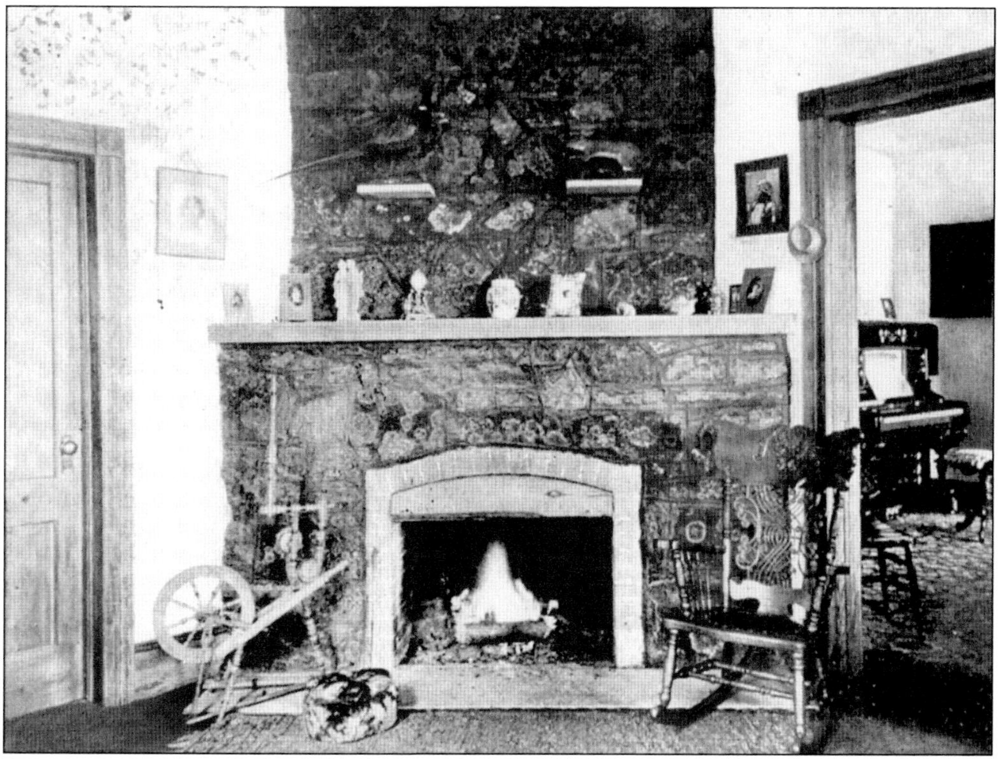

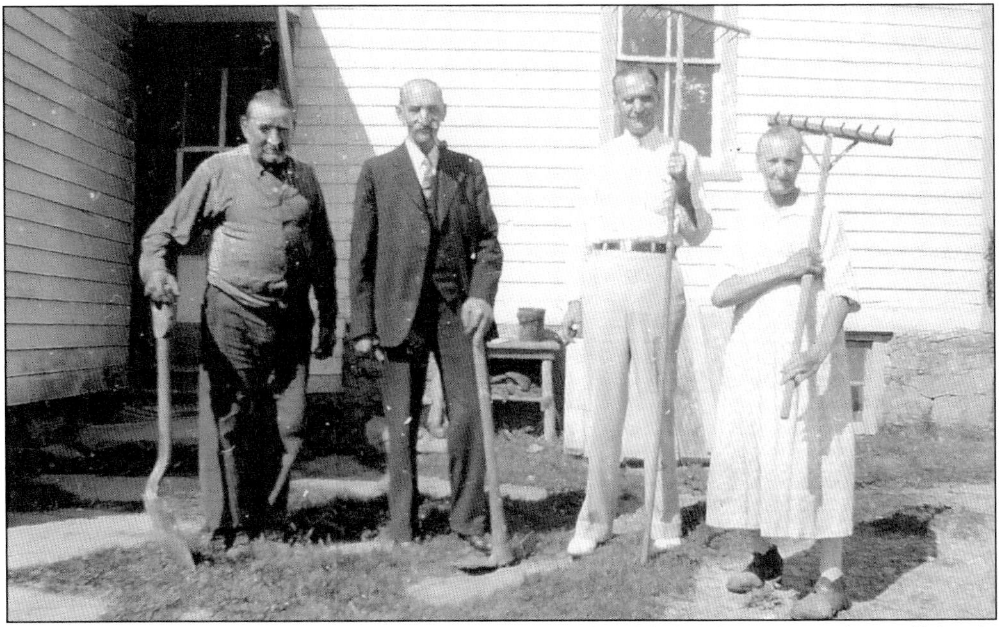

Everyone was always ready to work the fields, including the old plow horse. On a farm, all family members were expected to pitch in to get the work done. Below, Tillie MacDonald shows that she can manage the horse as well as her brothers could. Tillie married John MacDonald, a train conductor, and lived in Port Jervis until her death at age 98.

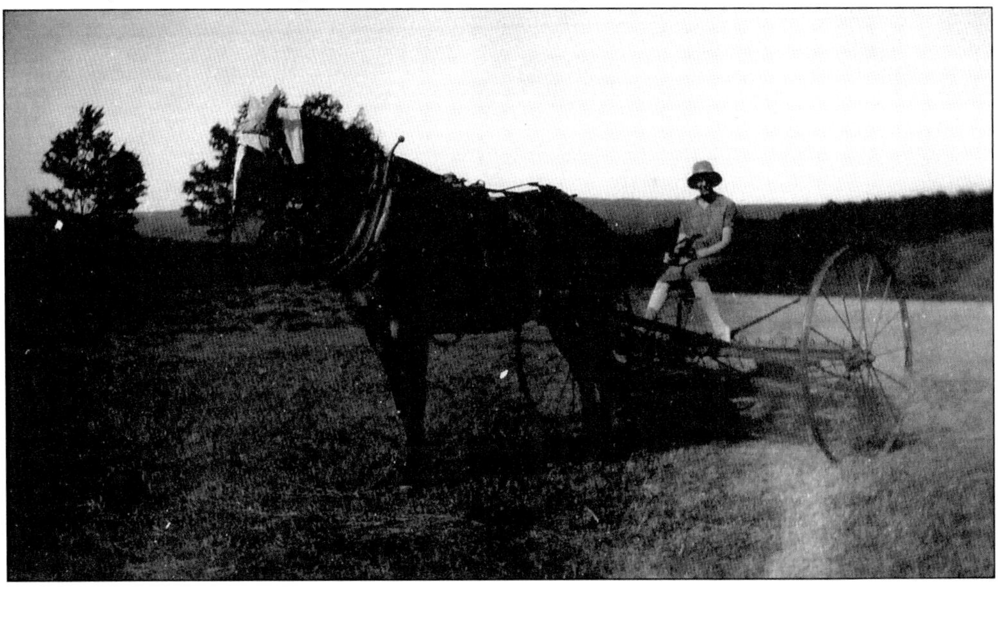

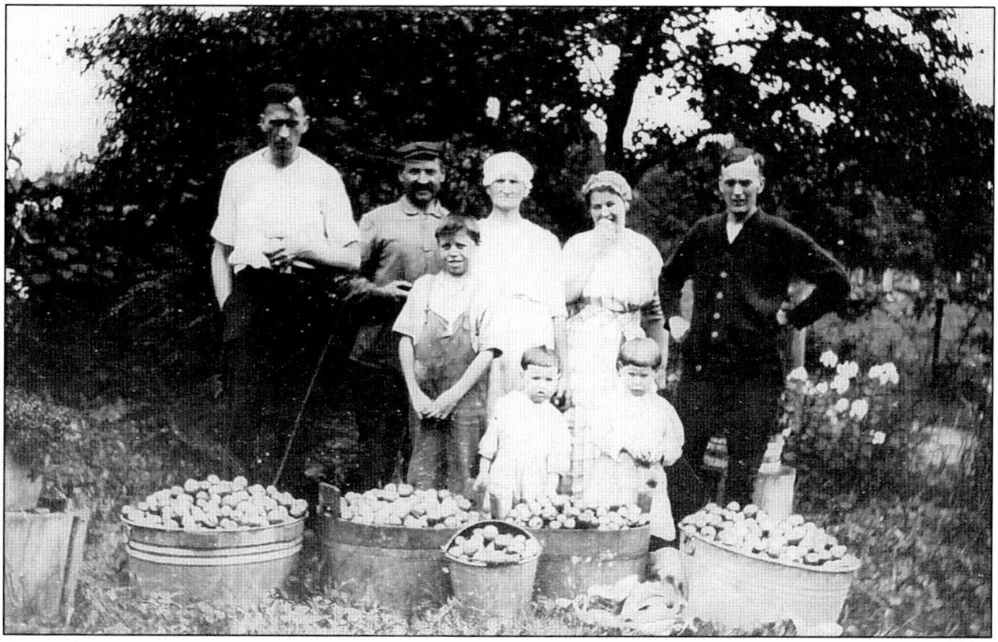

A good year meant a good harvest, and this year the apple crop was "sehr gut." Below, the Stretz family gets to visit their grand-aunt Augusta Carpenter (known as Gussy).

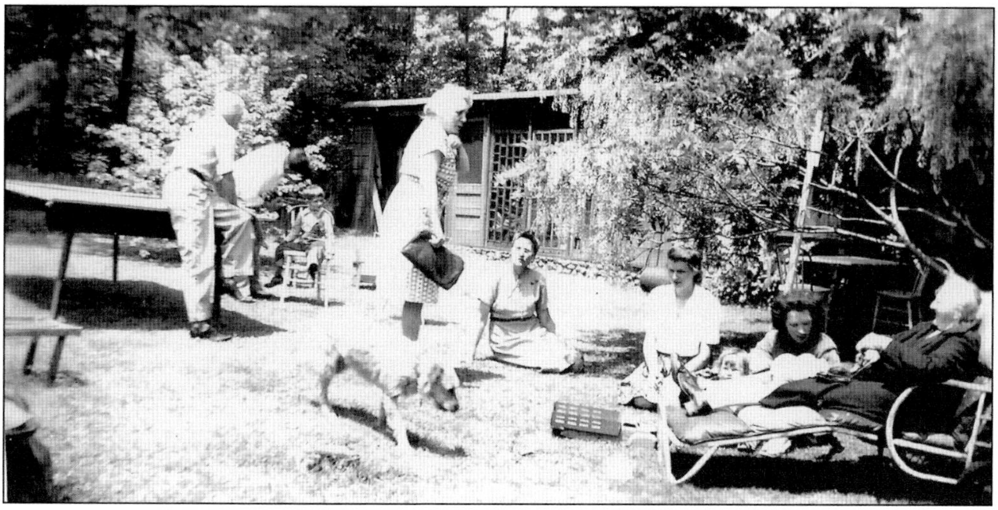

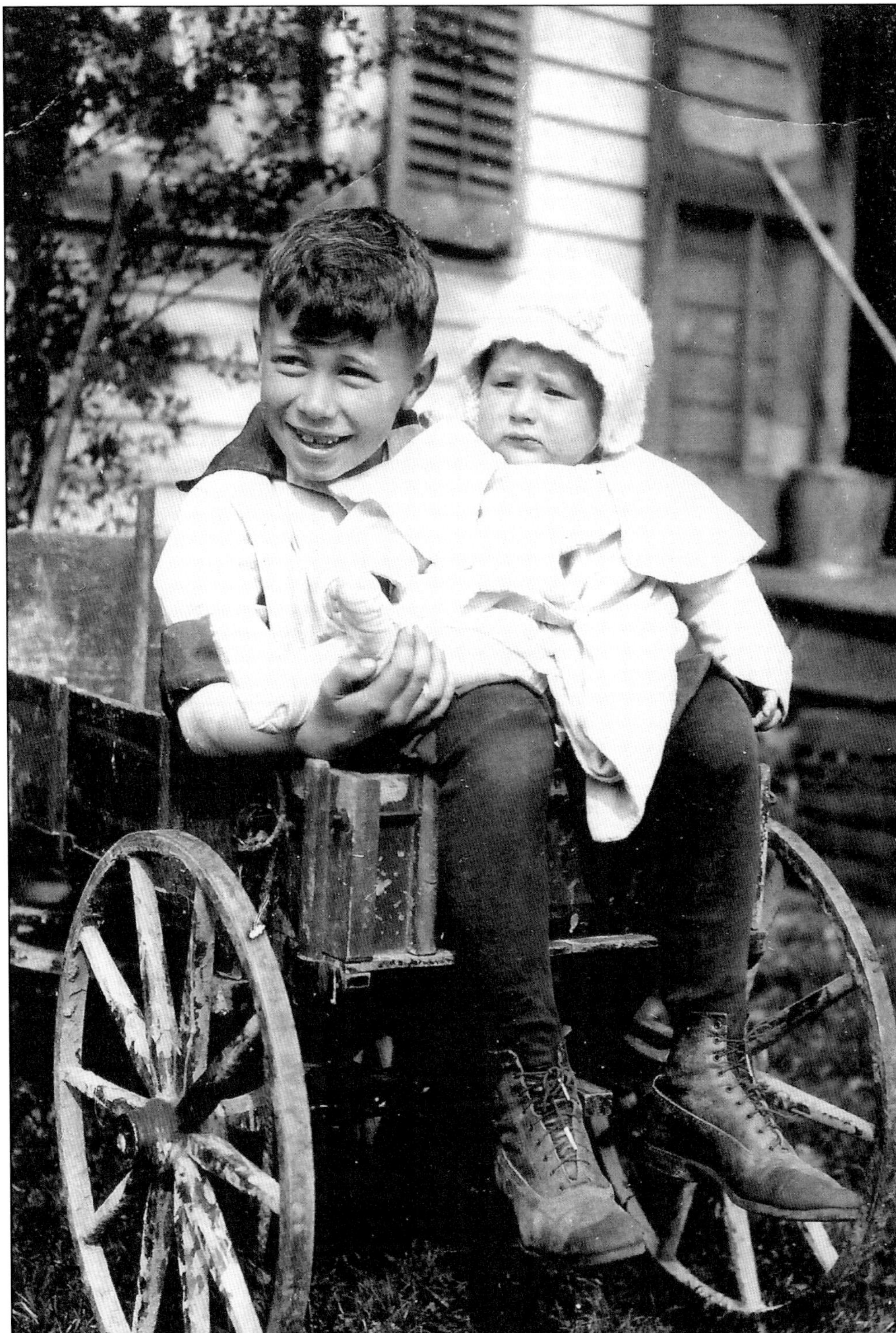

A young lad holds his sister for a pose in a garden cart. A goat or large dog may have pulled this cart. All able bodies, including the animals, were enlisted in helping with the chores on a farm.

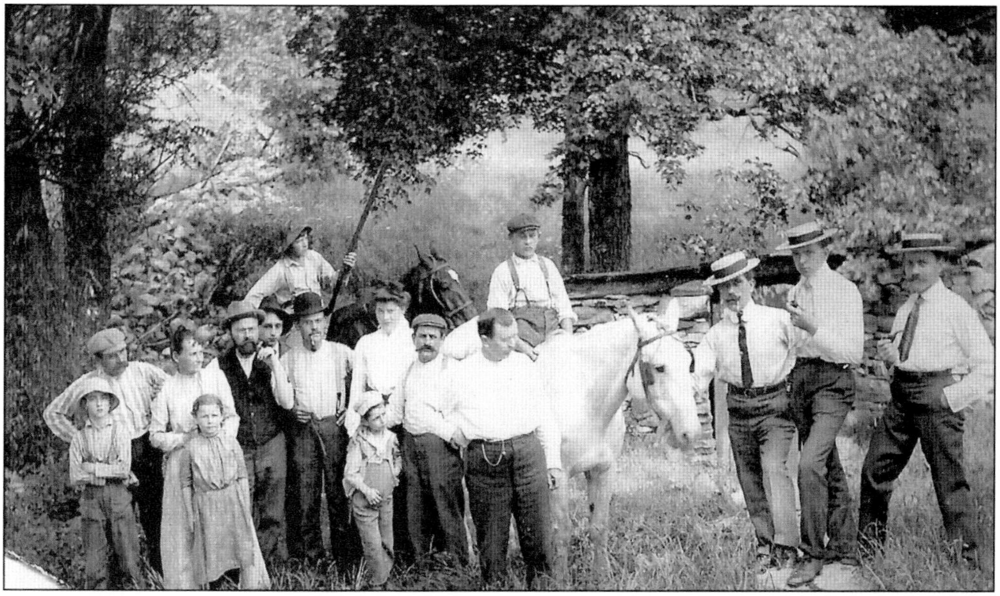

The photograph above was taken on the Fieg farm, on Schocopee Road in Milford, c. 1902. From left to right are two unidentified people; Emilie Bohler Fieg and her husband, Carl Fieg; the Feigs' daughter Emilie Fieg (Case), in front; daughter Martha Fieg and son Victor Fieg, in front; Lothar Fieg, on dark horse; and Max Fieg, on white horse. The five other people are unidentified. The photograph below was taken on the farm c. 1905. From left to right are mother Emilie Bohler Fieg, daughter Emilie Fieg (Case), Bertha Fieg, father Carl Fieg, son Max Fieg, and son Lothar Fieg. (Courtesy of Carol Ramagosa.)

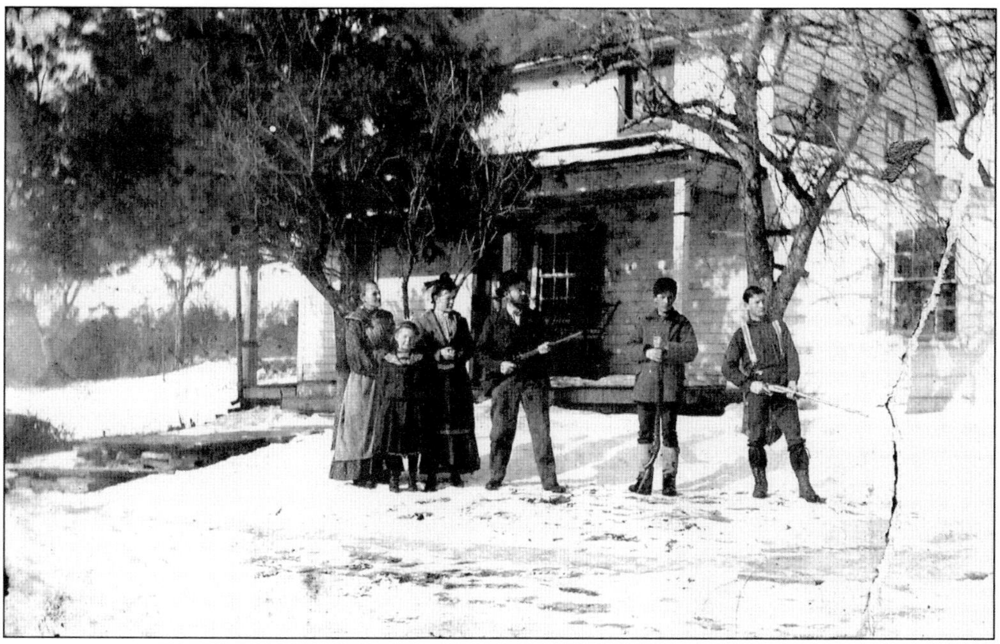

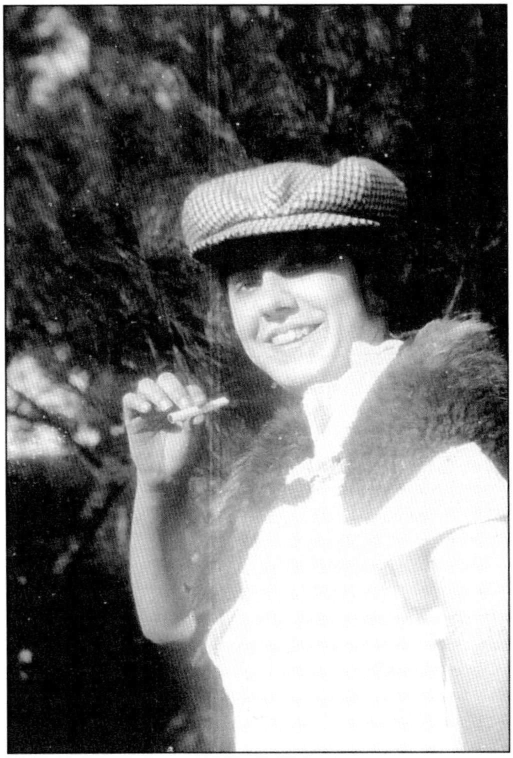

How are you going to keep them down on the farm? By the 1920s, women were more independent. Many young farm women worked in the local towns or went into New York City to work. Tillie (below) worked in New York City as a parlor maid when she was 16 (in 1910) and later worked in the silk mill in Port Jervis. She got married when she was 30 years old, and the marriage lasted 50 years.

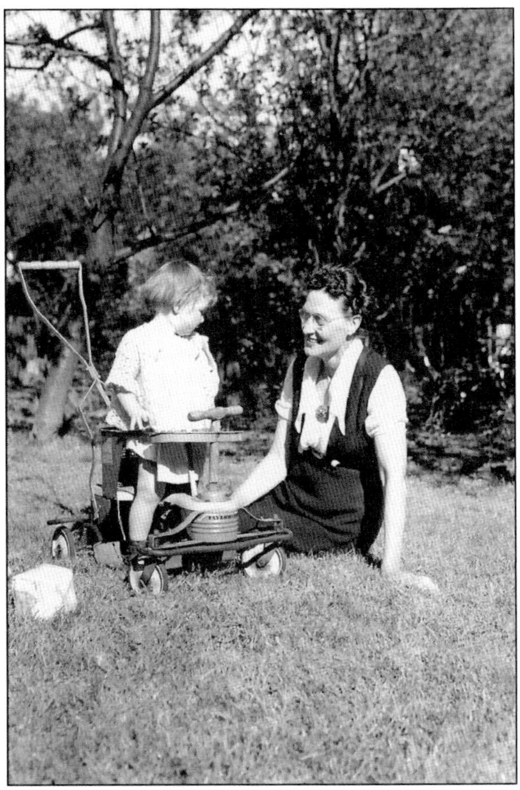

Three

Places and Faces

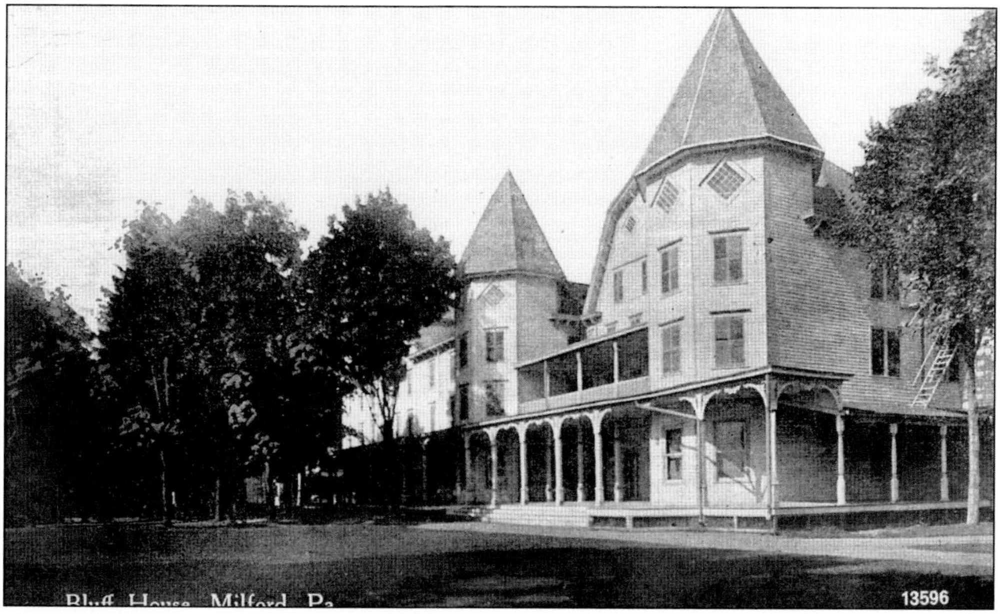

The Bluff House, in Milford, was a prominent structure that accommodated up to 350 visitors and staff from far and wide. It towered above the Delaware River and hosted a swimming hole and beach. Built in 1876 by H. B. Wells, it gained a reputation for elegant atmosphere and the latest amenities under the proprietorship of Paul and Kitty Bournique. A spectacular fire consumed the structure in 1947.

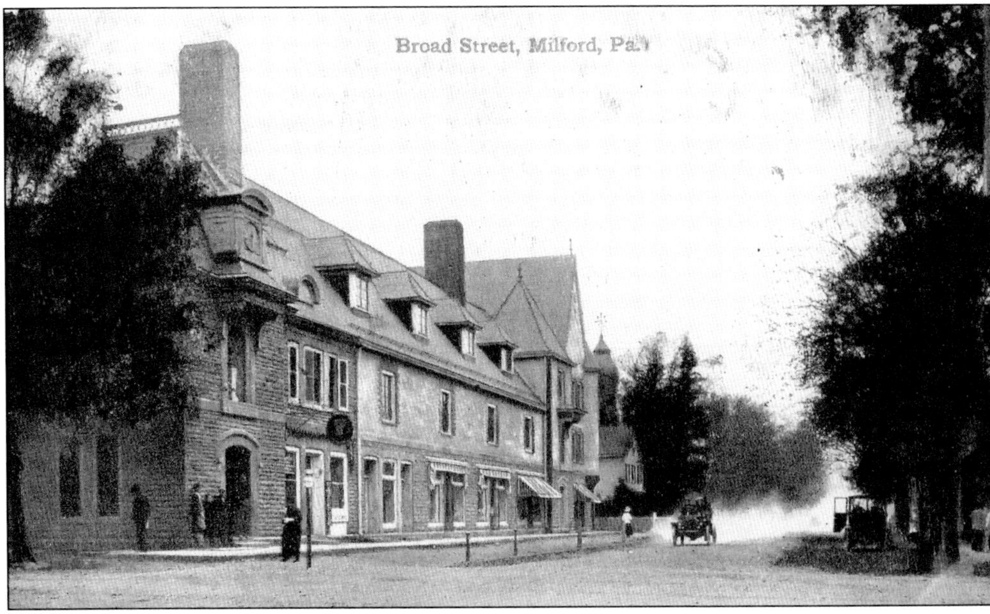

Broad Street has always been considered the main street of Milford. It has been graced by Forest Hall (left), Community Hall (now the Milford Library), the Tom Quick Inn, the Fauchere, the courthouse, the county jail, and a building known as the Columns (the home of the Pike County Historical Society).

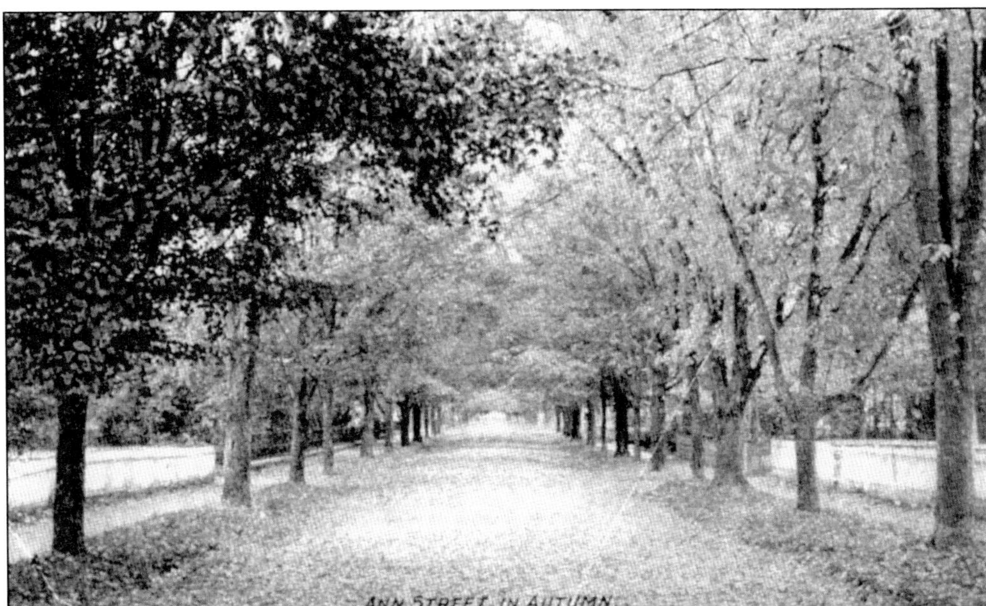

A view of Ann Street in autumn shows that the city planners had the foresight to lay out wide streets and to set houses back from the road. These features are still evident today in Milford and contribute to the village's charm.

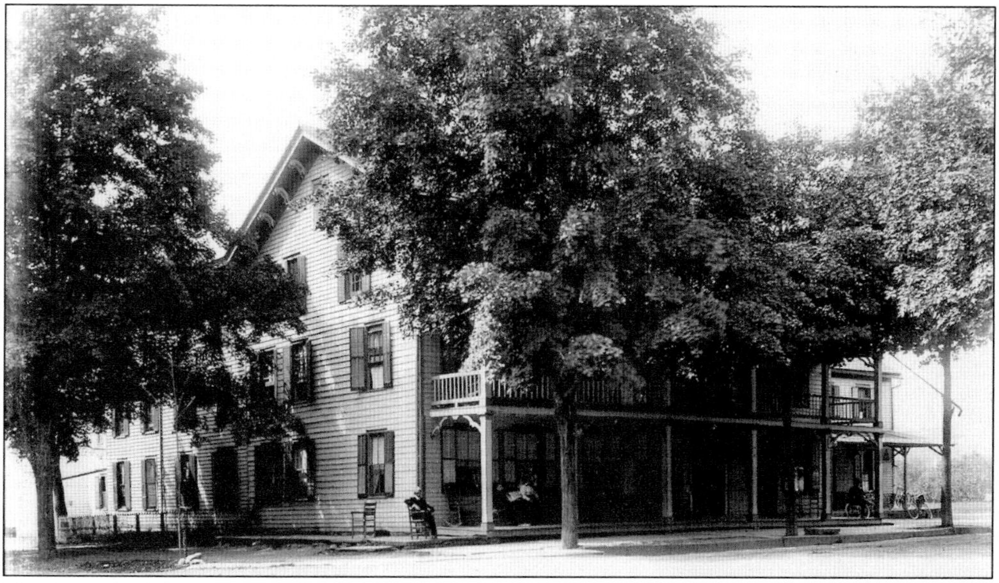

The beauty of the area attracted many visitors, and inns flourished. Timothy Candee built the Crissman House on the corner of Harford and Broad Streets (where the Rite Aid is now) before 1820. It was purchased in 1853 by Cyrus Crissman and was later operated by his son Frank. An inscription over the open fireplace in the dining room reads, "As ancient is this hostelry, As any in the land may be." The hotel burned down in 1960. The blaze was so high that houses within a block away had to be evacuated because of fears the fire might spread. Evacuated children slept on the floor and on couches in Dr. Harvey Klaer's living room until the danger had passed. Seen below, the Terwilliger and its twin structure next door, the Centre Square, now make up the Tom Quick Inn. Both buildings were built in 1882 by George Dauman and were popular stopping points for travelers who enjoyed the fine cuisine. (Above, courtesy of the Pike County Historical Society; below, courtesy of Diane Banach.)

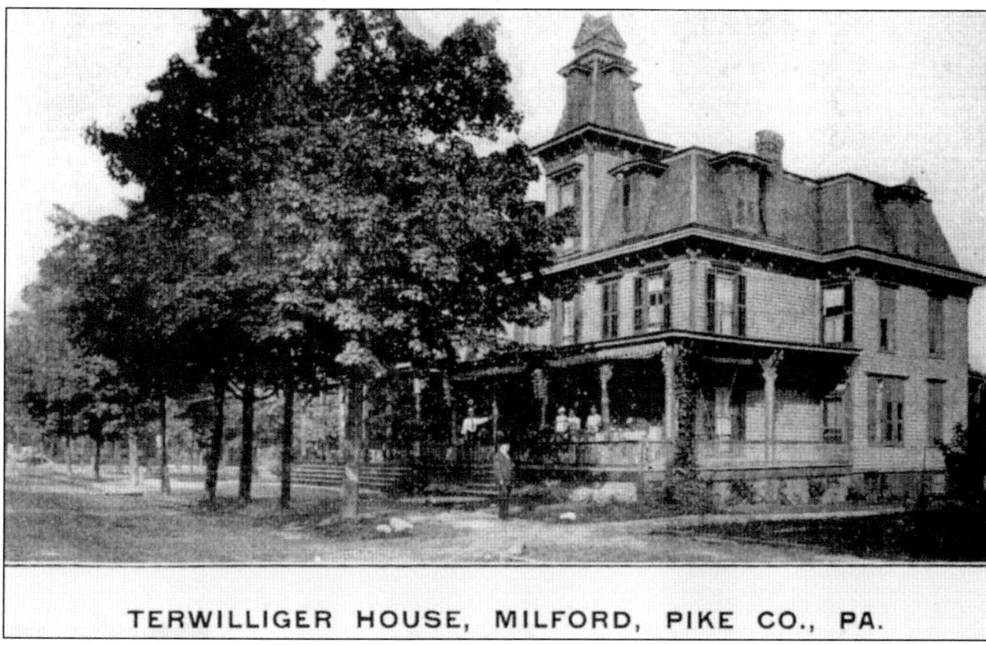

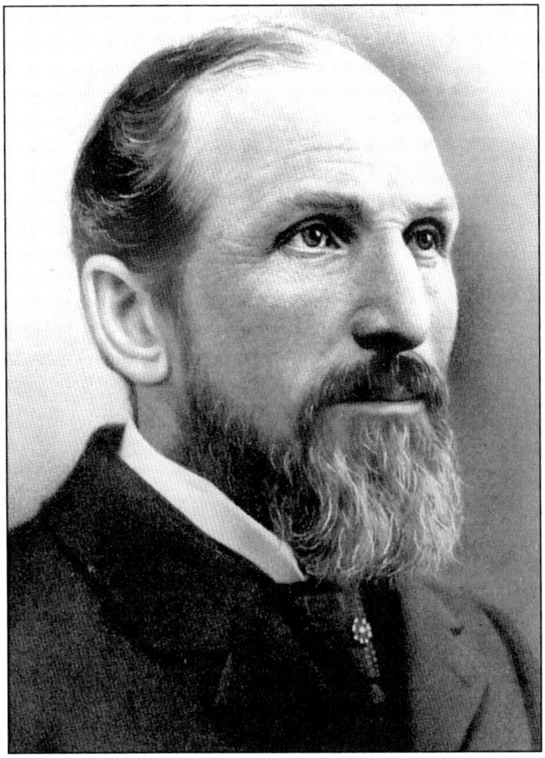

Jacob Klaer, the father of Jacob (left), came to America in 1840 from Germany at the age of 22. He worked in New York City for four years and then bought a farm in Dingman's, where he worked for eight years. He then sold the farm and moved to Milford, where he engaged in various mechanical endeavors. In 1858, he refitted Judge John Biddis's old woolen mill on the Sawkill, and his spoke and hub business flourished. His success gave him the means to purchase the gristmill next door, the Sawkill Mill. That building burned down, and he rebuilt it to the most modern standards of the time. Jacob Klaer, the son, was born in Dingman's. He took over his father's mill and successfully operated it until 1897, when he sold out and purchased 1,000 acres along the Delaware known as the Ross Farm. He served the community in various public offices and became an associate judge in 1896.

Henry B. Wells was a talented Milford carpenter. The area now occupied by Milford was originally named Wells Ferry after the ferry that the Wells family operated between Milford and New Jersey. Henry Wells, a direct descendant of one of the three Wells brothers who settled in Milford, can be considered one of the earliest developers in Milford. He purchased land while its price was low during the Civil War and began building houses, one at a time, to rent or sell. Henry B. Wells has been credited with building more than 50 houses between Milford and Port Jervis. In 1873, he built the Bluff House with 90 rooms and continued to add on to the establishment until 1896, when it reached a capacity 350 guests and staff in 214 rooms.

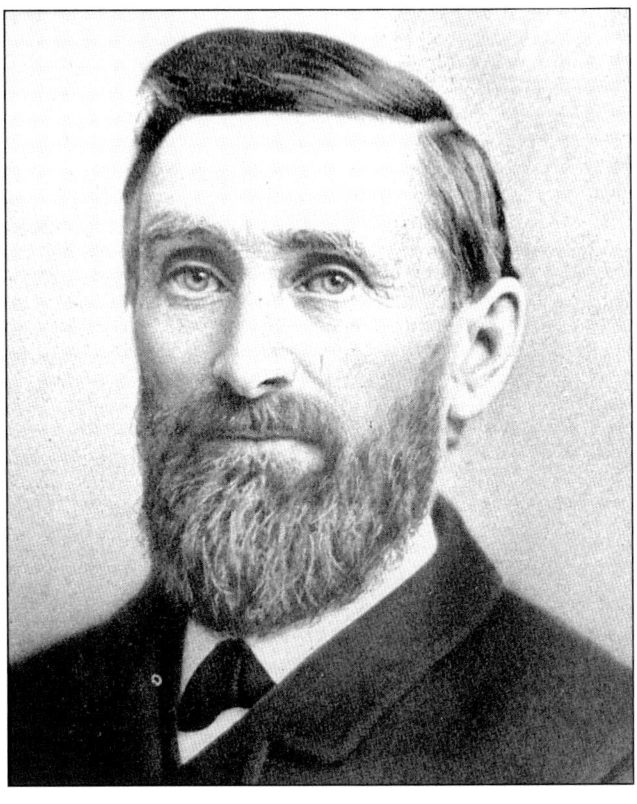

Milton Dimmick Mott was the longtime editor of the *Dispatch* and held various public offices. He was born in 1852 to an old Milford family and lost his father when he was 12 years old. His father's early death forced the young man to take odd jobs in the newspaper, where he learned the printer's trade. After working for several county newspapers, he was able to purchase the *Herald* and renamed it the *Dispatch*. Under his guidance, the *Dispatch* became one of the premier county newspapers in the commonwealth.

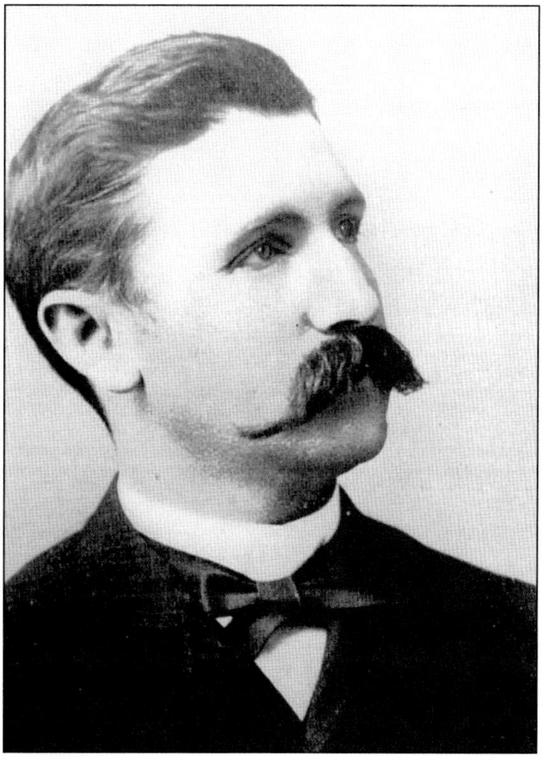

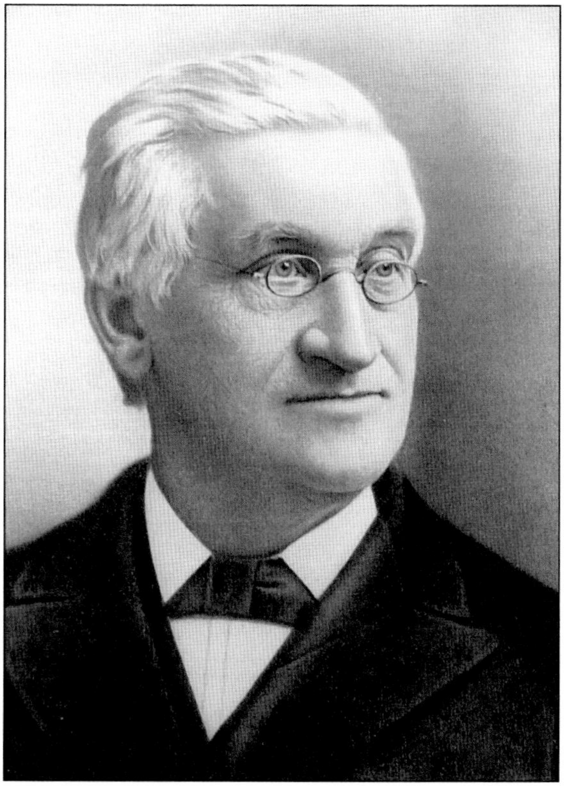

Charles H. Van Wyck came from an old distinguished American family that had numerous representatives fighting for the cause in the Revolutionary War. Many of his ancestors served in high public offices, and Charles Van Wyck was no exception. He was born in 1824 in Poughkeepsie, New York. After graduating from Rutgers College, he joined the Union army as a colonel and achieved the rank of brigadier general before the war ended. He was elected to Congress for four terms and removed to Nebraska, where he served that state faithfully for three terms in the state senate. He was finalizing plans to purchase the Ross Farm, near Elizabeth Street in Milford, when he passed away in 1895. His wife completed the purchase, and many of his descendants still reside in the area.

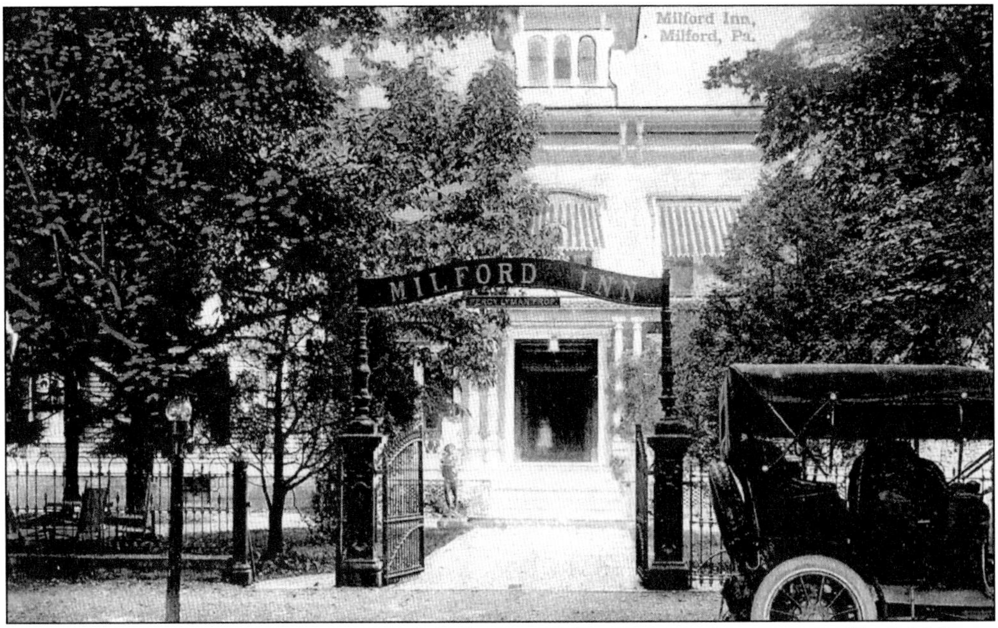

The Milford Inn was a grand example of the beauty of the accommodations in Milford. Millions of words on the printed page were available to the citizens of Milford in the public library. The library's central location provided access to all, and it was often the first place a parent would let their child go for their first solo outing. It was considered a sign of growing up when your parents took you there to get your own library card. (Above, courtesy of Diane Banach; below, courtesy of the Pike County Historical Society.)

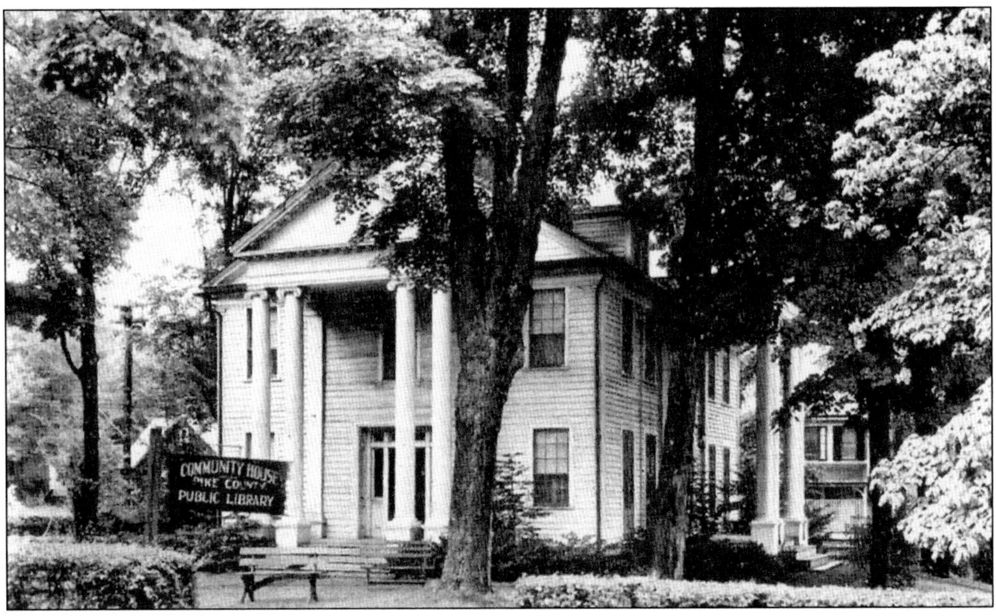

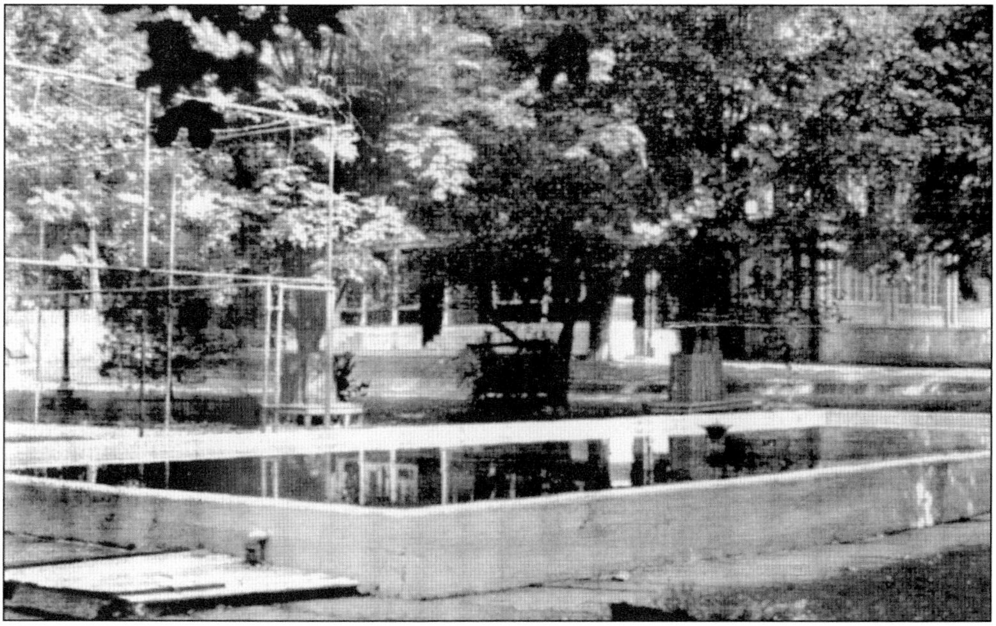

The Coachman's Inn (previously the Mayflower Hotel) was known for its fine cuisine. Located on Harford Street, it had one of the few swimming pools in town and a tennis court. The author's father, Fred Titus, bought the hotel in 1954 and converted it to a private residence. The author lived here with her five brothers in a blended family from 1956 to 1962, when the family moved to Stroudsburg. Her brothers, the Heery boys, discovered that they could travel between the walls from the attic to a space above the kitchen in the first floor and listen to their parents' conversations. The floors were built with three-foot spaces between them. The boys also built a tremendous three-story tree house in the large oak tree next to the house. In the 1960s, the inn burned down, and the lot stands vacant today. In the photograph below, taken in 1957, Fred Titus spends some time with his daughter Susan in the backyard of the former Coachman's Inn. (Courtesy of the Titus-Heery family.)

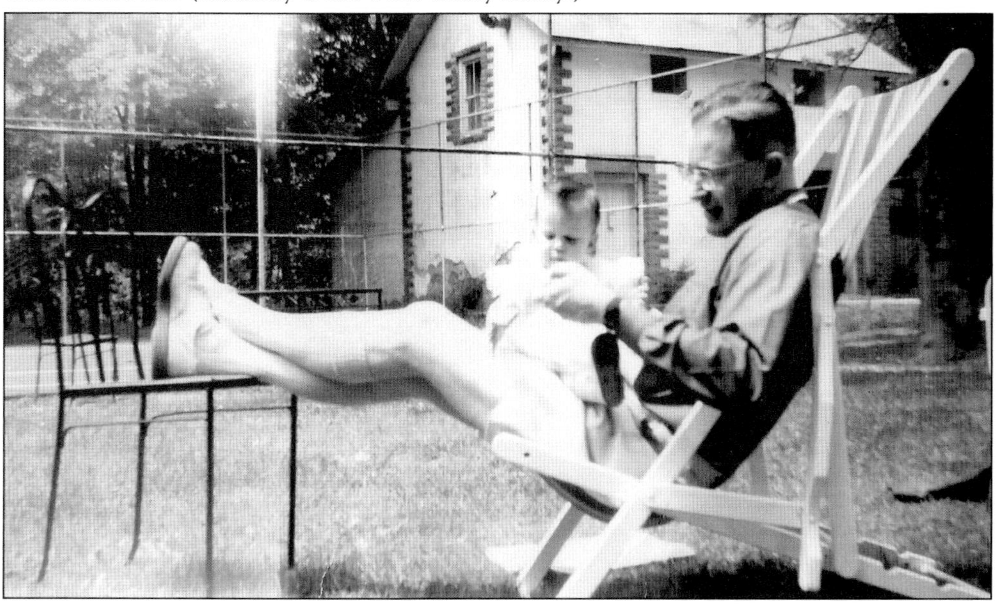

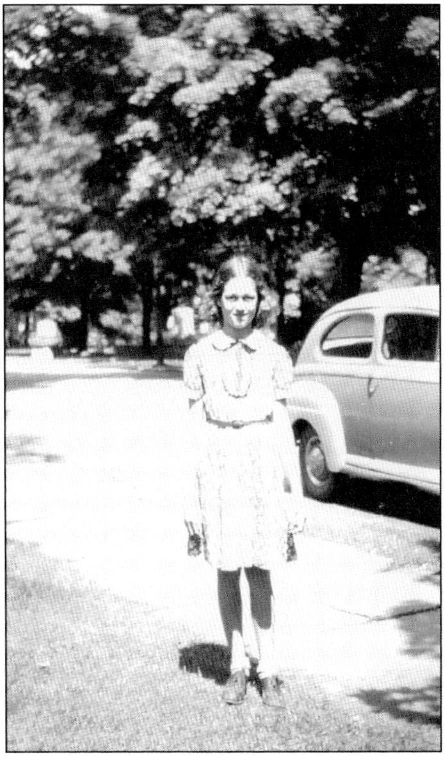

A visit to the park in Milford was always desired by the youth in town. It sported a baseball field, basketball courts, and many playground structures such as a merry-go-round, sliding board, swings, and teeter-totters. To the left, Criss Crosby poses before she visits the park. Below, children play in the park. (Left, courtesy of Criss Crosby Stone.)

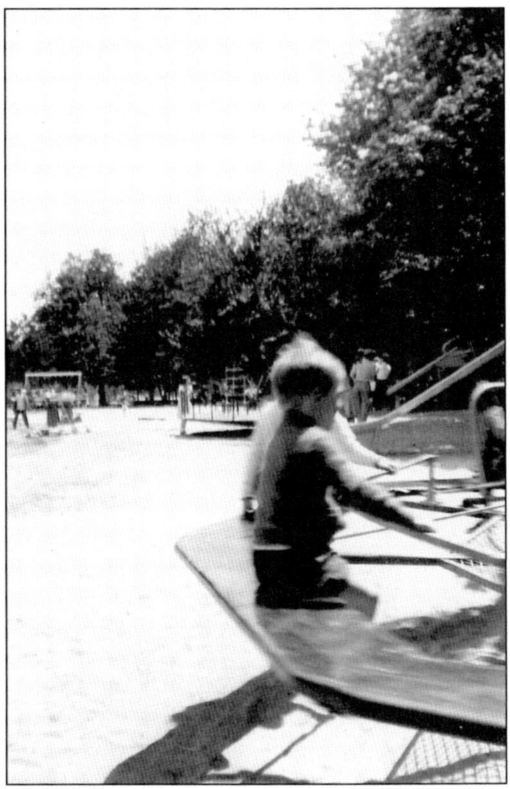

Criss Crosby married George Stone in 1949. Here they pose on the street just south of the Hotel Fauchere. (Courtesy of Criss Crosby Stone.)

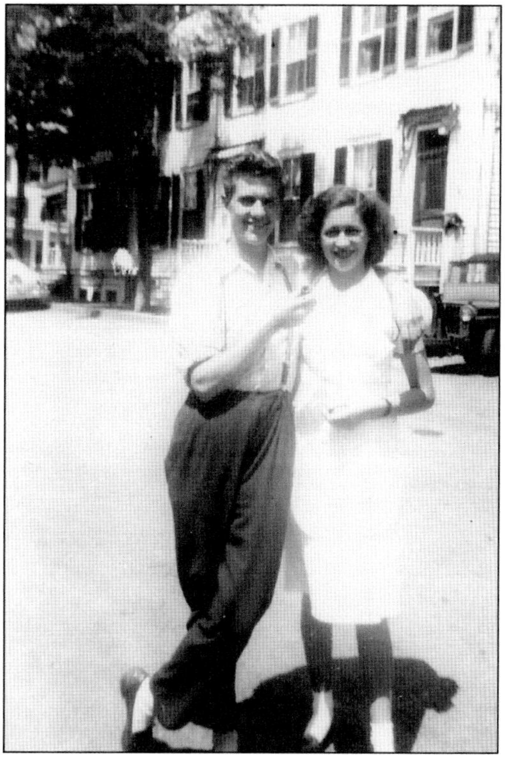

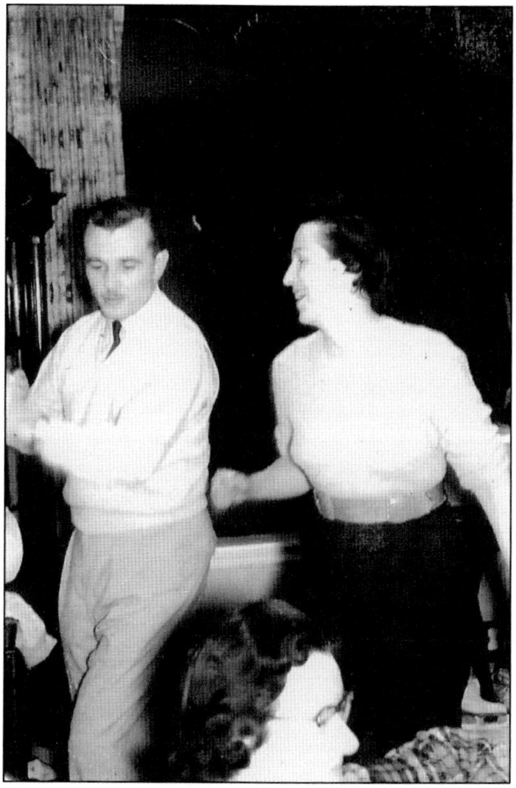

Realtor Allen Titus dances with his sister-in-law, Irma Titus. His wife, Gene Anne Buchanan Titus, can be seen sitting in the foreground.

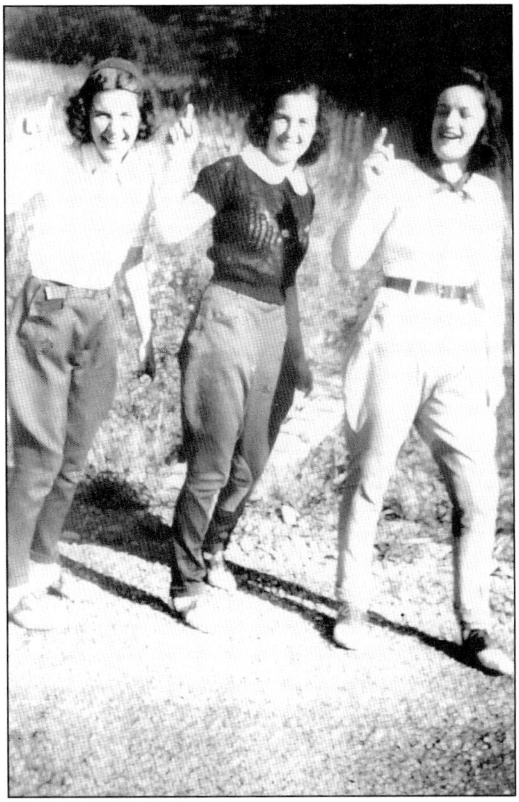

Irma Stretz visits Milford with her friends, Fran and Mary.

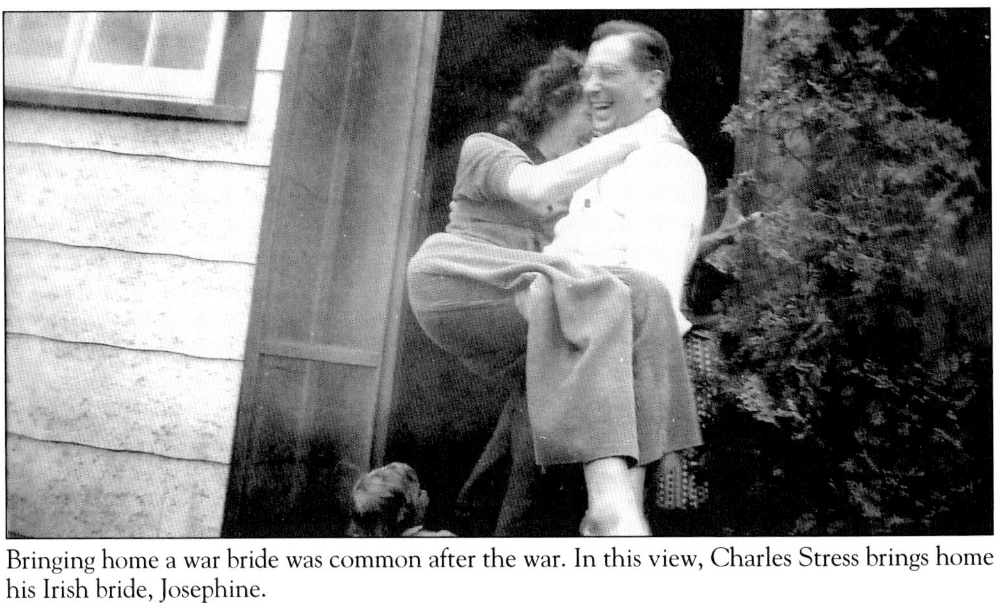

Bringing home a war bride was common after the war. In this view, Charles Stress brings home his Irish bride, Josephine.

Criss, George, and Gail Stone pose for a shot in one of the neighborhoods in Milford. Most driveways at the time were unpaved, and the village had a rustic feeling. Many couples found that Milford was a wonderful place to raise their children. "It takes a village" was a prevailing community spirit, and many parents felt comfortable allowing children as young as five years old to walk home from school and ride their bicycles through the alleys to the candy store or to a friend's home.

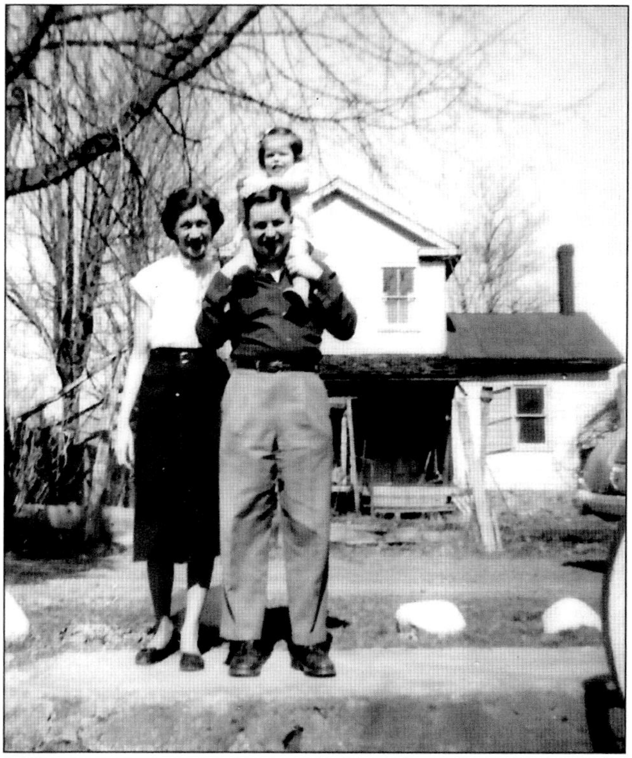

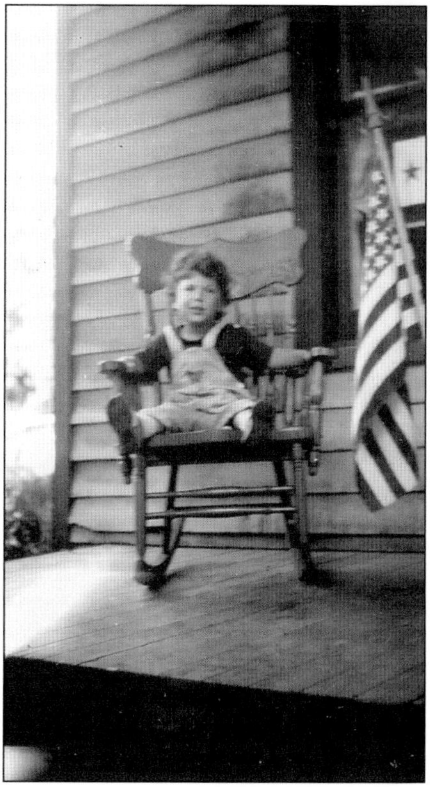

A young boy enjoys rocking on his porch while watching the world go by. The service star in the window denotes that a family member was serving in the war. (Courtesy of Criss Crosby Stone.)

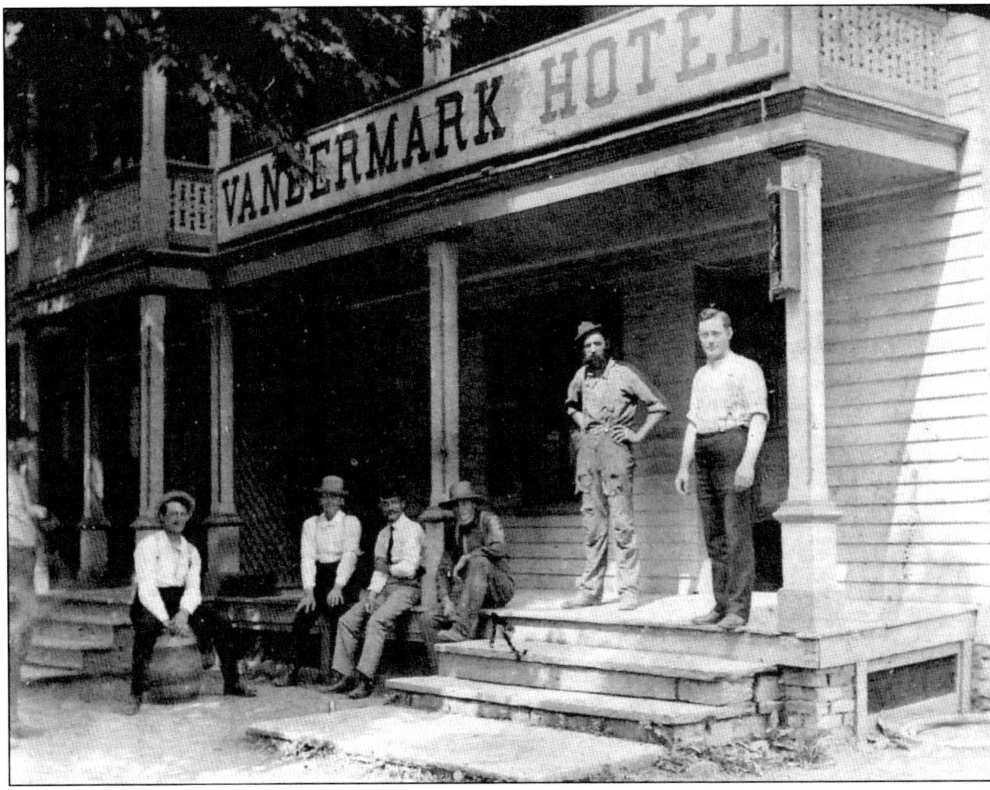

The Vandermark Hotel was built in 1785 next to the old courthouse. It hosted many jurors and hunters. Noted guests were William Jennings Bryan and James T. Corbett. As seen below, even private estates in town offered beautiful parklike settings such as Foster's Hill. This was a favorite sleigh-riding hill for all the children in town through the 1960s. (Above, courtesy of Criss Crosby Stone.)

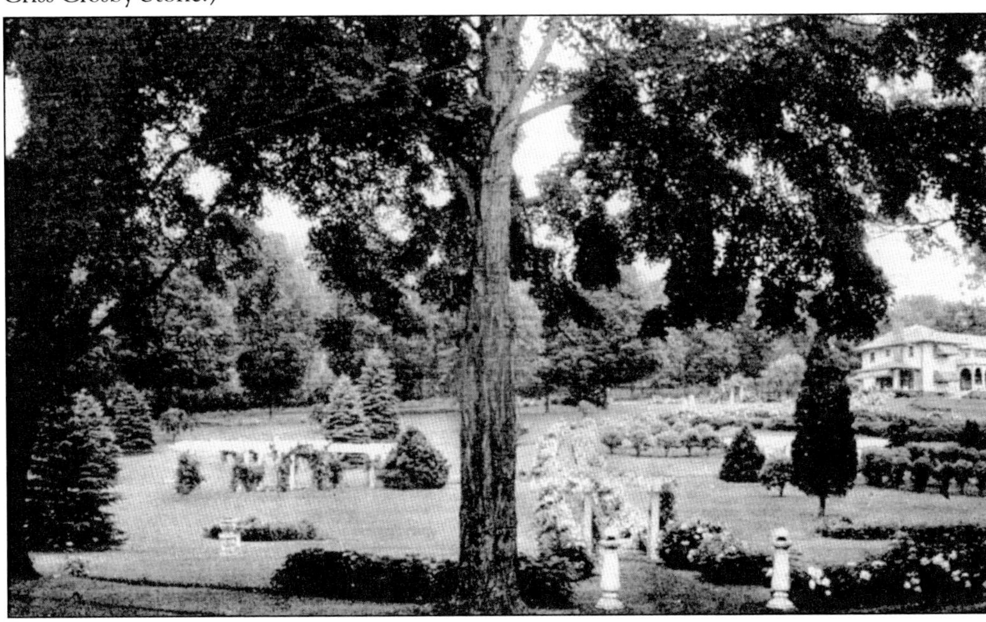

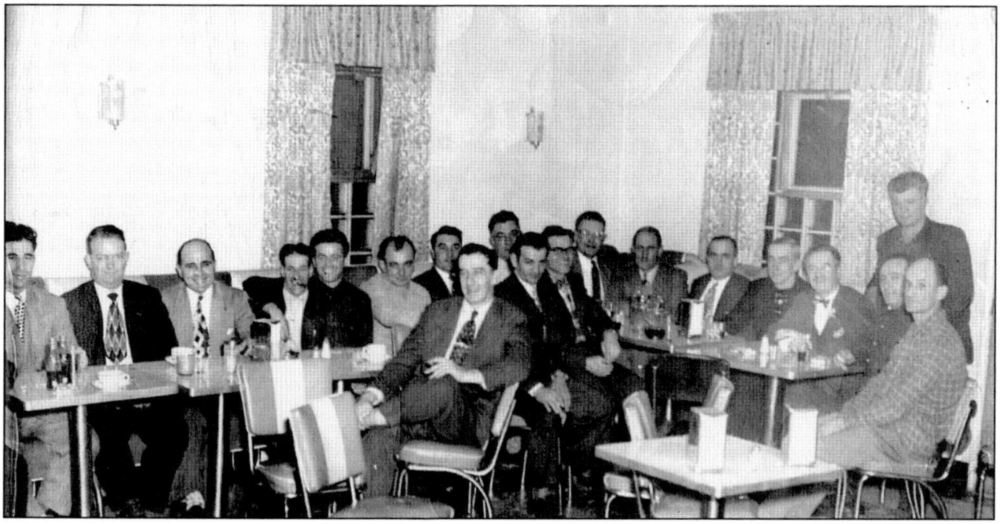

The Wilderness Hunting Club (above) had an active membership that organized hunting trips near and far. This photograph, taken in 1954–1955, shows the membership, who represented most of the sportsmen in Milford and the Minisink. In the back corner, the man with the glasses is Fred J. Titus, who was the president that year. Seen below, in a photograph taken by John Lohman in June 1951, is another organization meeting. From left to right are the following: (first row) ? Maureaux, Josie Kiesel, Papa Kiesel, Pearl Kiesel, and two unidentified people; (second row) unidentified, Silvia Lauer, Mrs. Henry Emery, Henry Emery, Phil McCarty Sr., Henry Kleinstuter, Tina McCarty, and Charles Kurtz. (Courtesy of the Pike County Historical Society.)

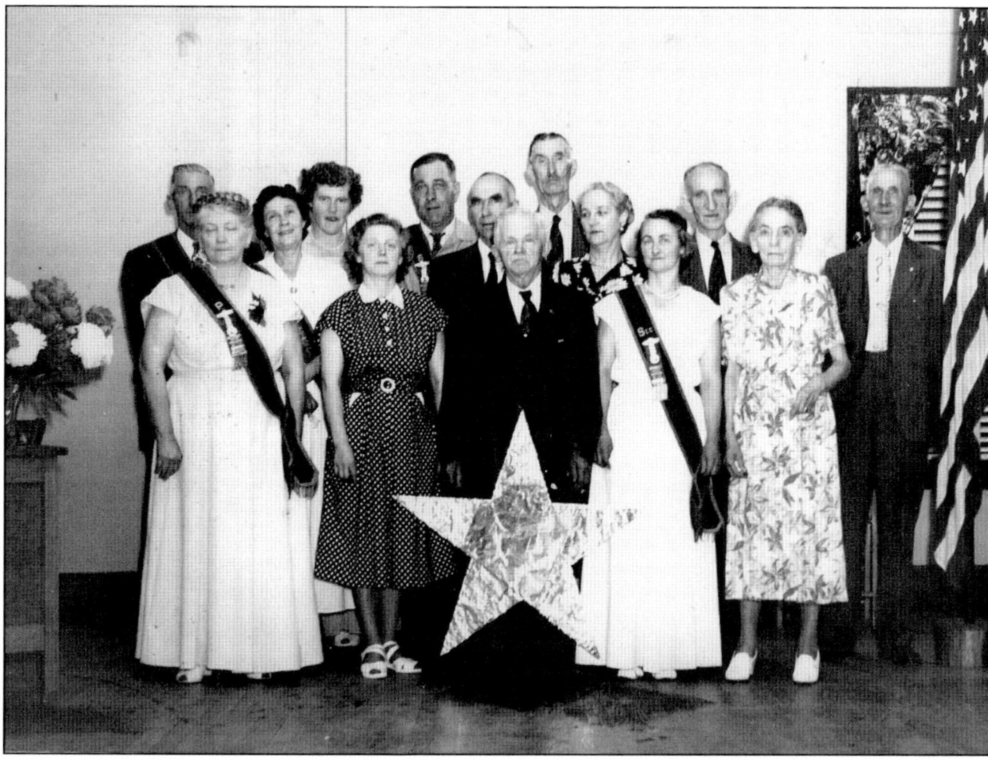

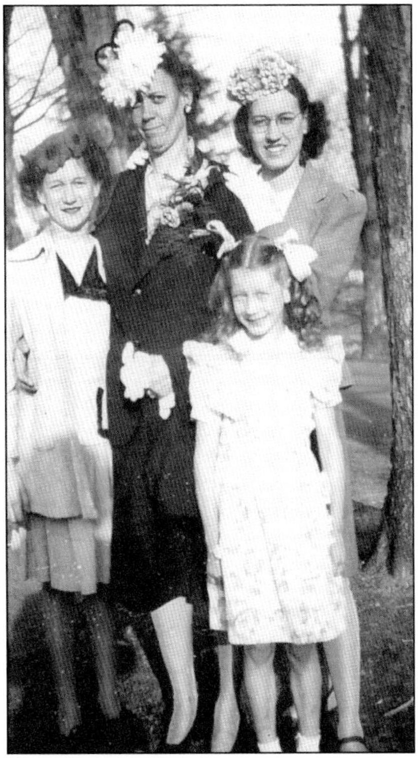

The women of Milford are a sharp-looking bunch in what is probably their Easter attire. From left to right are Criss Crosby, Mildred Higgins, Annabelle Crosby, and Grace Crosby. (Courtesy of Criss Crosby Stone.)

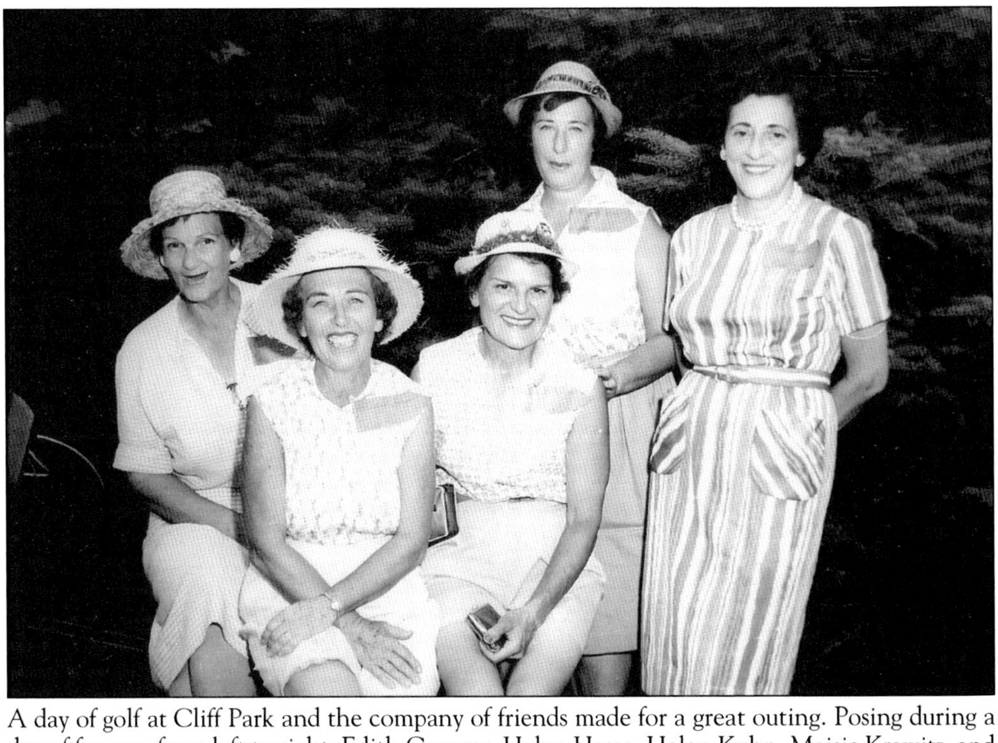

A day of golf at Cliff Park and the company of friends made for a great outing. Posing during a day of fun are, from left to right, Edith Gregory, Helen Hesse, Helen Kuhn, Maisie Krawitz, and Shirley Riordan. (Courtesy of Barbara Buchanan.)

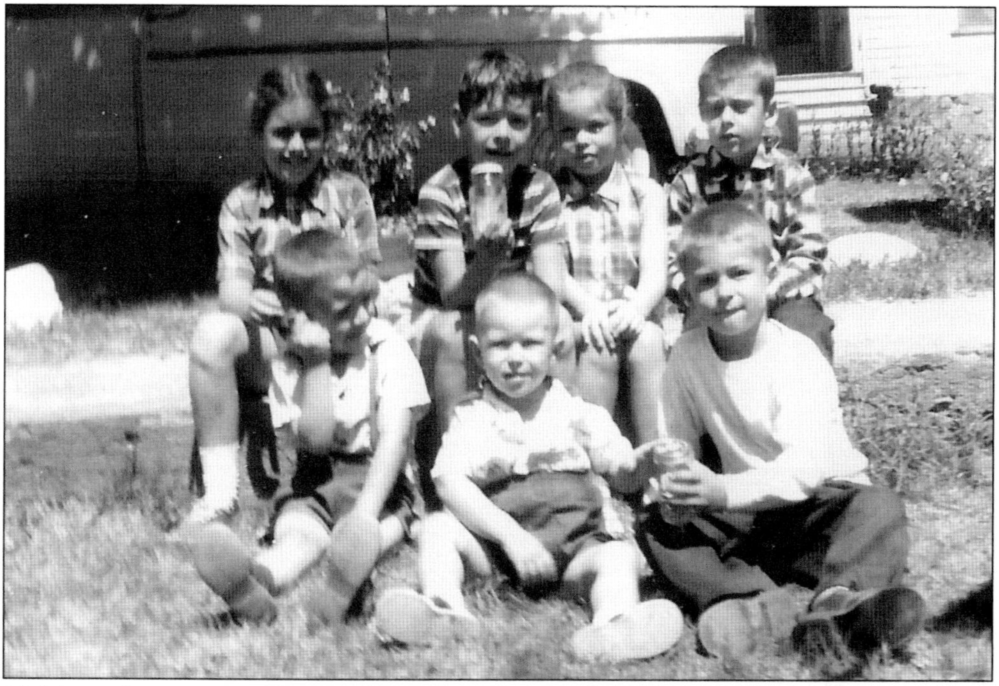

Children take a moment during a family event to pose for a photograph. From left to right are the following: (first row) Johnnie Probia, Gregg Stone, and Donnie Stone; (second row) Norma Hotalen, Ed Hotalen, Gail Stone, and Billie Stone. (Courtesy of Criss Crosby Stone.)

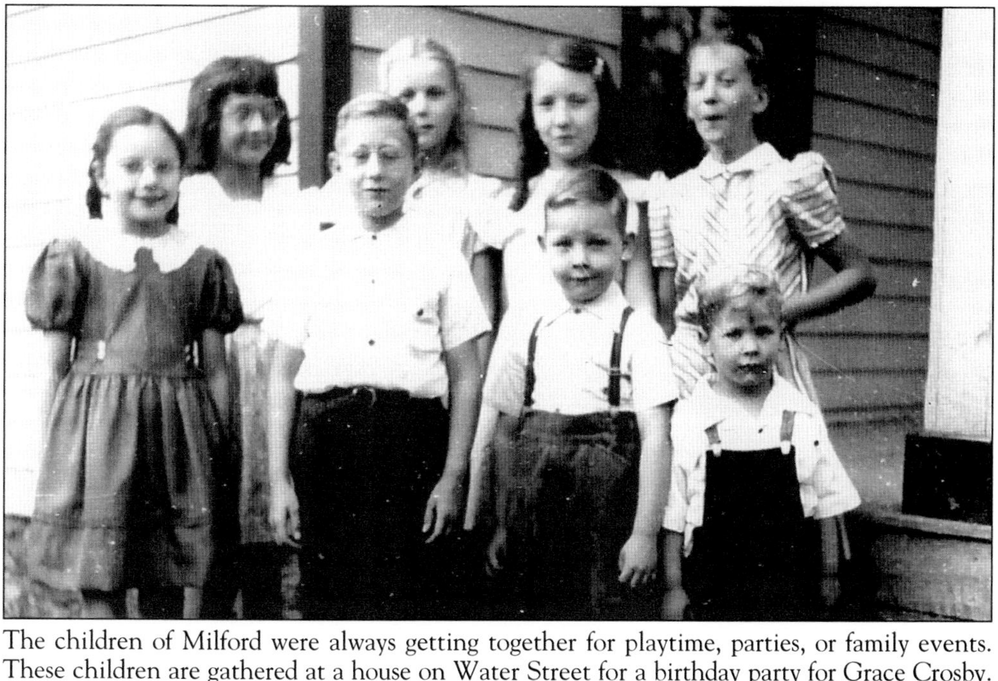

The children of Milford were always getting together for playtime, parties, or family events. These children are gathered at a house on Water Street for a birthday party for Grace Crosby. From left to right are the following: (first row) Cecile Santos, Eddie Anchel, Craig Moureaux, and Vaughn Maureaux; (second row) Mary Anchel, unidentified, Sheila Orban, and Grace Crosby. (Courtesy of Frances Hotalen.)

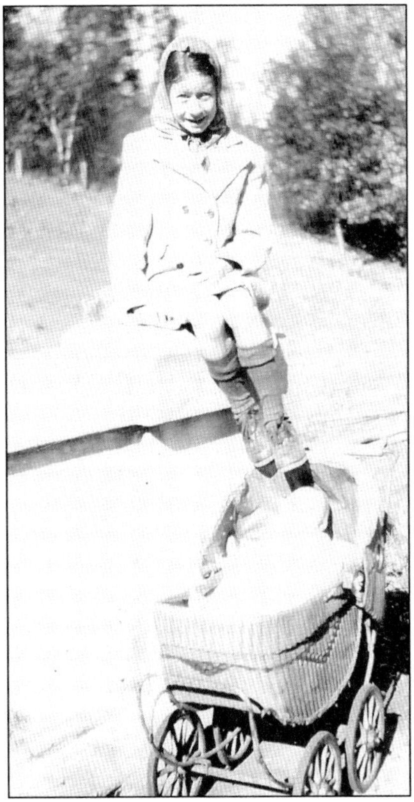

A young girl, Grace Crosby, enjoys a walk with her doll in a beautiful wicker stroller. Walks through town were a common pastime and brought neighbors together. (Courtesy of Frances Hotalen.)

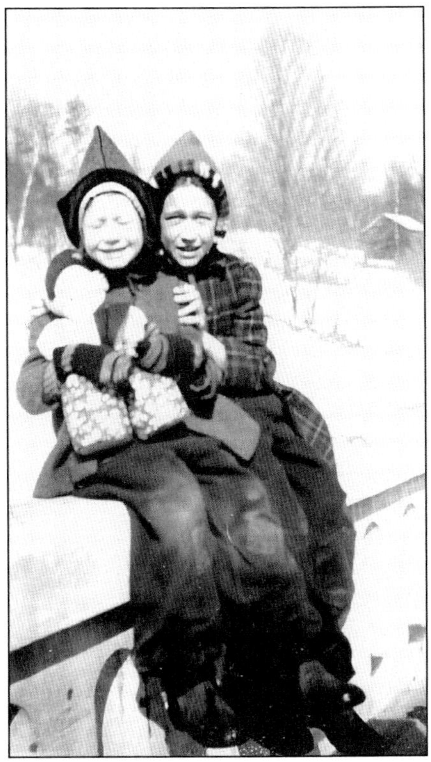

Bundled up, Criss and Grace Crosby enjoy a winter outing. Snow-covered hillsides in town were targets of sleigh riders and snowball fighters. (Courtesy of Frances Hotalen.)

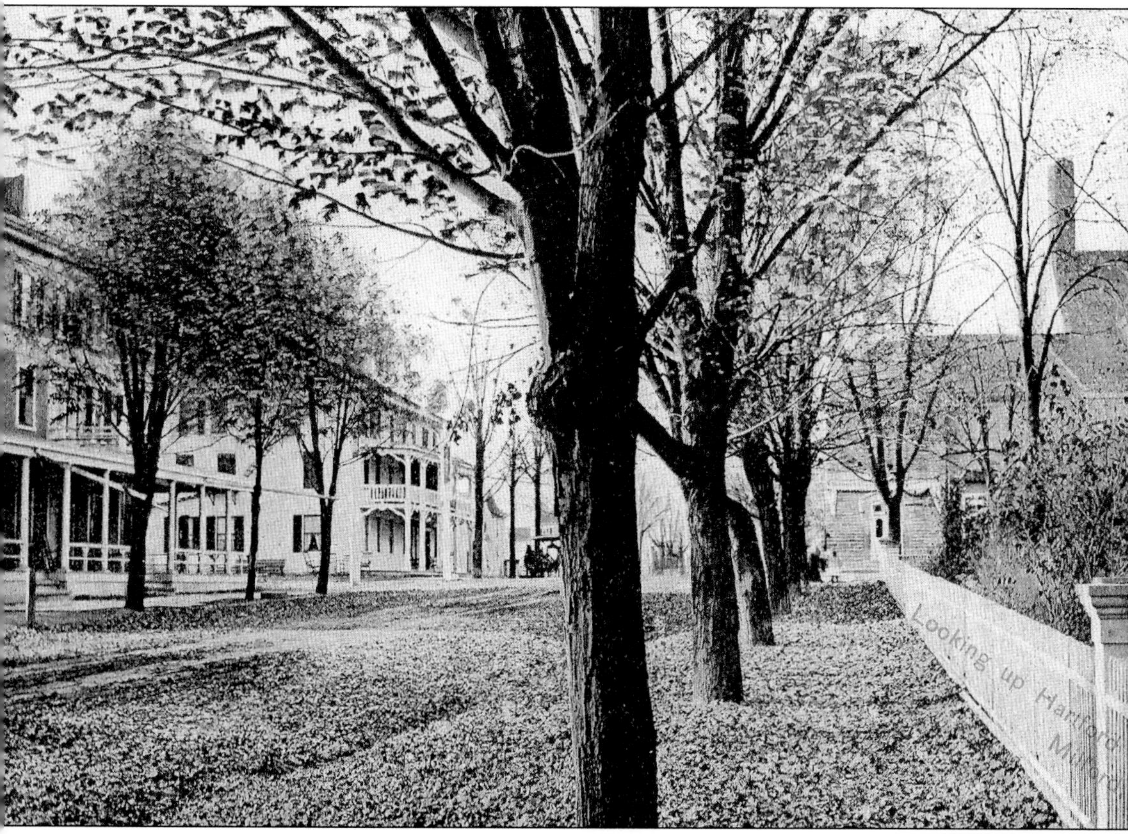

Harford Street (Route 209) approaching Broad Street is seen here in the horse-and-buggy days in autumn. A line across the road shows where the community placed plank-board walkways to help pedestrians travel clear of the mud on rainy days.

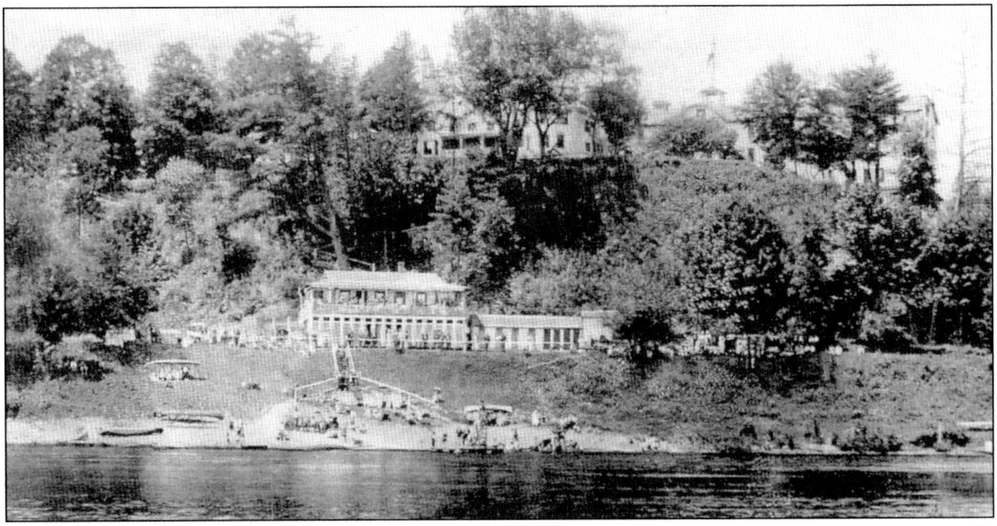

The bathing beach at the Bluff House has always been a prime swimming hole in town. It was located in a spot where the river widens and the waters flow peacefully south through the Minisink Valley.

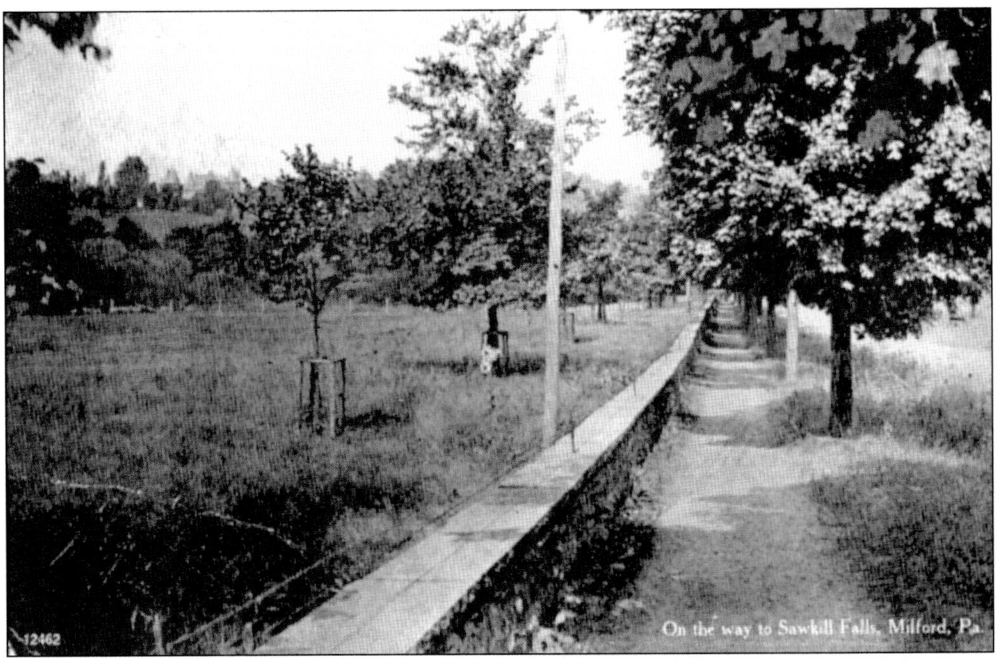

Many visitors and locals traveled walkways on foot, horse, or bike to view one of the area's beautiful waterfalls, such as the Sawkill Falls. (Courtesy of Diane Banach.)

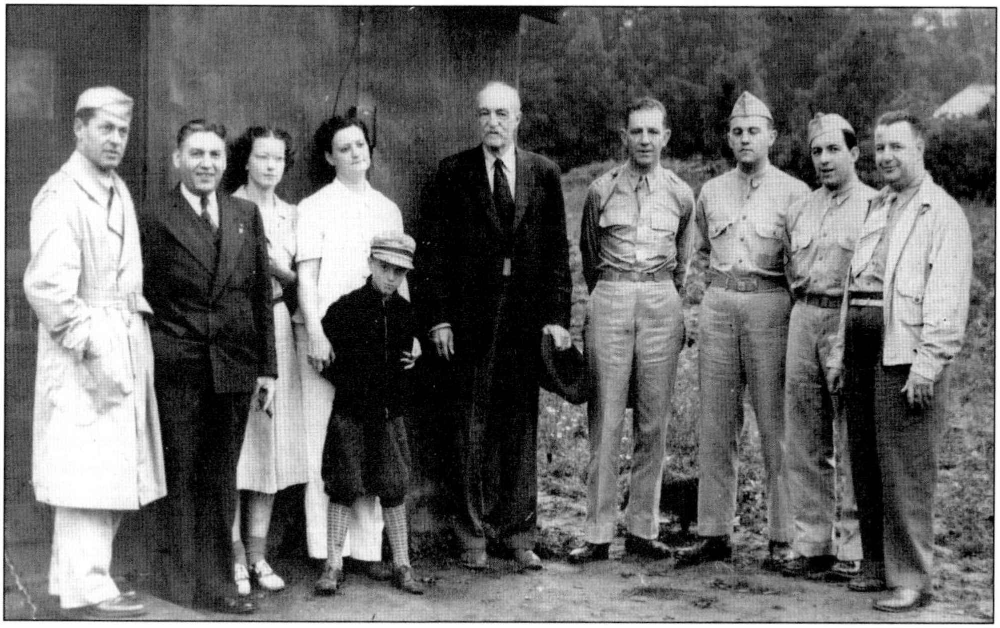

Gov. Gifford Pinchot (center) poses above with members of the Milford Spotting Post, which was set up to spot enemy planes in the skies over Milford. From left to right are Maj. Robert "Bobby" Jones, Hall of Fame golfer John Kololias, Madeline Lohmann, Matilda Drake, Godfrey Drake Jr., three unidentified people, and civil-defense director Dr. H. D. Jones. Below is a view looking south on Broad Street. The Dimmick Hotel is on the right. (Courtesy of the Pike County Historical Society.)

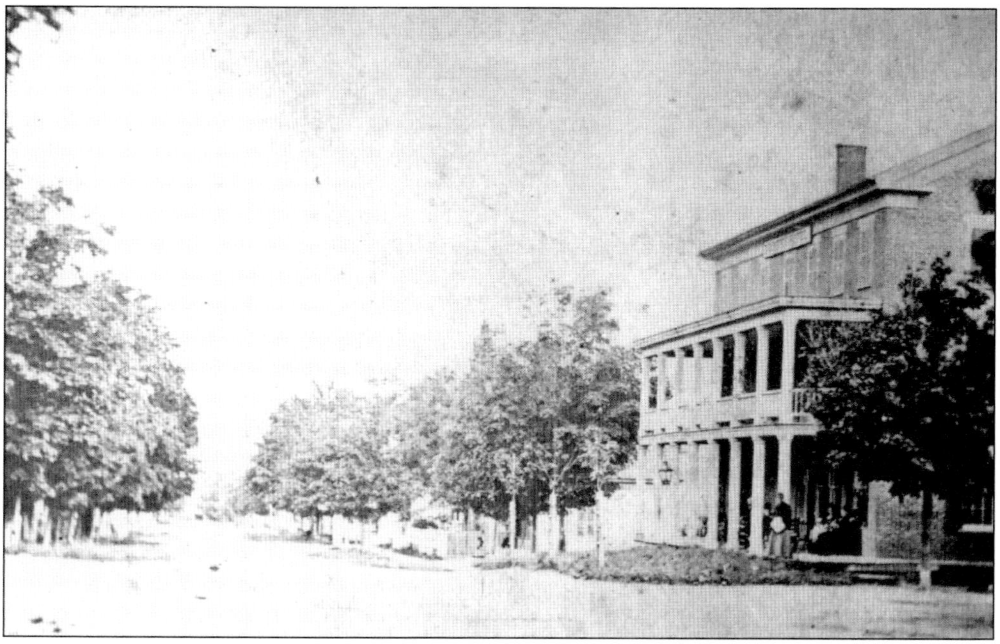

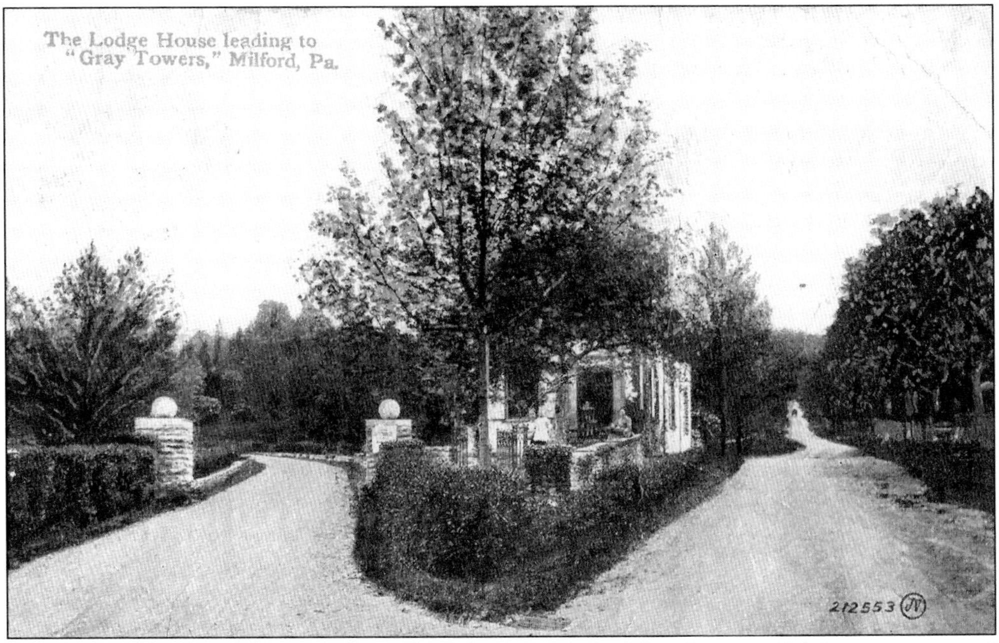

Gray Towers was a stately manor house built by Gov. Gifford Pinchot in 1886. It was recognized by John F. Kennedy as the birthplace of the U.S. Forestry Service and was dedicated as the Pinchot Institute for Conservation Studies just two months before Kennedy's assassination. The mansion and the beautifully landscaped grounds and walks are a tribute to Pinchot's sense of nature. The architectural style of its designer, Richard Morris Hunt, and his experience designing stone structures, such as the base of the Statue of Liberty, are illustrated in this beautiful home. Today, Gray Towers is a National Historic Site run by the National Park Service. (Courtesy of Diane Banach.)

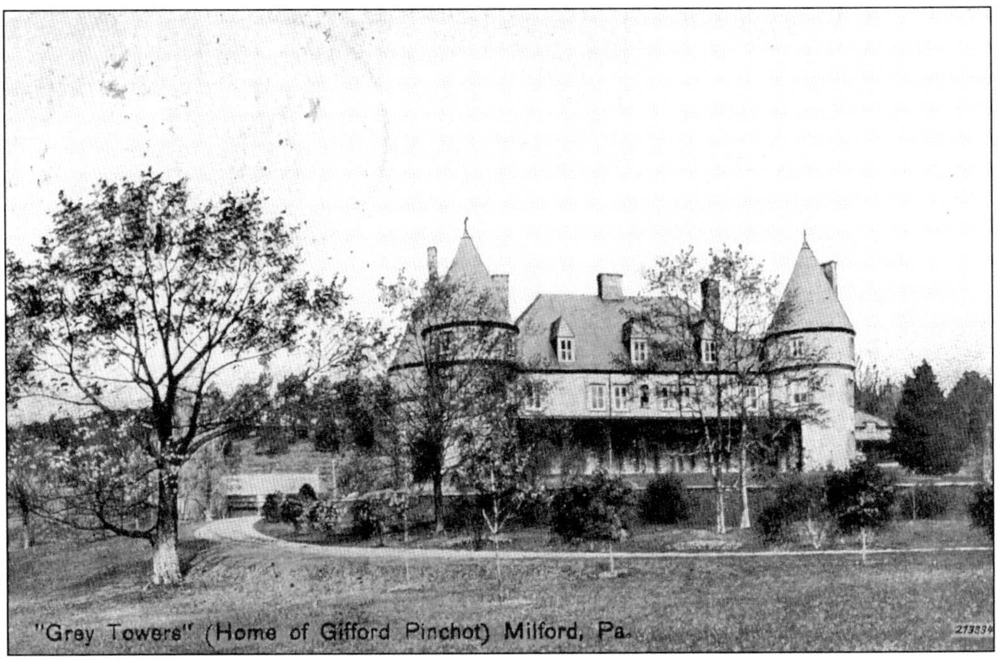

Four

Dingman's Ferry

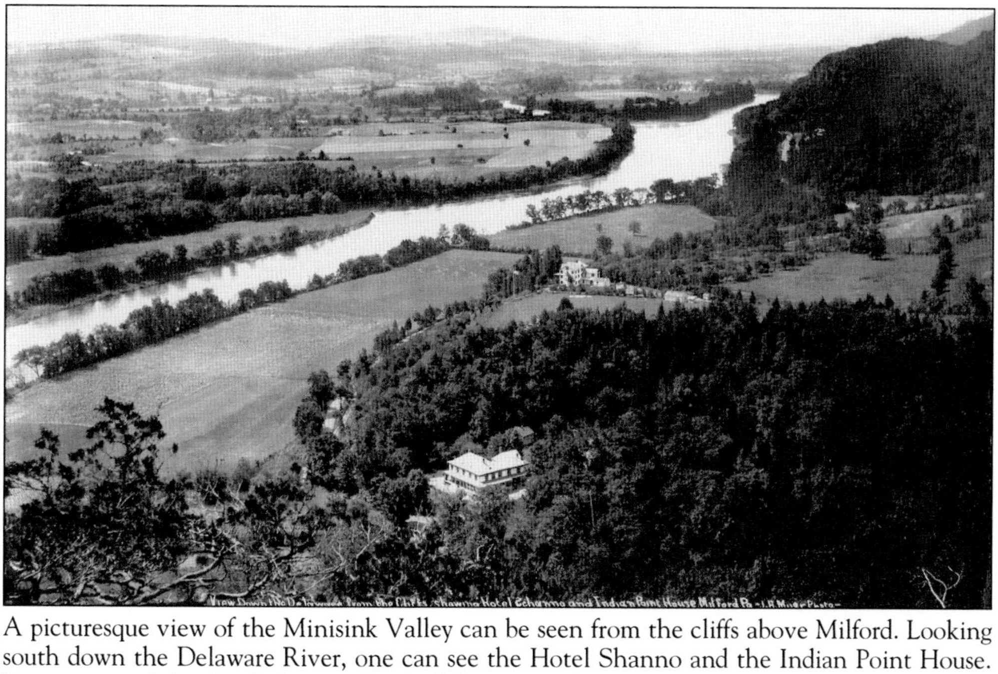

A picturesque view of the Minisink Valley can be seen from the cliffs above Milford. Looking south down the Delaware River, one can see the Hotel Shanno and the Indian Point House. Farmers prized the fertile bottom land of the Minisink, and those lucky enough to possess it thrived with many years of cash crops such as corn, wheat, and garden crops. Minisink Island, located where the river forks in the distance, was prized by both natives and settlers for its rich soil and protected location. The portion of the Minisink Valley in New Jersey can be seen across the river to the left. The Old Mine Road, one of the oldest roads in America, runs along the river on the Jersey side. The natives, and later the Dutch, used it to access the copper mines in the Minisink Valley. It was an important route for troop and supply movement during the French and Indian and Revolutionary Wars.

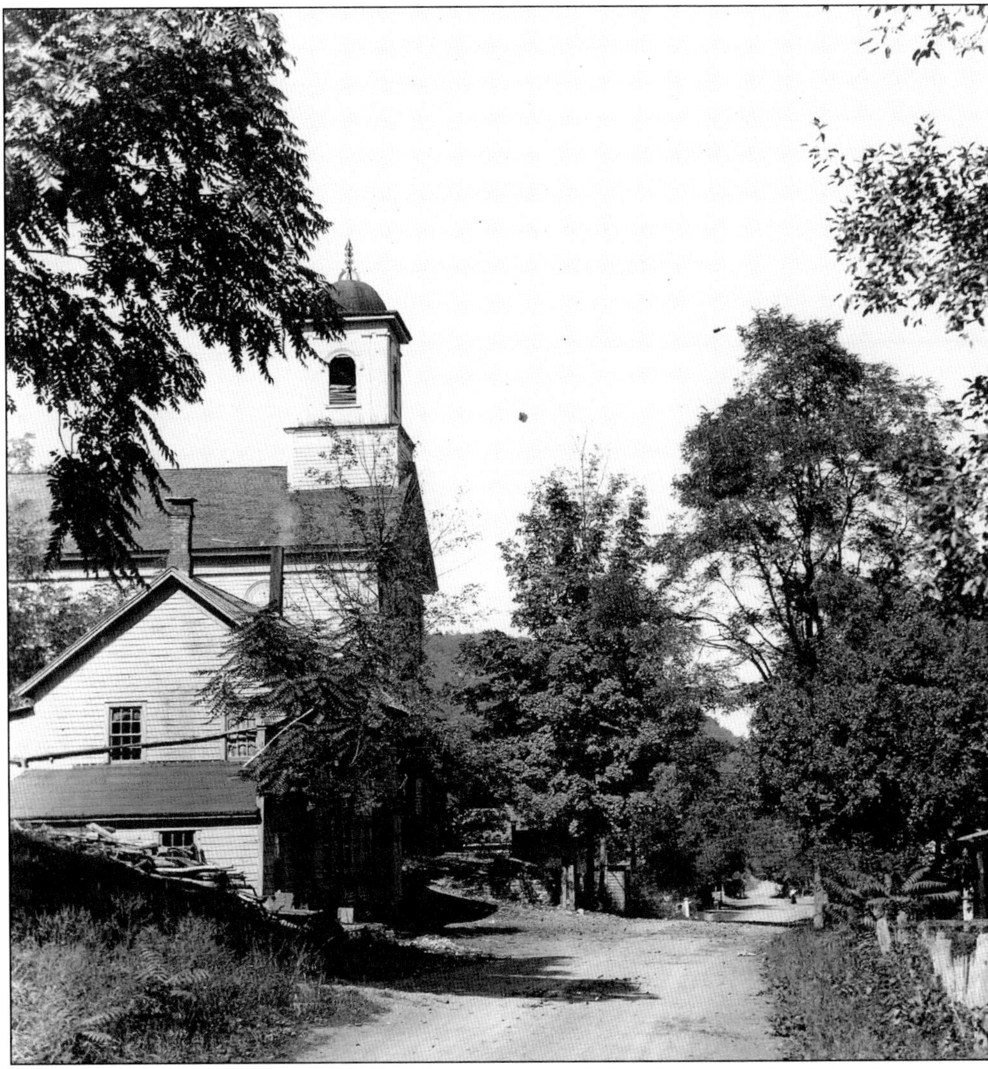

The Minisink homelands along the Delaware provided rich bottom land for farming and profitable timber resources as well as scenic attractions for tourists. By 1889, Dingman's Ferry had became a thriving village. It boasted one of the few ferries that crossed the Delaware to the New Jersey side. Many travelers, tourists, and merchants relied on this ferry to access all points east. (Courtesy of the Pike County Historical Society.)

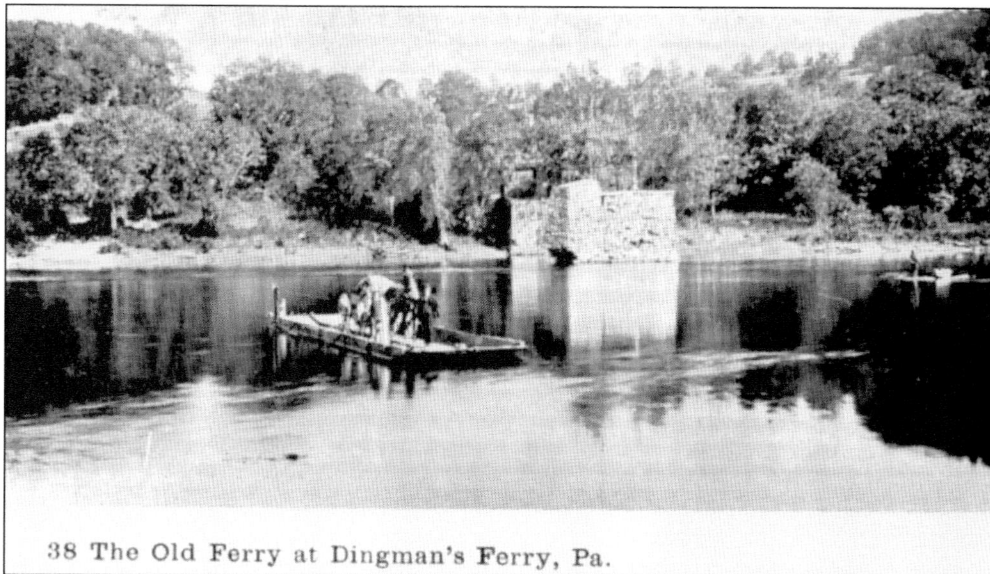

The ferry could transport horses and wagons in one load. The Dingman family started it in 1735. They operated it until 1836, when they replaced it with a private toll bridge. It was pressed back into service after a fall flood in 1903 took out most of the area's bridges. The Pumpkin Flood, as it was called, swept away the area's pumpkin crop, and the pumpkins could be seen bobbing down the river. Below is another means of transportation—a team of oxen. (Above, courtesy of Diane Banach; below, courtesy of the Pike County Historical Society.)

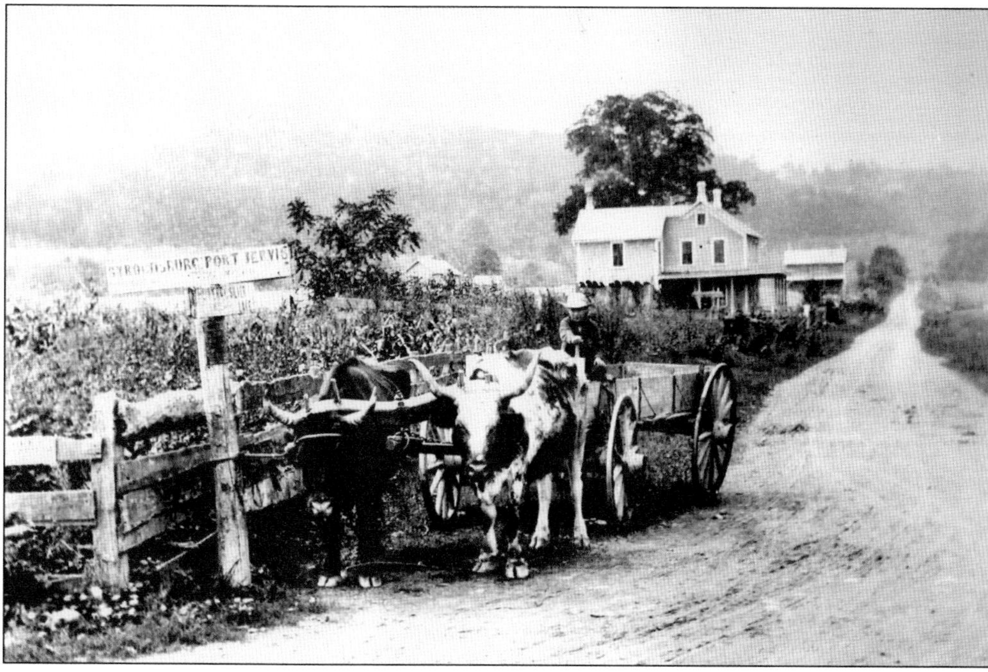

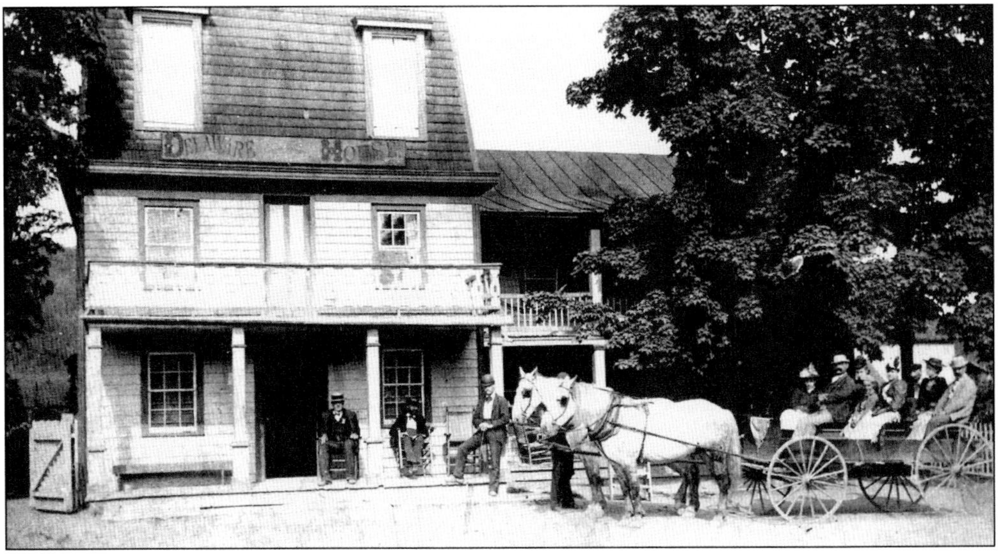

The Delaware House was a popular meeting place for all the local residents and was a convenient stop for coaches. (Courtesy of the Pike County Historical Society.)

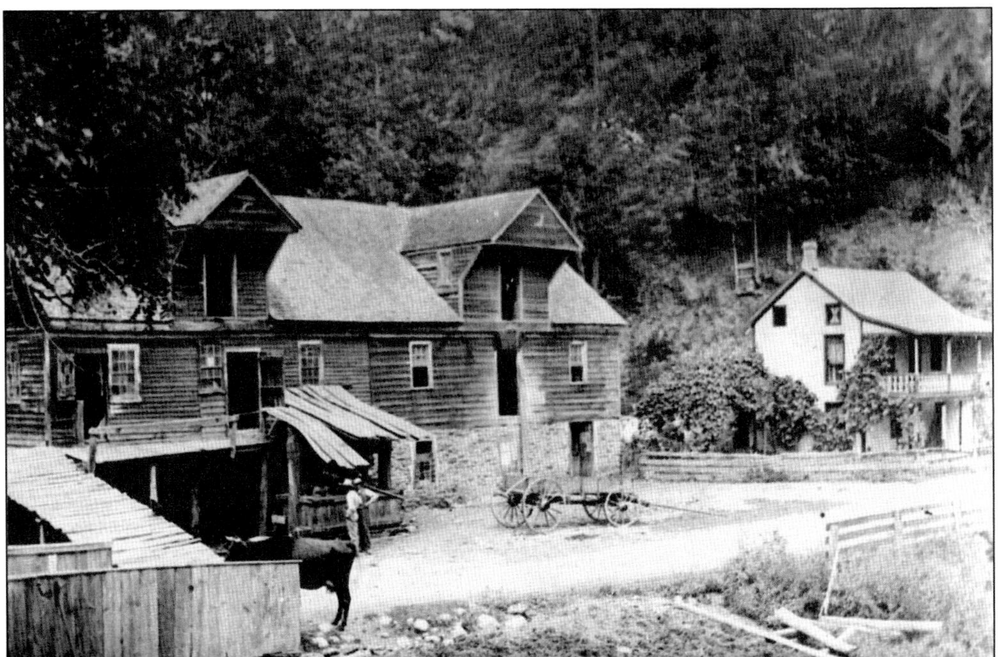

The mill in Dingman's Ferry was where farmers took their grain to be processed and sold. It was also the source of seeds for next years' crops. (Courtesy of the Pike County Historical Society.)

Alfred Stoll Dingman was a prominent politician and businessman in the county. He was born on the original family homestead in Dingman's Ferry in 1837. He is a direct descendant of Andrew Dingman, who came to the Minisink Valley in 1735 and settled on a site he called Dingman's Choice. He built the first log house in the area and cleared the first farm and operated the first ferry. Alfred Stoll Dingman served in the Civil War and, upon his discharge, embarked on a career in the mercantile business in Dingman's. At one point, he worked in Milford at the store of John F. Pinchot.

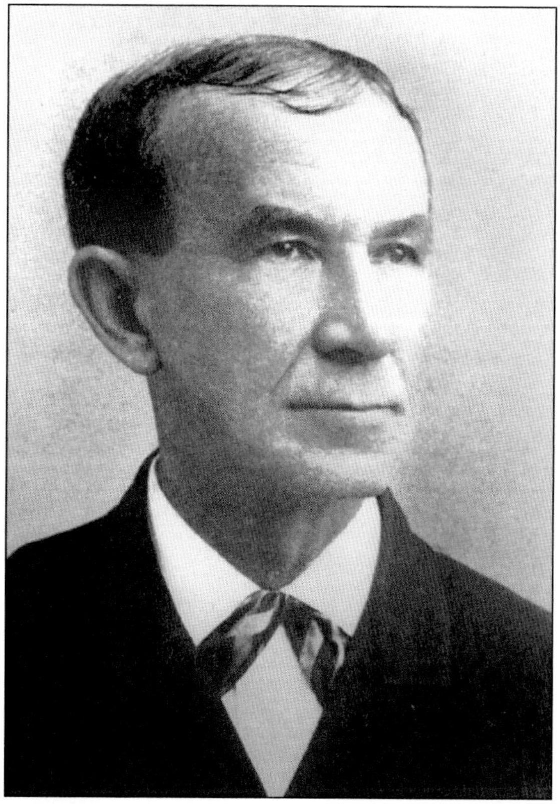

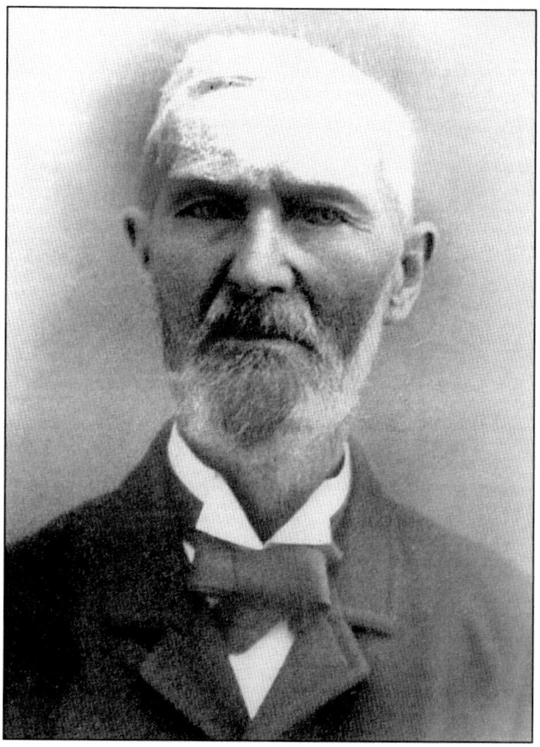

John Coolbaugh Westbrook is descended from another pioneer family well represented in the Minisink Valley. The first Westbrook came to America prior to 1630, and Anthony Westbrook settled in the Minisink Valley prior to 1737. The Westbrook and Dingman families intermarried throughout the years, and both families married into the Van Auken and Van Etten, who were descendants of some of the earliest Dutch settlers in the valley. Over the generations, the Westbrooks worked as successful farmers, lumbermen, and merchants in Dingman's Ferry and Blooming Grove. John Coolbaugh Westbrook took over his father's store in Dingman's Ferry. He was a partner with his brothers in the lumber business and built a sawmill and gristmill. In 1850, he married Jane Wells, another descendant of a pioneer family.

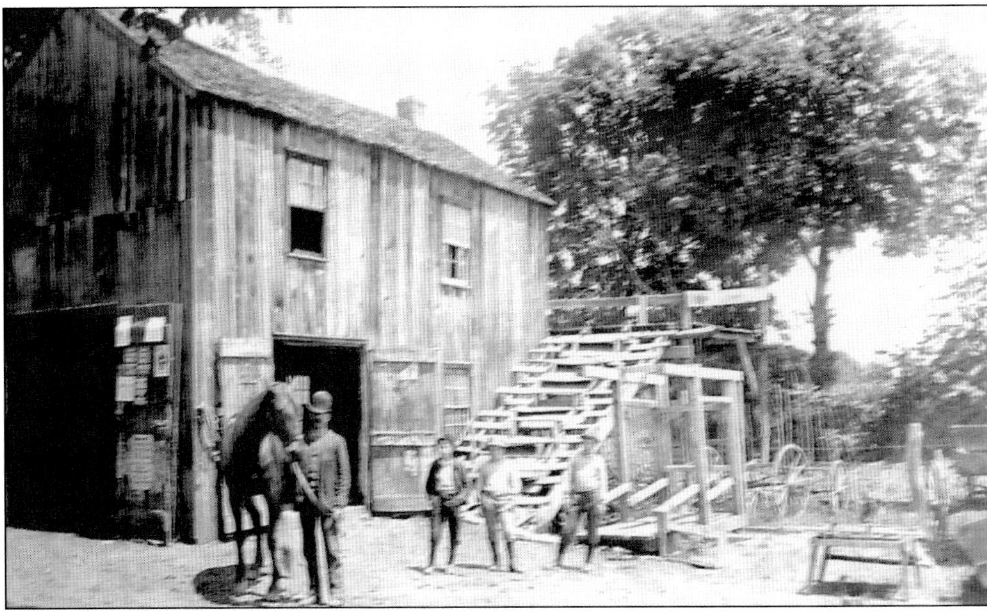

The blacksmith's shop in Dingman's Ferry was a busy and essential establishment in 1889. Horses' feet were shod, harnesses were repaired, pots and pans were mended, farm implements were fixed, and broken wagon wheels were restored. When the automobile began to dominate the roads, the building was torn down and replaced by an automotive garage. As seen below, boardinghouses thrived in the beautiful valley, and establishments in Dingman's were no exception. The Dingman House was a popular and well-run boardinghouse in town. (Courtesy of the Pike County Historical Society.)

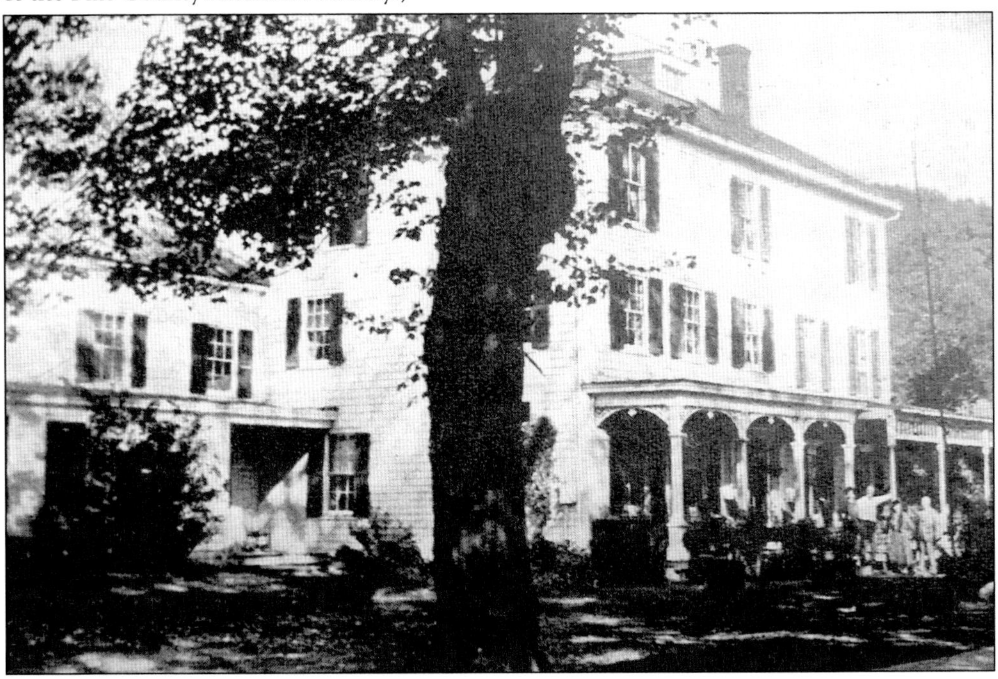

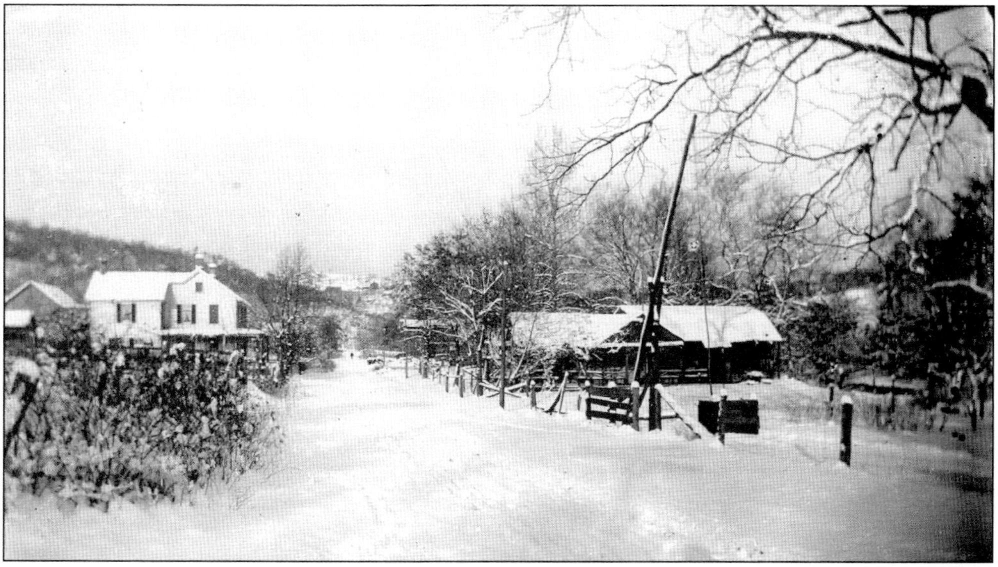

A beautiful scene of winter in the Minisink Valley shows Dingman's Ferry with the old oak bucket well on the right along the fence line. Wintertime was a time to settle down in front of a warm fire, mend clothes, repair equipment, and enjoy a good book. On Christmas Eve, a tree would be cut and decorated with painted walnuts, pine cones, popcorn and cranberry garlands, and lighted candles. Most farm girls were happy to receive a new dress for their favorite doll and enjoyed the songs and thankful feast with their family. Floods were a great threat to the Minisink farmers. They were often caused by ice jams such as the one seen below, near Matamoras. (Courtesy of the Pike County Historical Society.)

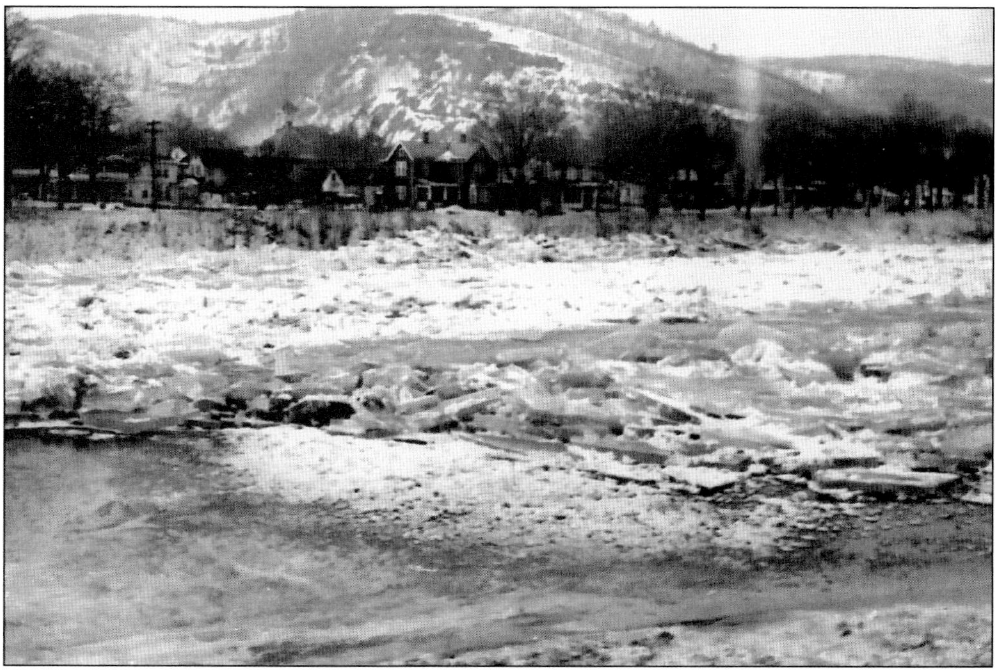

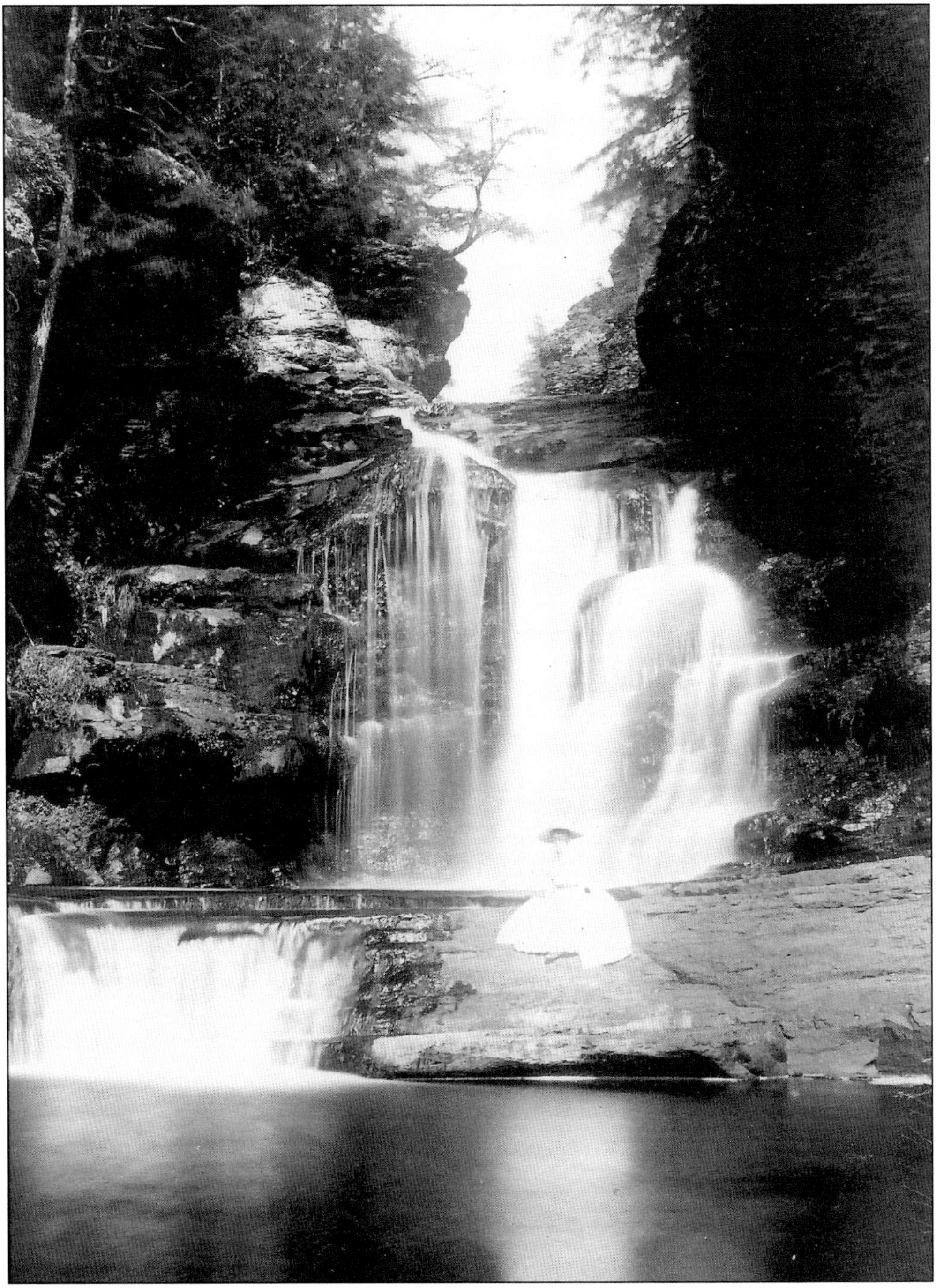

Among the features that attracted visitors to the Minisink Valley were its waterfalls. Photographers, movie directors, tourists, and the local residents all enjoyed hiking up the mountain paths to take in the beautiful site of the cascading waters. One can imagine the Native Americans passing by the waterfalls on their way to their winter camp in the Wyoming Valley and taking a long look at the falls with hopes that they would return safely in the spring. (Courtesy of the Pike County Historical Society.)

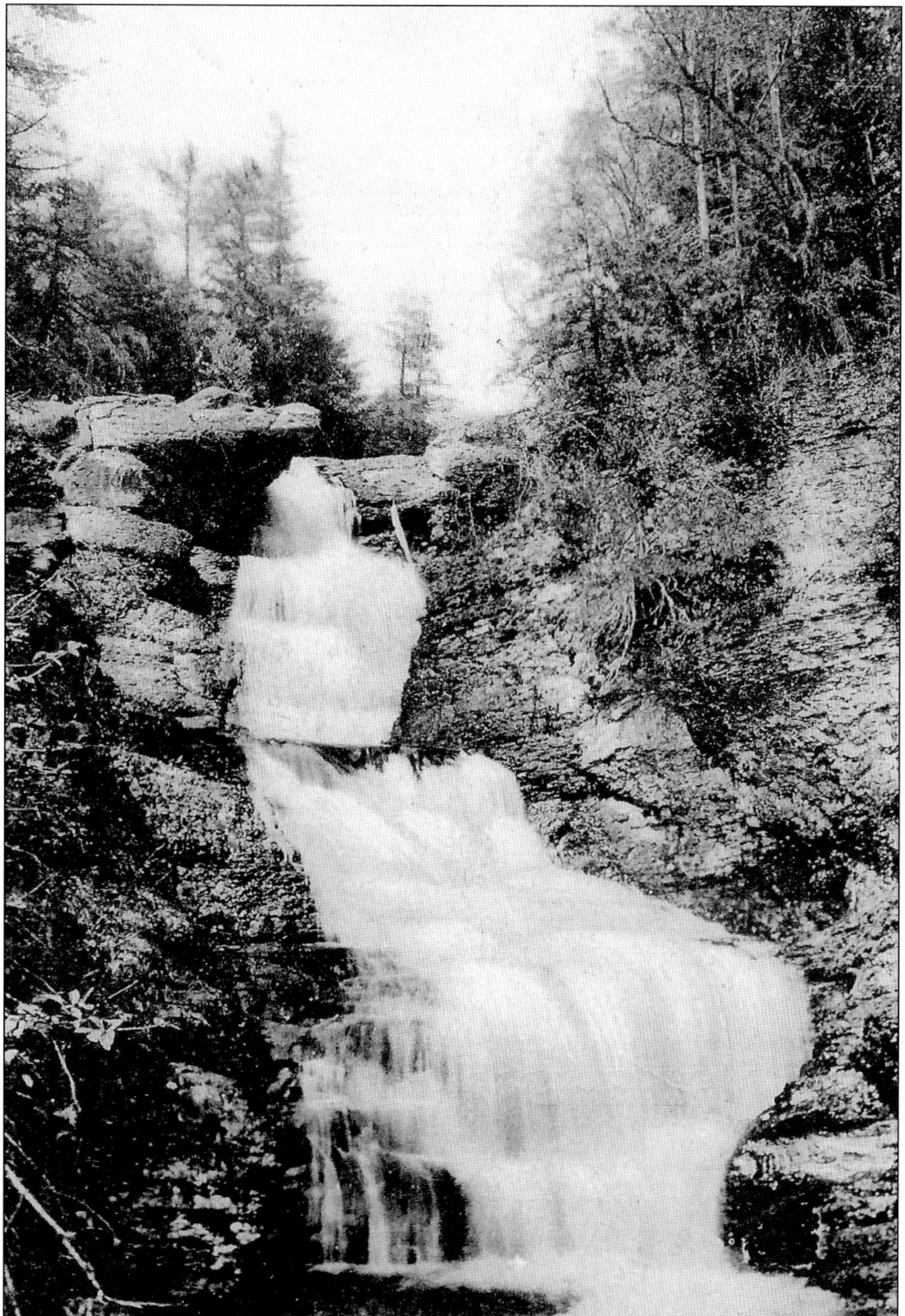

The Minisink Valley was blessed with many waterfalls fed by streams flowing from the high mountains and cliffs above the Delaware. (Courtesy of the Pike County Historical Society.)

The rich bottom land of the Minisink Valley was the prized possession of the farmers who were blessed to own it. The reign of the farmers ended when the federal government purchased or condemned the farms to make way for the Tocks Island Dam project. Hundreds of structures were destroyed as part of the project, and only a few buildings still stand today. The project was abandoned after many years of controversy because the engineers could not design pilings that could support a dam of that size. Today the area is owned by the National Park Service. The habitable buildings that remain are leased to farmers

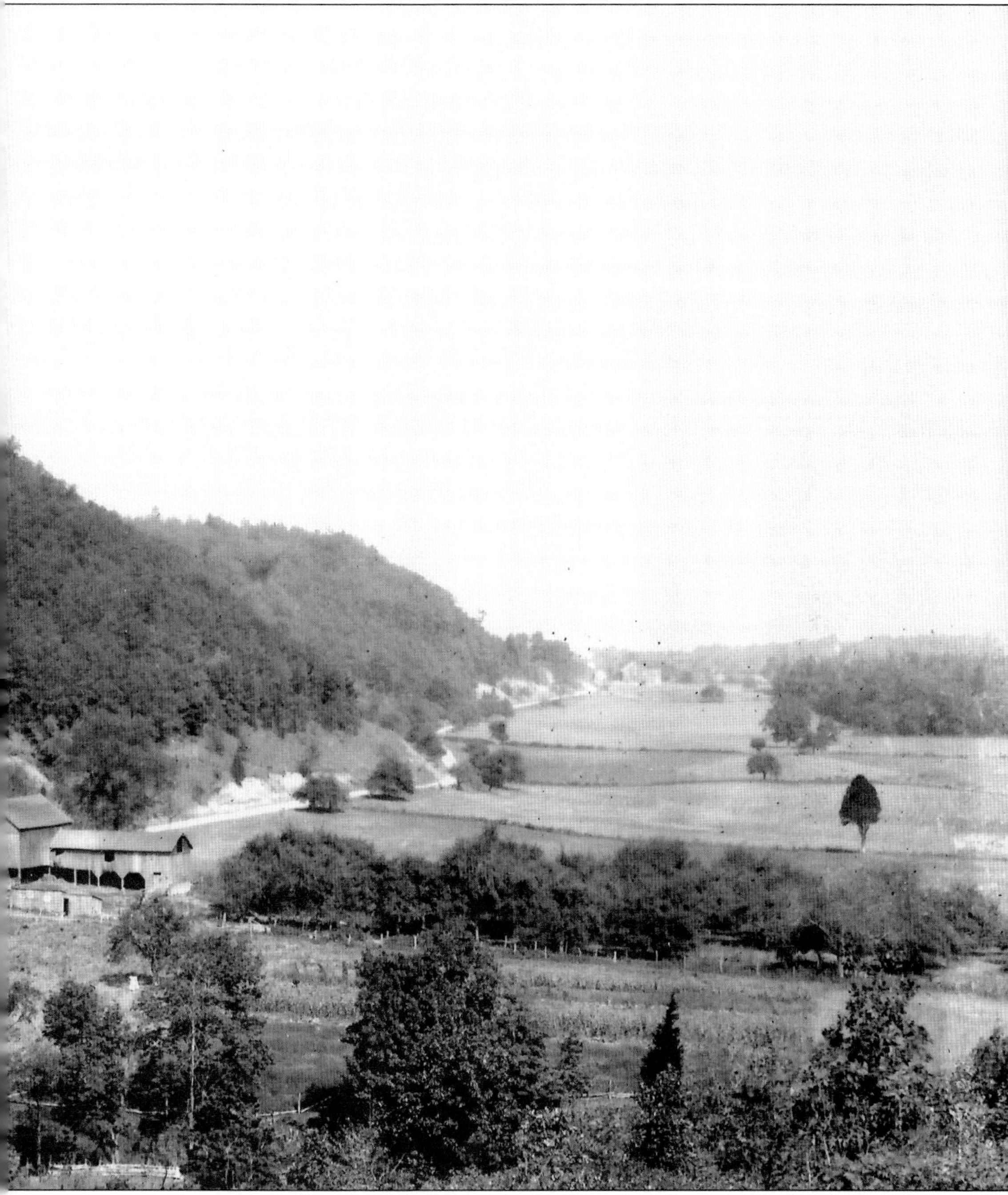

or businesses or are used by the National Park Service staff. Most of the tourist trade in the area diminished as automobile sales increased. The automobile created a new era of exploration by the American populace as they went longer distances from the cities for their vacation thrills. One popular destination became Niagara Falls. Recently, the Milford area has realized resurgence in popularity because of its convenient location to the cities. The area has even been nicknamed "the Hamptons of the West." (Courtesy of the Pike County Historical Society.)

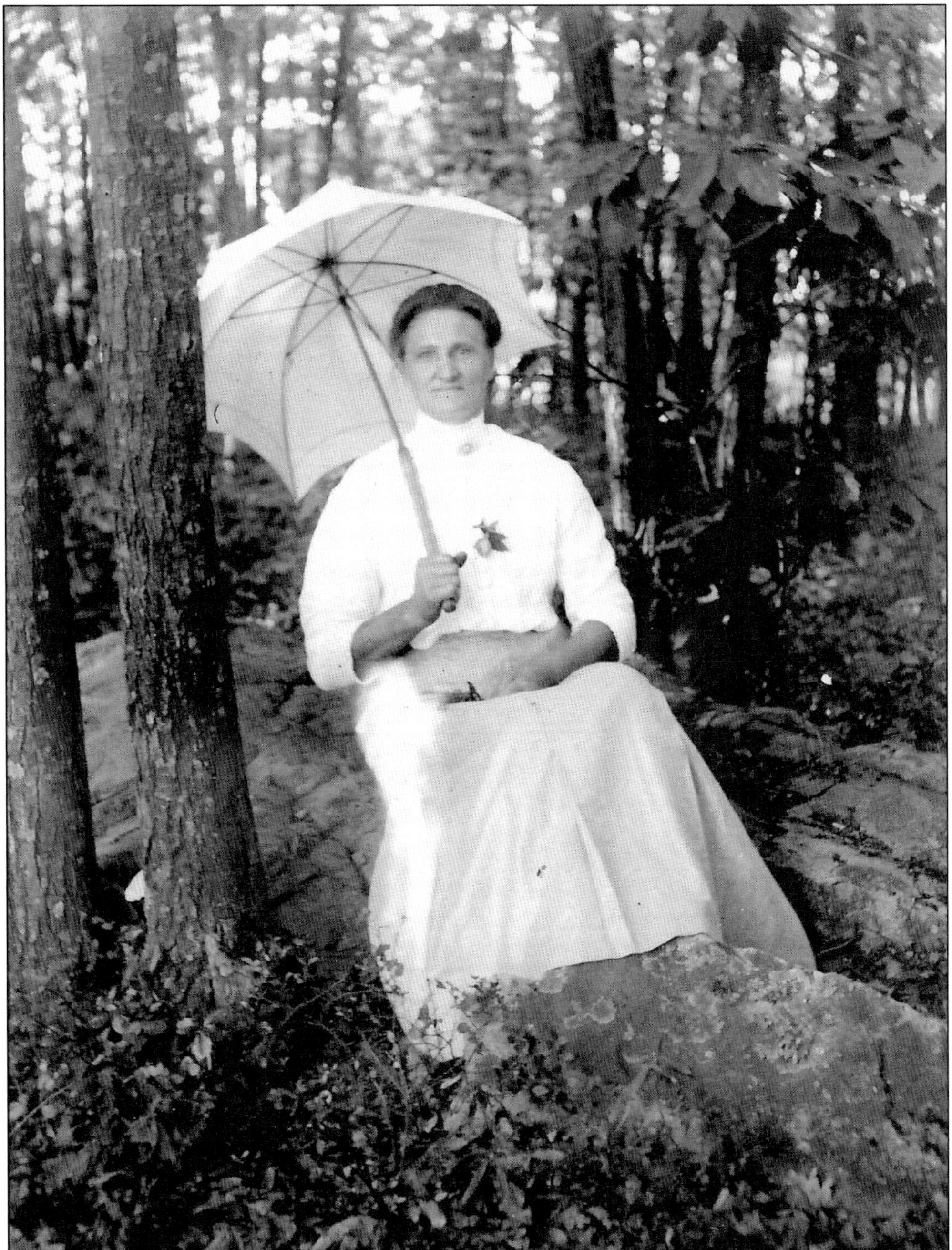

A repose in the shade of the woods was a sought-after experience by many visitors who came out of the hot city to enjoy the refreshing country air. The woods were not plagued with poison ivy, as was the area south of the Delaware Water Gap. This made the area more favorable to hiking and exploring by visitors.

Five

EDUCATION

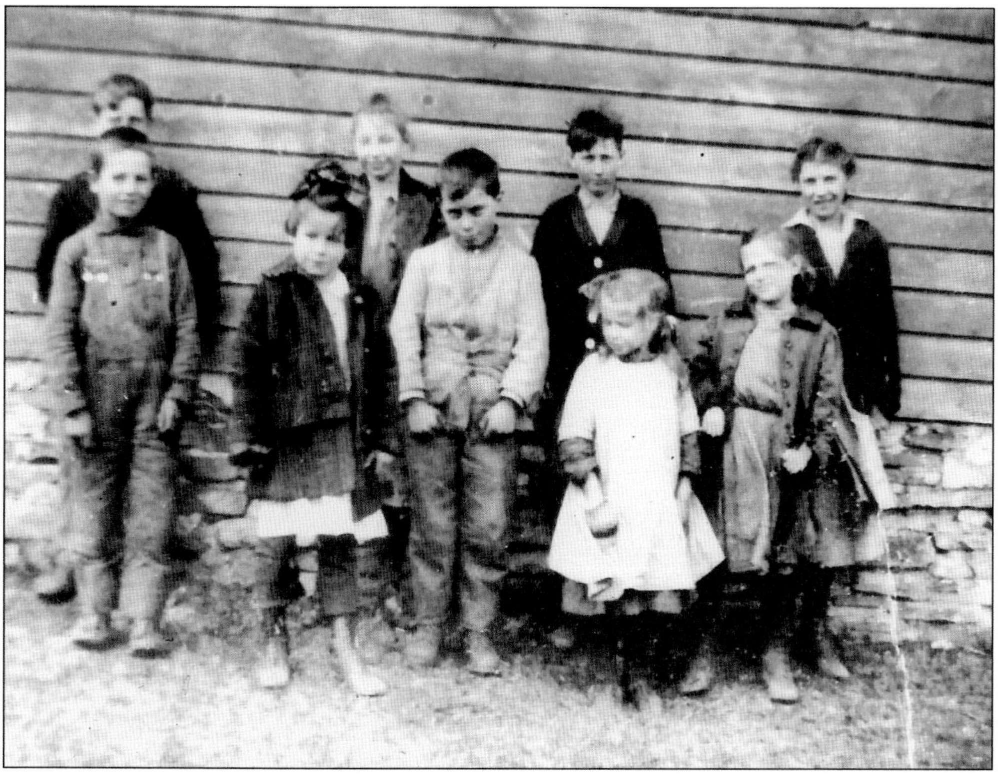

This Dark Swamp School photograph was taken in 1918. From left to right are the following: (first row) John DeGroat, Arlene Simons, Albert Simons, Kaska Kirby, and Grace Farr; (second row) Arthur DeGroat, Margaret Farr, Spenser DeGroat, and Hilda Farr. The teacher was Charles Fowler, who served the District No. 23 School, in Dingman's Ferry. (Courtesy of the Pike County Historical Society.)

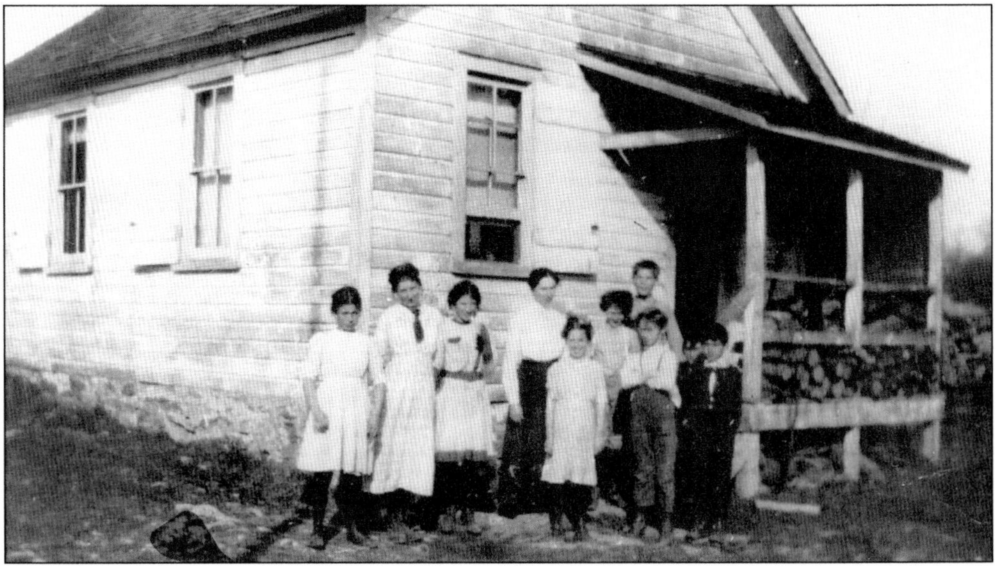

Above is a 1919 photograph of the German School, in Dingman Township. From left to right are Amy Lauer, Arlene Simons, Jane Greening, Ross Kleinstuber (rear), Harry Antaner, Jess Newfield, Joseph Greening, and Albert Simons. The teacher is Hazel Orben. Below is the Greeley School, District No. 1, which had a school year that ran from September 4 to April 2 *c.* 1900. Hattie Bradford was the teacher. The students included Margaret Tumm, Albert Vogel, Katie Hoocker, Jacob Werner, Mercella Dotter, Eugen Anderegg, Christine Knoedler, Jacob Eggenberger, Gussie Gronweldt, Paul Anderegg, Molly Vogel, Willie Loske, Ottiellie Tumm, August Pufahl, Frances Dotter, Rosie Anderegg, Bennie Steinke, Emma Goller, Louisa Eggenberger, Herman Gronweldt, Lizzie Knoedler, Gustav Tumm, Ella Loske, Marat Dotter, Annie Hoocker, Henry Goetz, Bertha Tumm, Koney Eddenberger, Freddie Pufahl, Charlie Tumm, Earnest Anderegg, Hermenie Eggenberger, Alfred Eichler, Charlie Loske, George Steinke, John Anderegg, and Lorence Goetz. (Above, courtesy of the Pike County Historical Society and Ross and Olive Kleinstuber.)

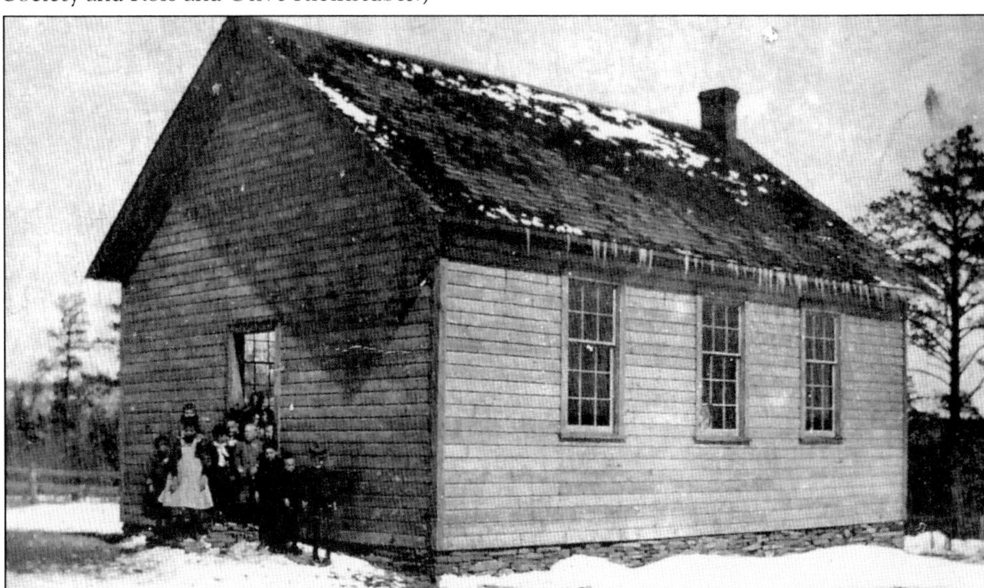

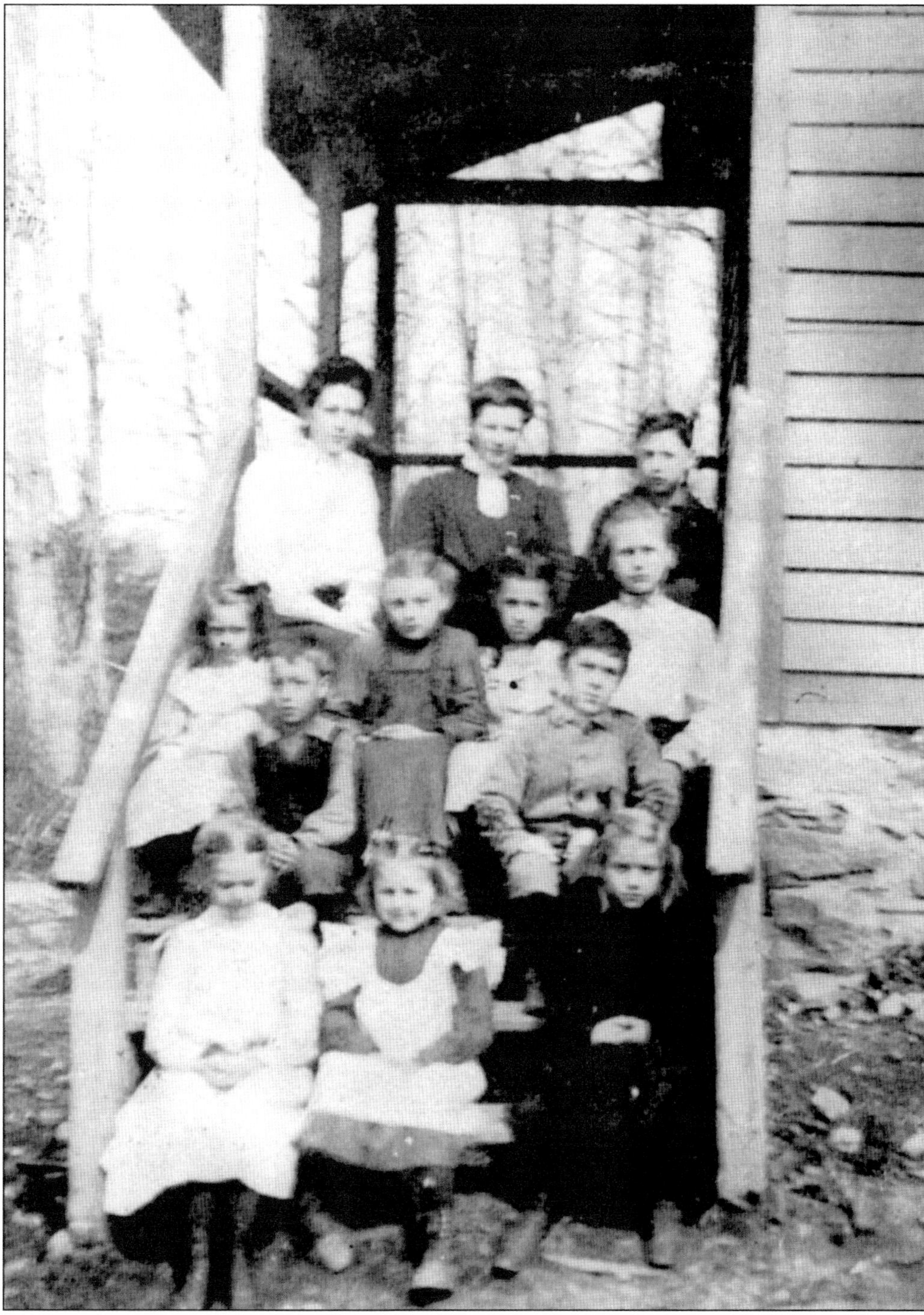

The Sawkill School was located in Dingman Township. Harriet (Bradner) Dierlumn, the teacher in 1910, was a resident of Woodtown, Twin Lakes, until her death in 1973. Pictured with their teacher are Lillie (Bridge) Badoud, Edward Doboise, Bertha (Quick) Badoud, Gertrude (Quick) Kellogue, Charlotte (Stark) Westbrook, James Stark, Lillian Hoffman, Ethel Stark, and ? Shields. (Courtesy of the Pike County Historical Society.)

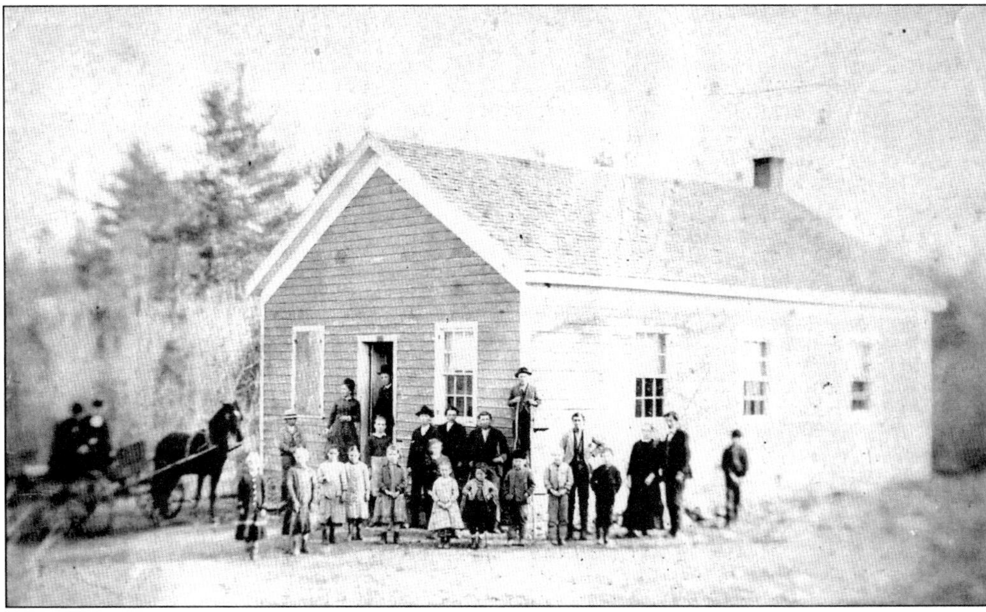

The Union School was located in Dingman Township. Included in this 1879 photograph are Charley Gebhardt, Mr. and Mrs. Ira Case (in wagon), Anna Case, Ida Case, Carrie Haffner, Nellie Clark, Katie Gebhardt, Lizzie Case, Charles Persival, Charles McCarty, George Hafner, Lewis Chattion, Sanders Persival, Lottie Persival, Ericka McCarty, Charles Case, Charles Gebhardt, Frank McCarty, Rose Lambert (teacher), Horton Woodward, Jennie Hafner, Fred Persival, Elmer McCarty, Alfred Chattlion, and John Case (on stilts). The Worzel School, pictured below in 1893, was located in Shohola. (Courtesy of the Pike County Historical Society.)

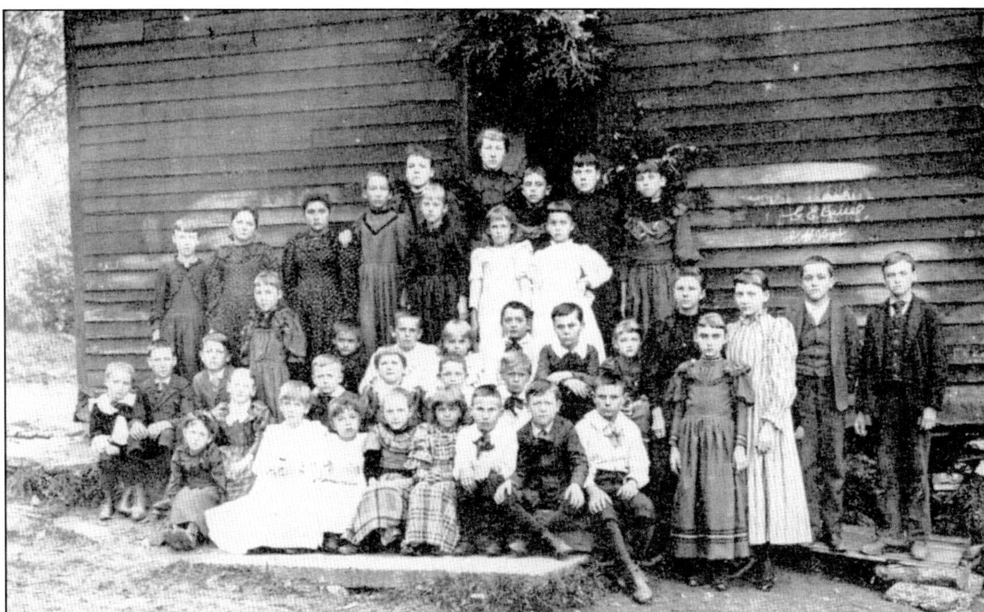

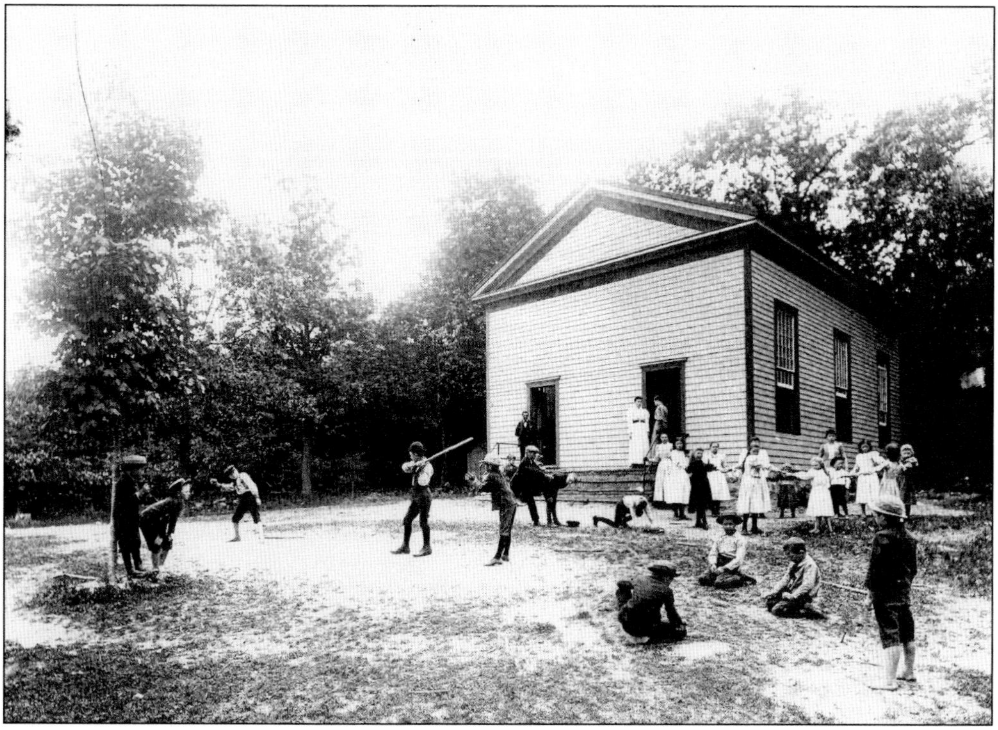

Recreation is not one of the three Rs but was included in the school curriculum. In this view, children of Dingman's Ferry are enjoying a reprieve from book learning. Shown in the 1866 photograph to the right is the Schocopee School at its original location, on Schocopee Road about one mile west of Firetower Road. This building has been relocated to Milford on Route 6 and has been restored by the Pike County Historical Society. (Above, courtesy of the Pike County Historical Society and Bill Henn; right, courtesy of the Pike County Historical Society.)

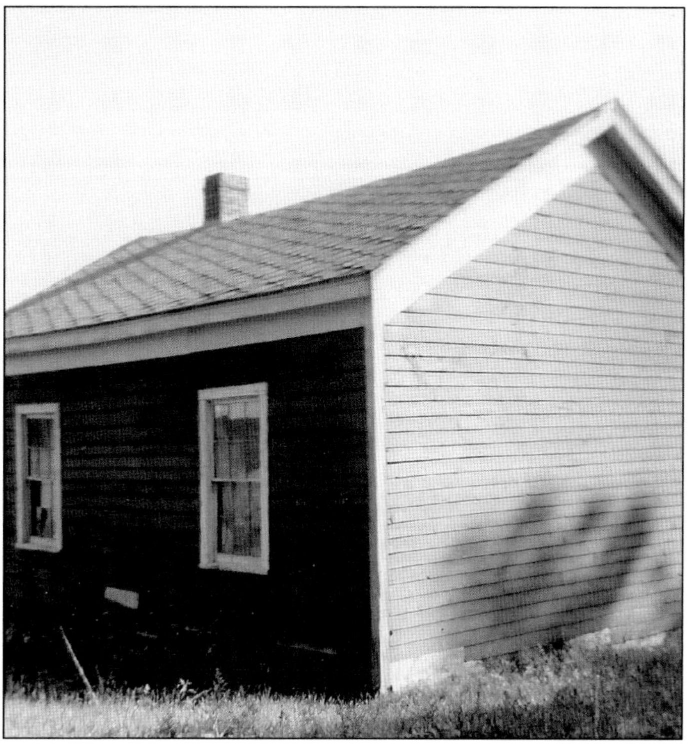

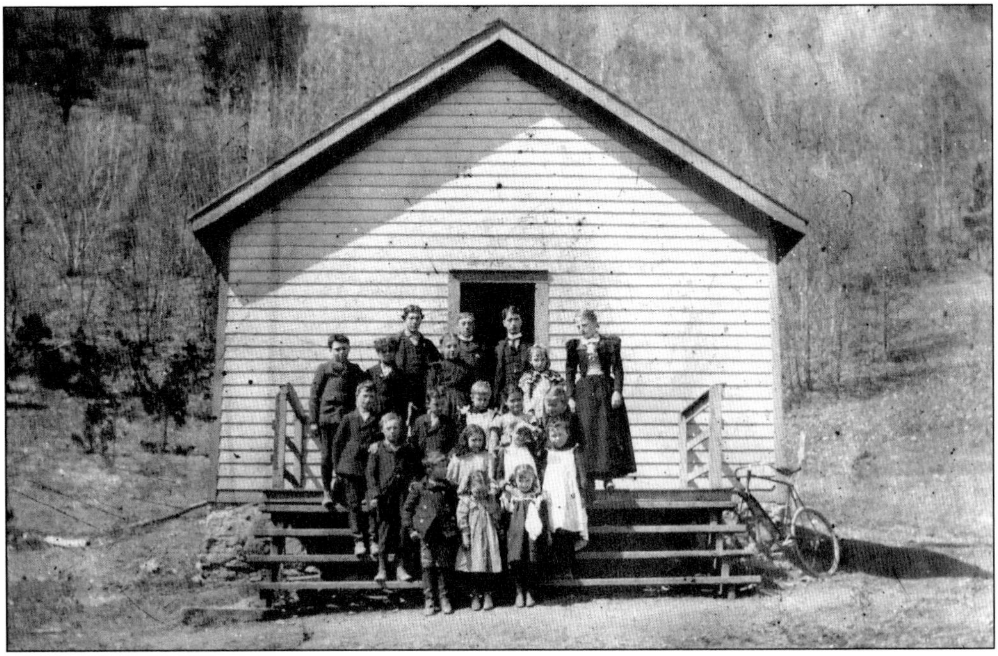

The Utter School No. 8 was located just below Milford on Route 209. This photograph was taken in April 1899. The school year would end in April so the children could help their parents with the spring planting. (Courtesy of the Pike County Historical Society.)

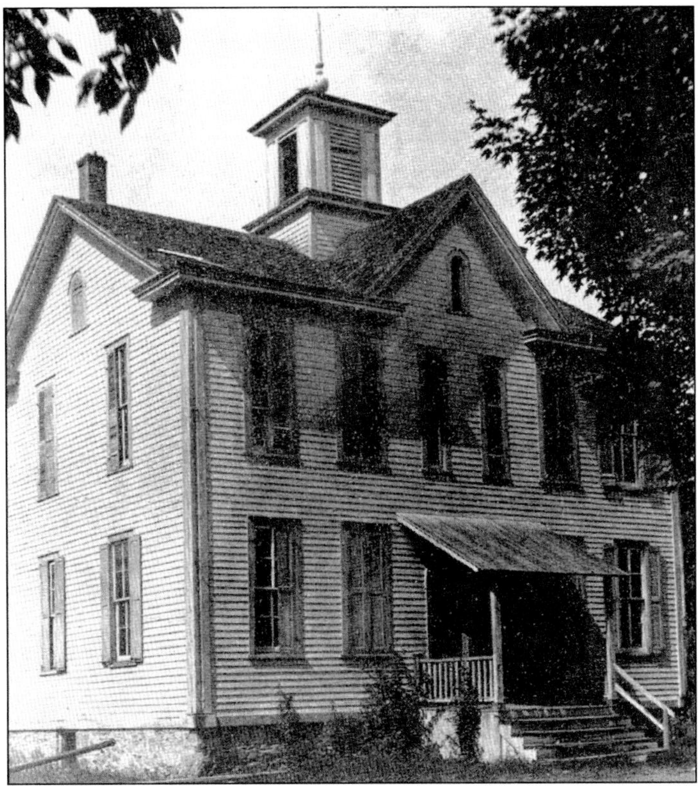

This photograph of the original Milford High School shows a good example of the shutters on Victorian-era buildings. The first-floor shutters were usually painted white or light colors and were solid to keep the heat and bugs out in the evenings when lights were in use. The second-floor shutters were louvered to allow airflow and were painted dark colors to detract bugs. (Courtesy of the Pike County Historical Society.)

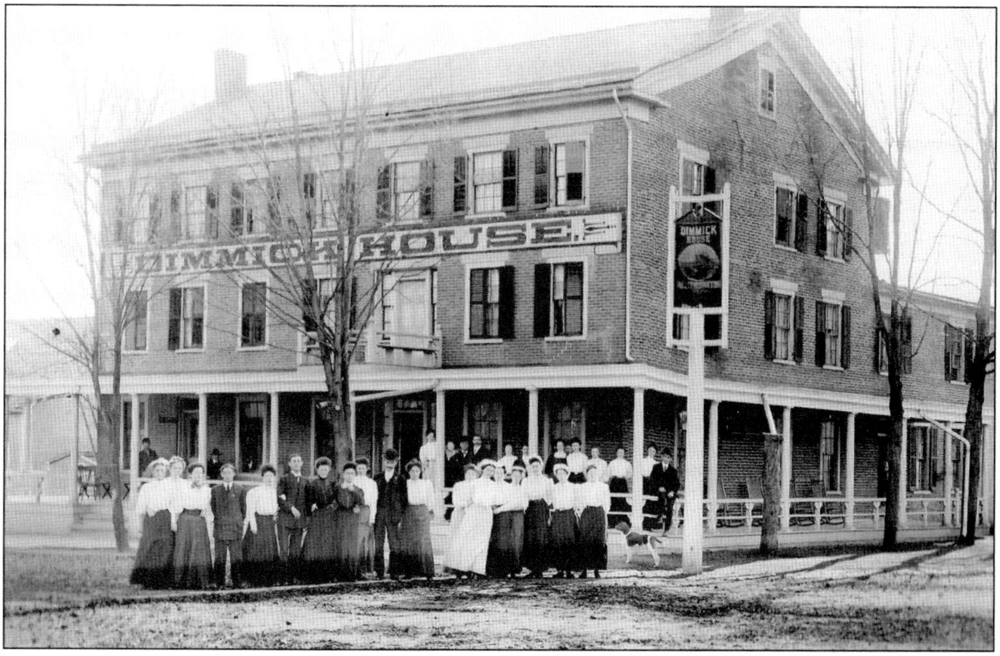

In the early 1900s, the teachers of Pike County attended a school institute at the Dimmick House. The man wearing the bowler is J. F. Molony. The man on rail is Howard Allen. The photograph below, taken by Howard Allen of Mill Rift, includes H. Allen, Olla Hazelton, Al Stage, and J. F. Molony. (Courtesy of Diane Banach.)

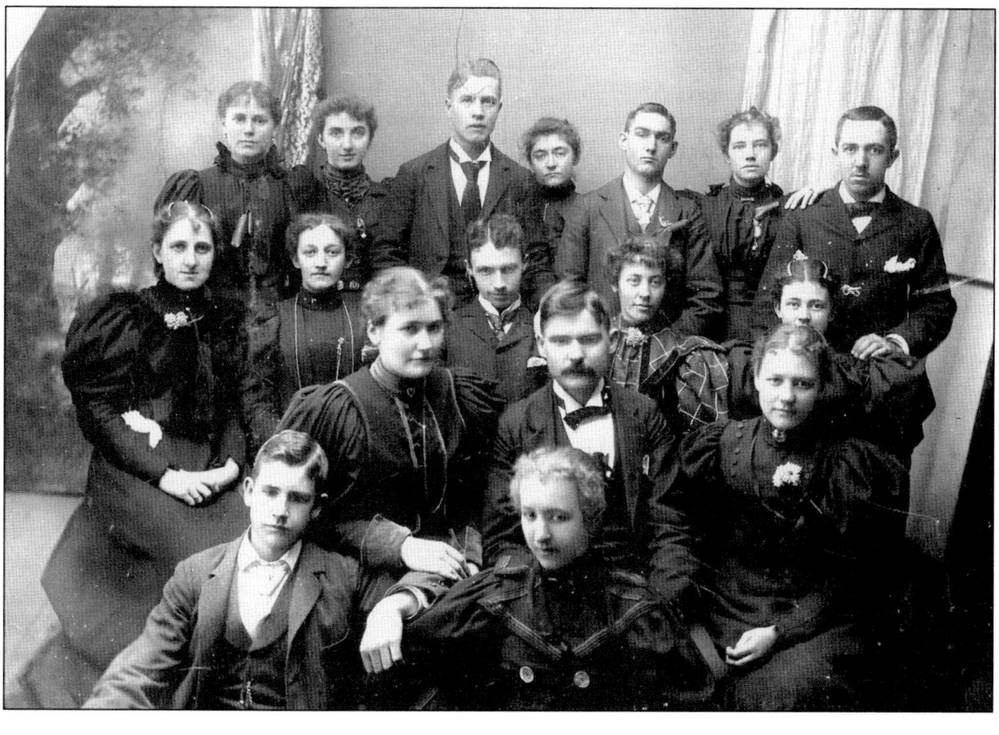

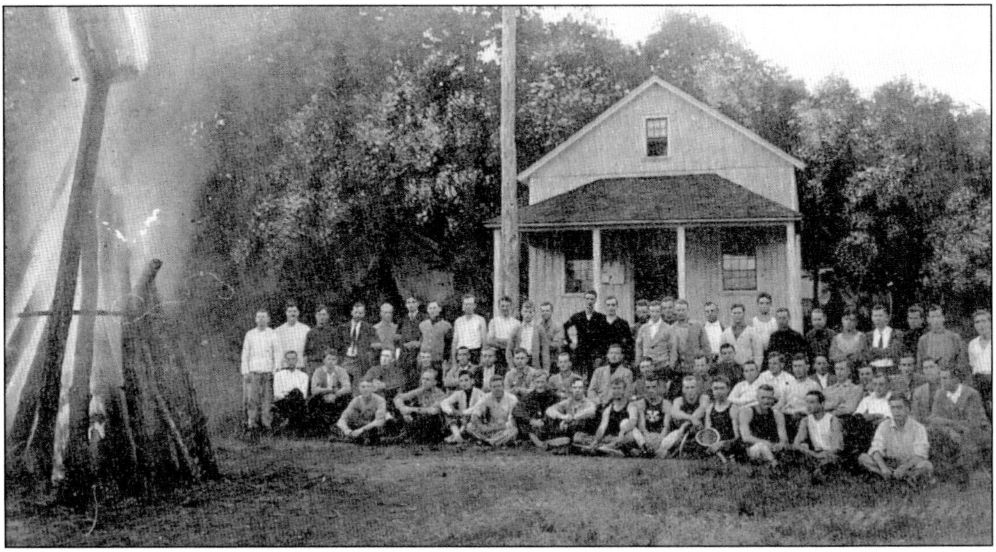

Above, members of the Yale School of Forestry Camp, in Milford, enjoy a bonfire. Below, the campgrounds of the summer school are well attended. The forests of eastern Pennsylvania were a good study for the forestry students.

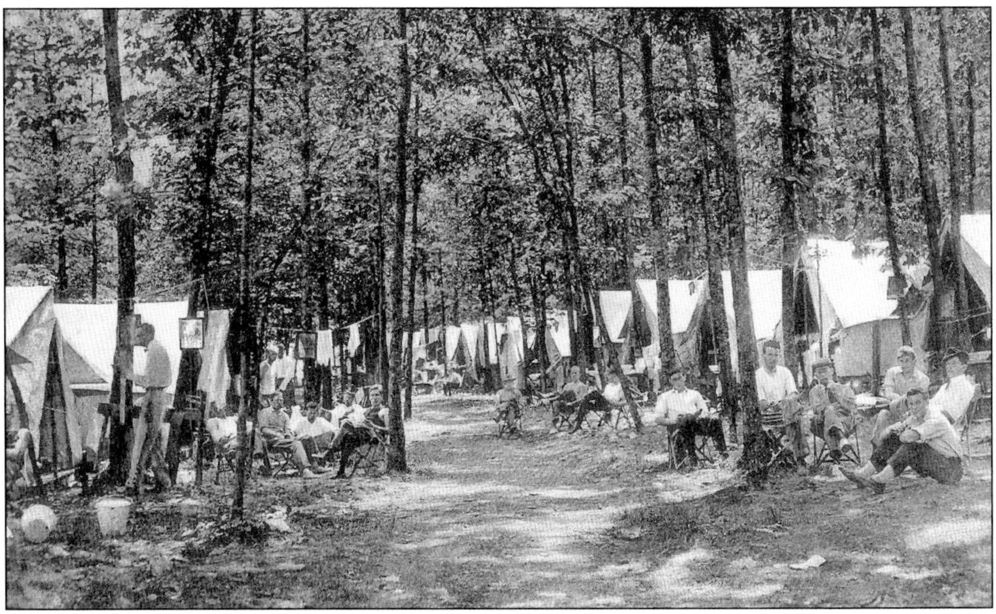

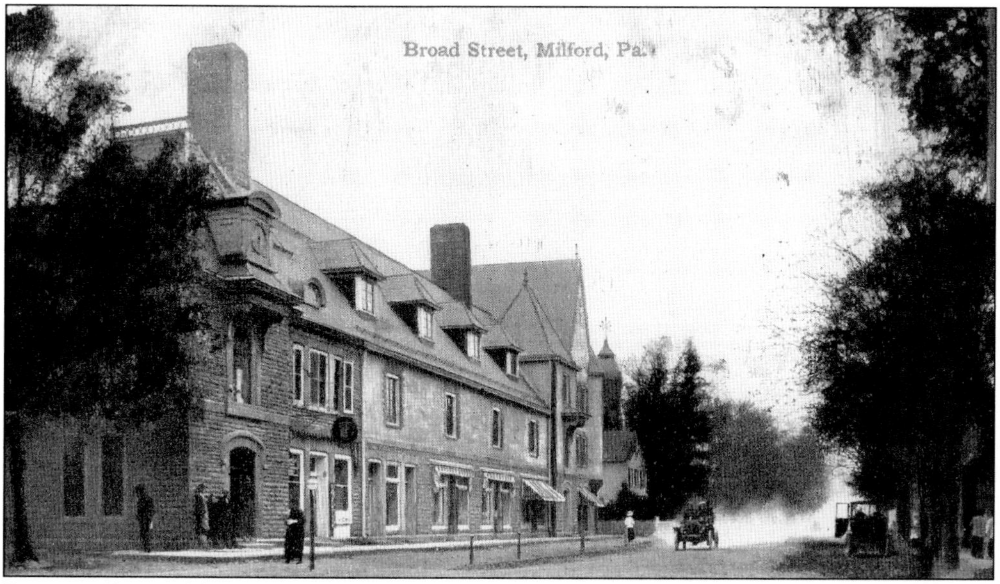

Forest Hall was added to the original building by Gov. Gifford Pinchot. He included classrooms on the second floor for the Yale School of Forestry's summer school.

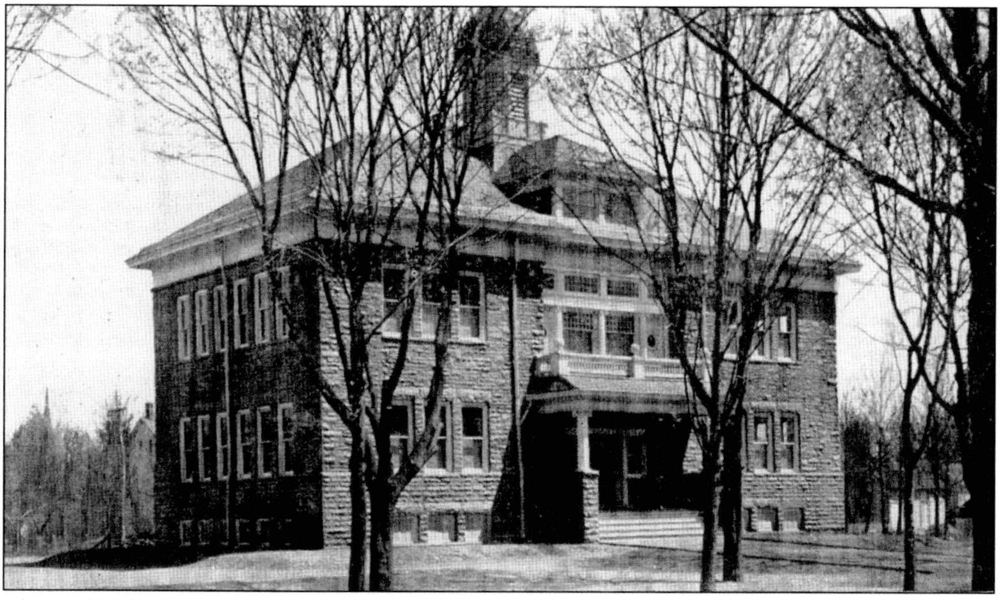

The Milford High School was the pride and joy of the town. Its central location made it the heart of community events and meetings. Built in 1904, it served as a high school and then as the elementary school (grades one through six) until it was sold to become a merchant center and commercial offices.

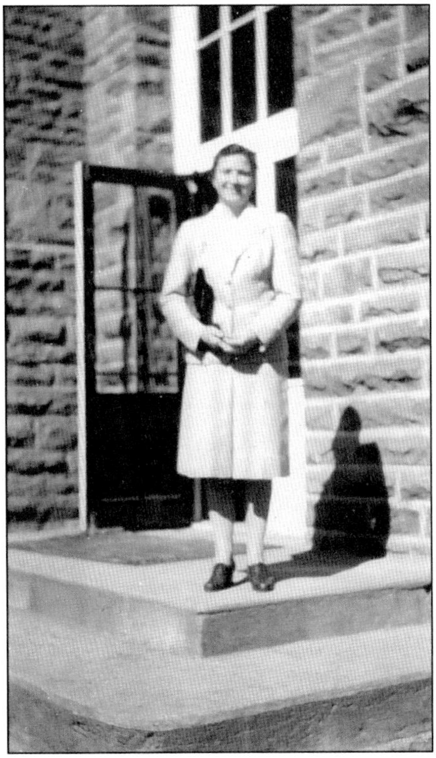

Alice Stevens, a teacher hired for the 1945–1946 school year, taught English and French at Milford School. (Courtesy of Criss Crosby Stone.)

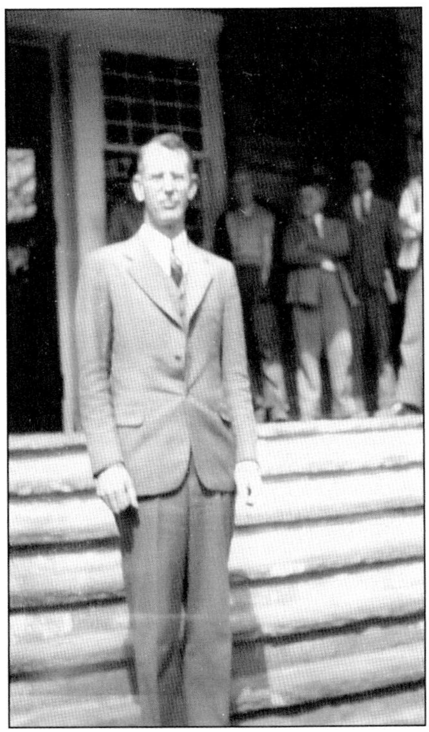

John Somes, hired in 1944–1945, taught math and health sciences in the eighth grade. (Courtesy of Criss Crosby Stone.)

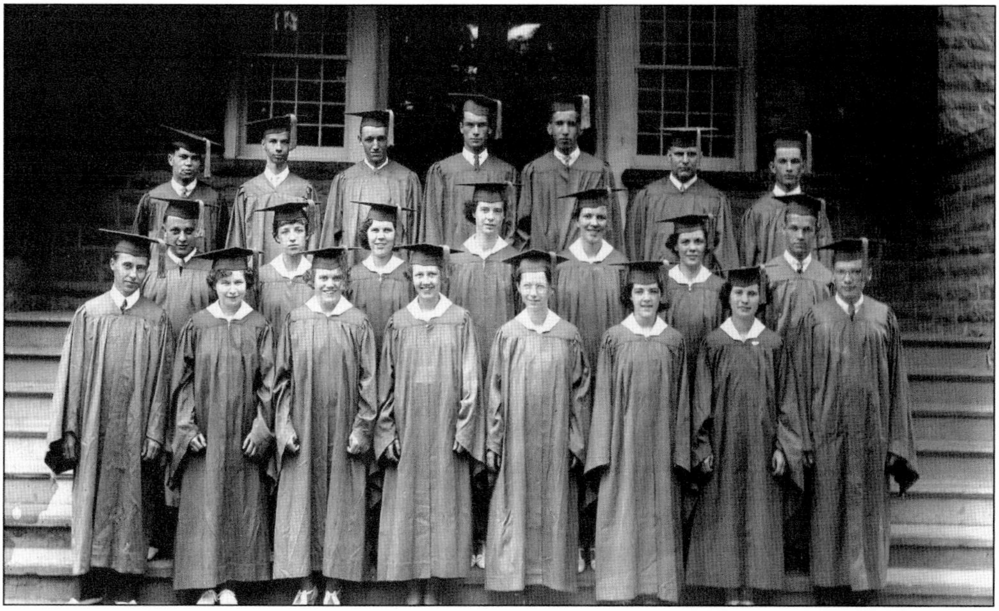

This photograph of the graduating class of 1937 shows, from left to right, the following: (first row) Otto Kittel, Elsie Kittel Bensley, Bernice Kellogg Hoehne, Victorine Spotts, Regina Castle, Maybelle Hotalen, Gladys Hess, and Kurt Nork; (second row) George Bopp, Virginia Daumann, Bertha Jagger Linsley, Dorothy Orben Cole, Lela Foster, Gertrude Nork Rosencrance, and Gifford Case; (third row) George Wyckoff, Albert Allgrumn, John Kurz, Lawrence Herman, Harley Hinkel, Willard Hinkel, and Andrew "Jim" Armstrong. (Courtesy of the Pike County Historical Society.)

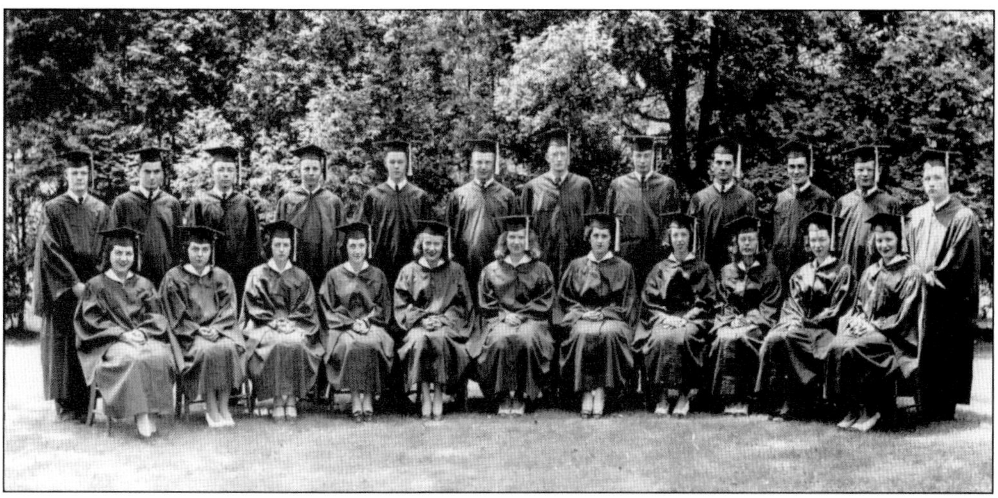

The graduating class of 1942 at Milford High School poses here. From left to right are the following: (first row) Patricia Goviolle, Virginia Quick, Dorothy Theurich, Genevieve Schnoir, Elsie Almer, Betty Depuy, Dorothy Takosh, Arlene Routte, Frances Crosby, Marilyn Boker, and Marcella Moureaux; (second row) Walter Case, Paul Altoner, Douglas Wolfe, Edward Naeglen, Walter Myer, Edson Helms, Jim Middough, Jim McKittrick, Robert Husson, Paul Gebhardt, Robert Stefenik, and Paul Vooux. (Courtesy of Frances Hotalen.)

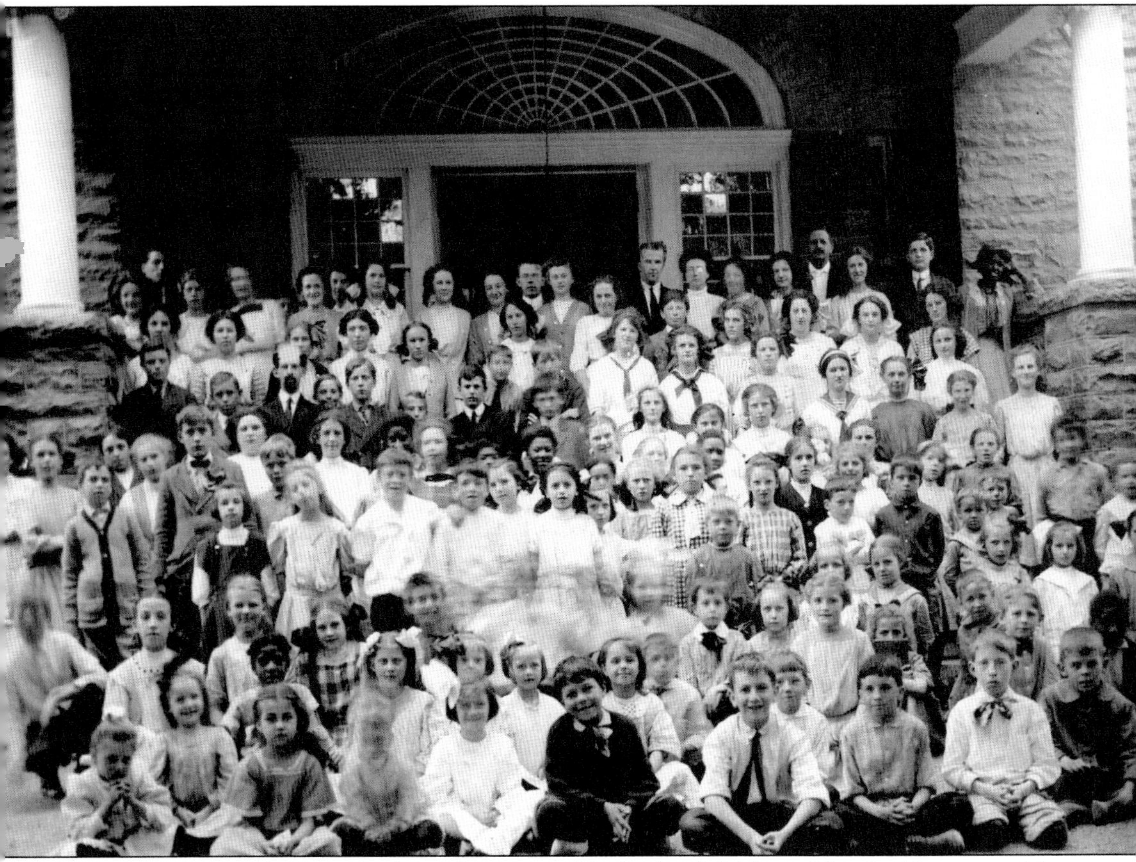

The *c*. 1920s photograph above features Milford schoolchildren. This building was able to accommodate grades 7 through 12 for many years. Eventually, a separate high school was built to meet the needs of the growing student population. The building became the home for grades one through six until the new elementary and middle schools were built on the Delaware Valley School District campus. (Courtesy of the Pike County Historical Society.)

Six

CELEBRATIONS

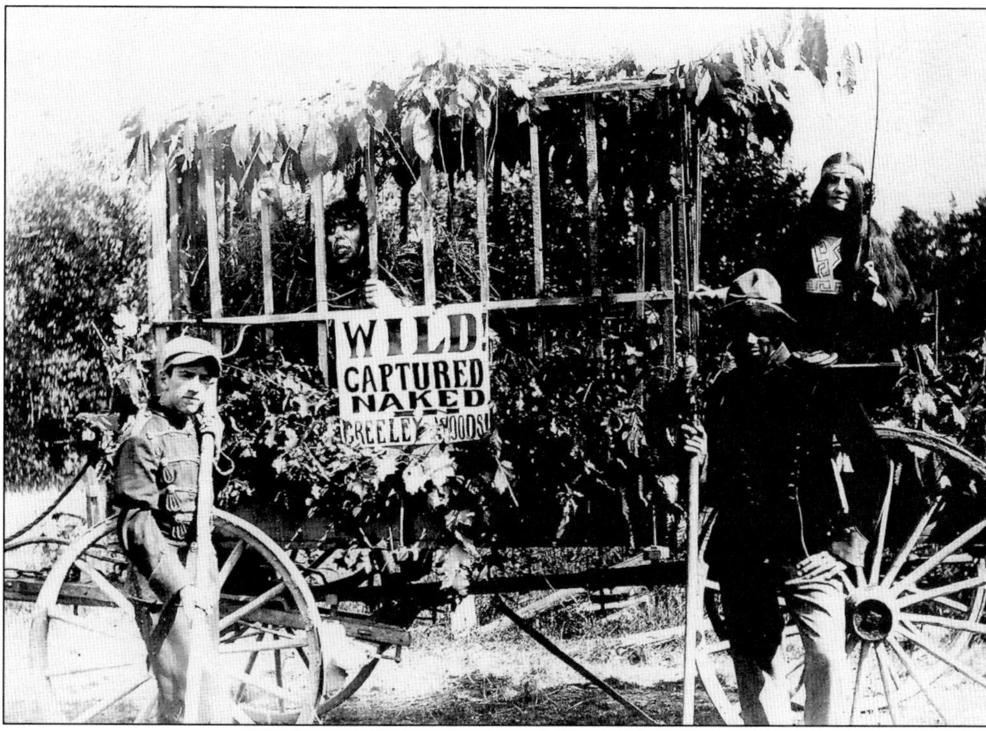

The fun and frivolity of a parade were always welcome. A parade was often a time for groups to band together to share their talents and tout their community spirit. "I Love a Parade" chimed up and down the streets as people lined the sidewalks to see what new spectacles the event would bring.

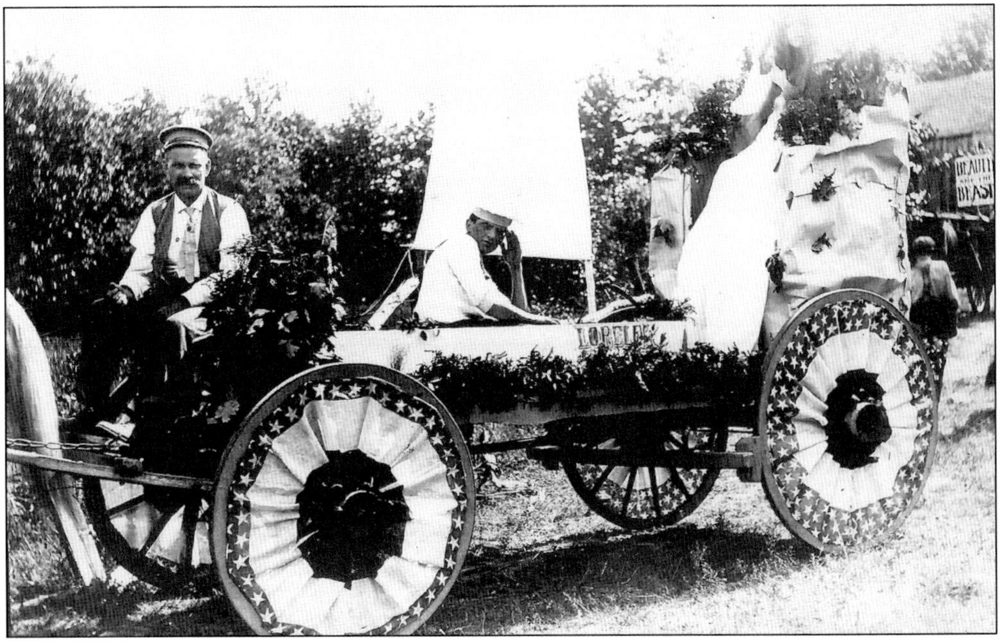

This patriotic horse-drawn float shows how the citizen groups went all out to decorate their wagons and floats. Uncle Sam was a frequent visitor during Fourth of July parades.

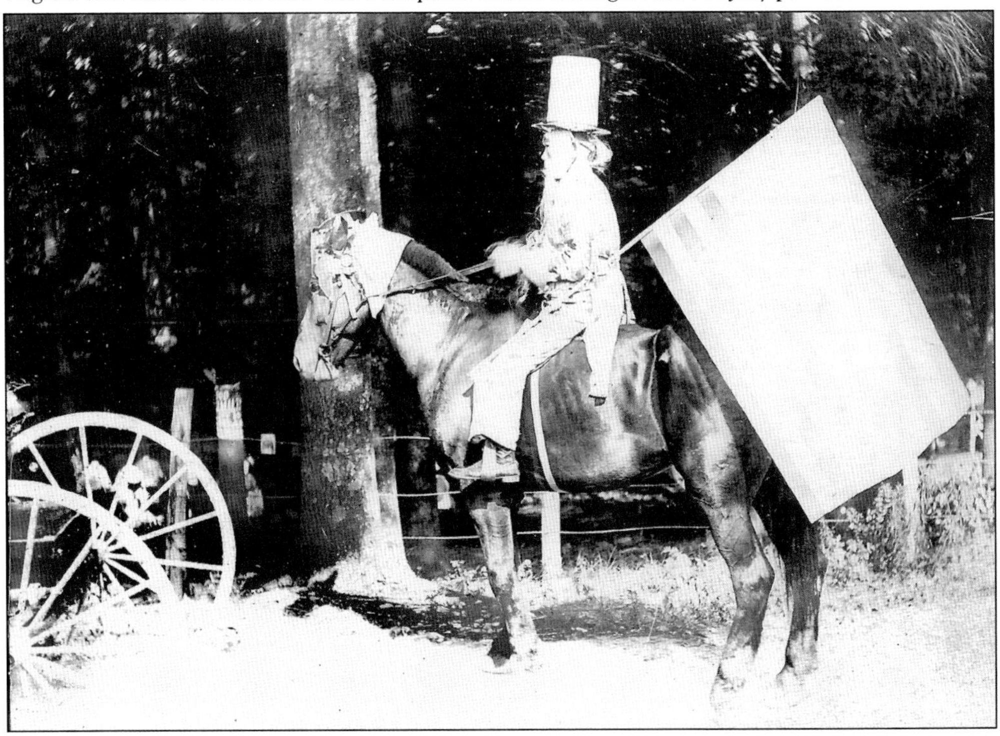

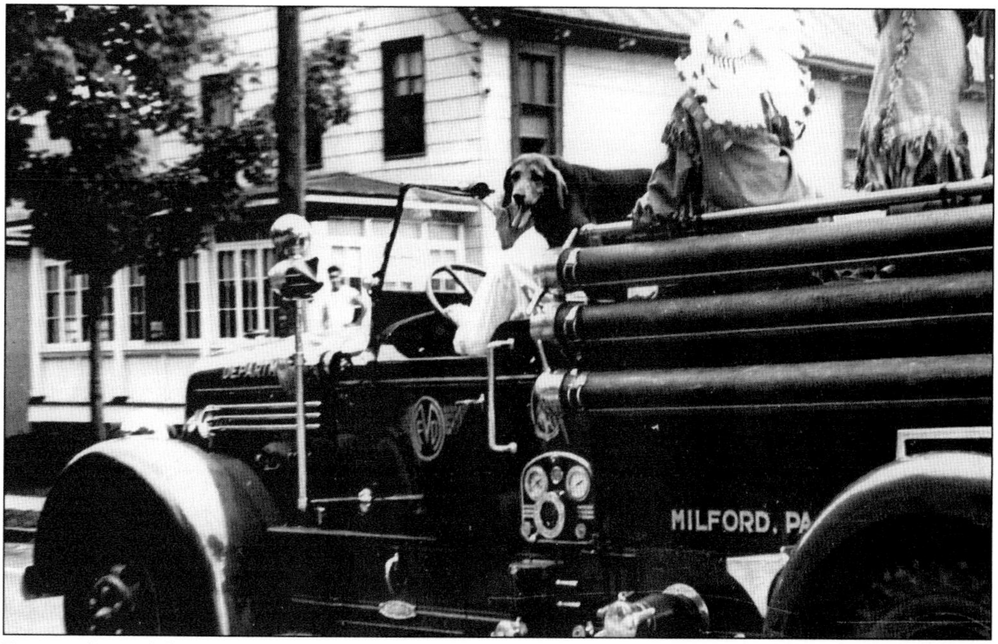

Fire trucks and the volunteers who manned them have always been important to the community. It was not uncommon for a businessman to leave a meeting mid-sentence or a teacher to leave a classroom when the sound of the sirens pealed through town. Three major fires in town were the Bluff House, the Crissman, and the Coachman's Inn. Several of these fires were captured by home movie cameras. (Courtesy of the Pike County Historical Society.)

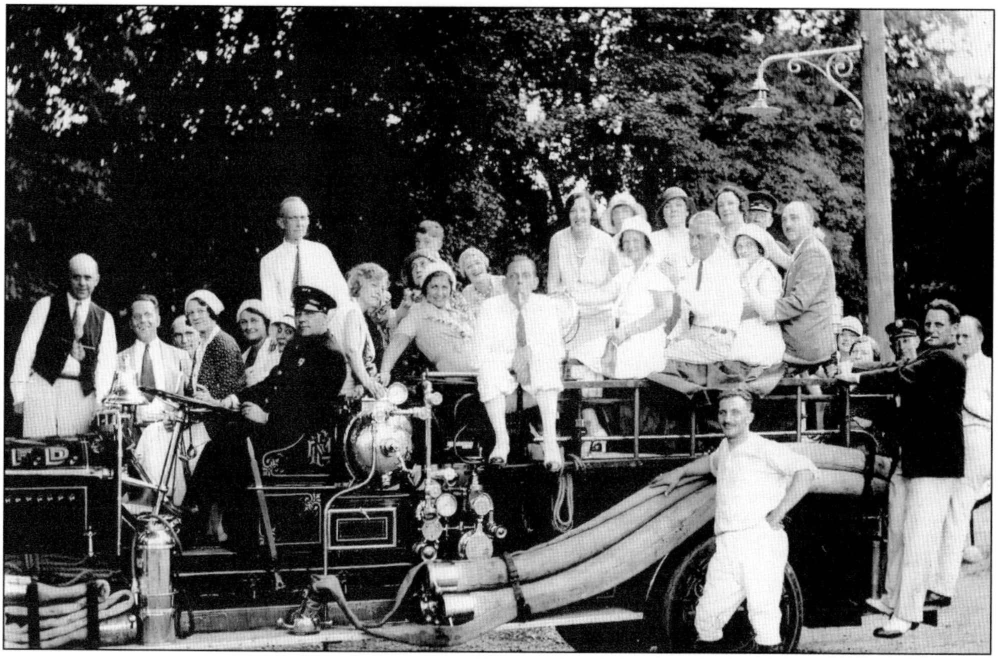

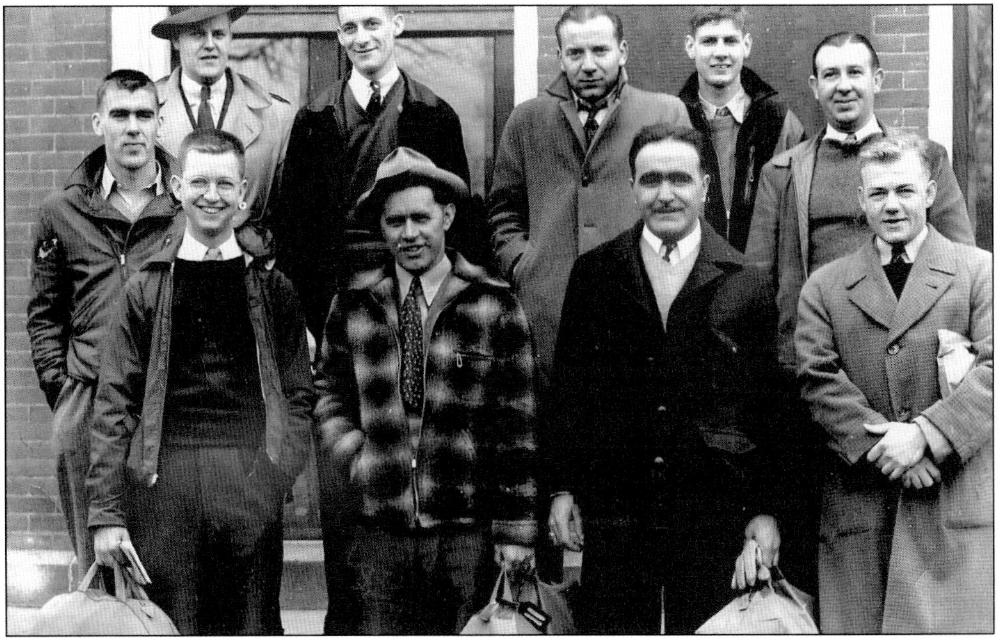

The citizens of Milford thanked their military heroes with special memorials and parades. The town also kept a photographic record of all the young men who went to war to defend our nation. These photographs show just two of the groups of inductees from Milford during World War II. The bravery of these men in time of war was an example of what made our country great. (Courtesy of Carol Ramagosa and the Pike County Historical Society.)

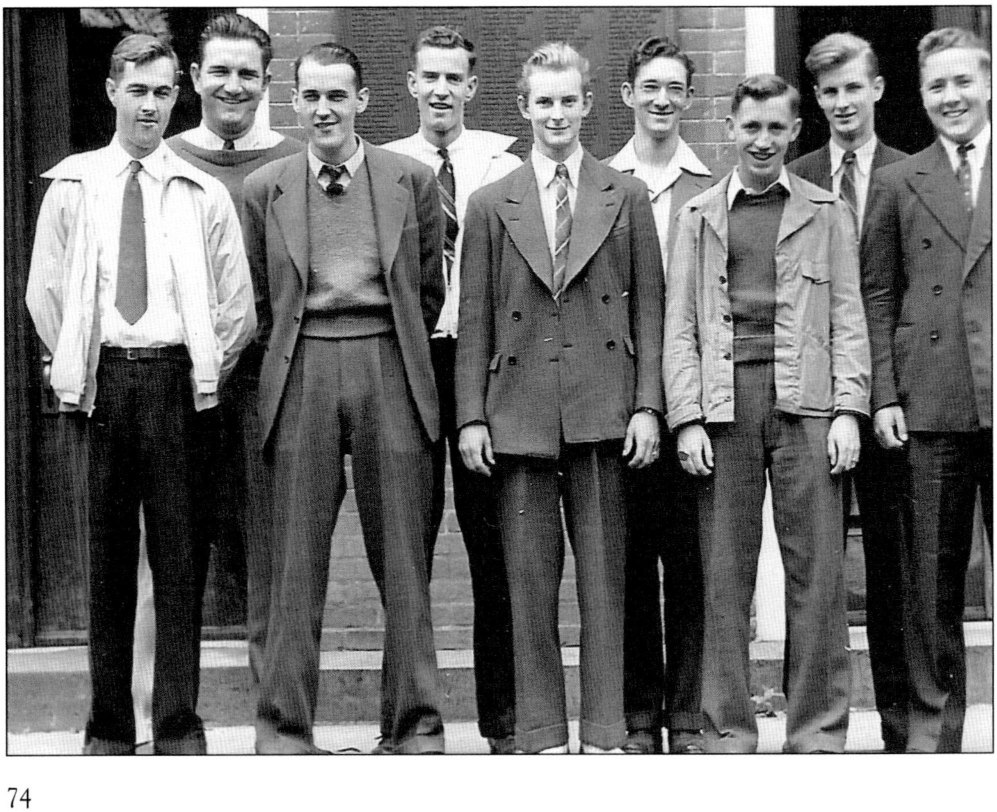

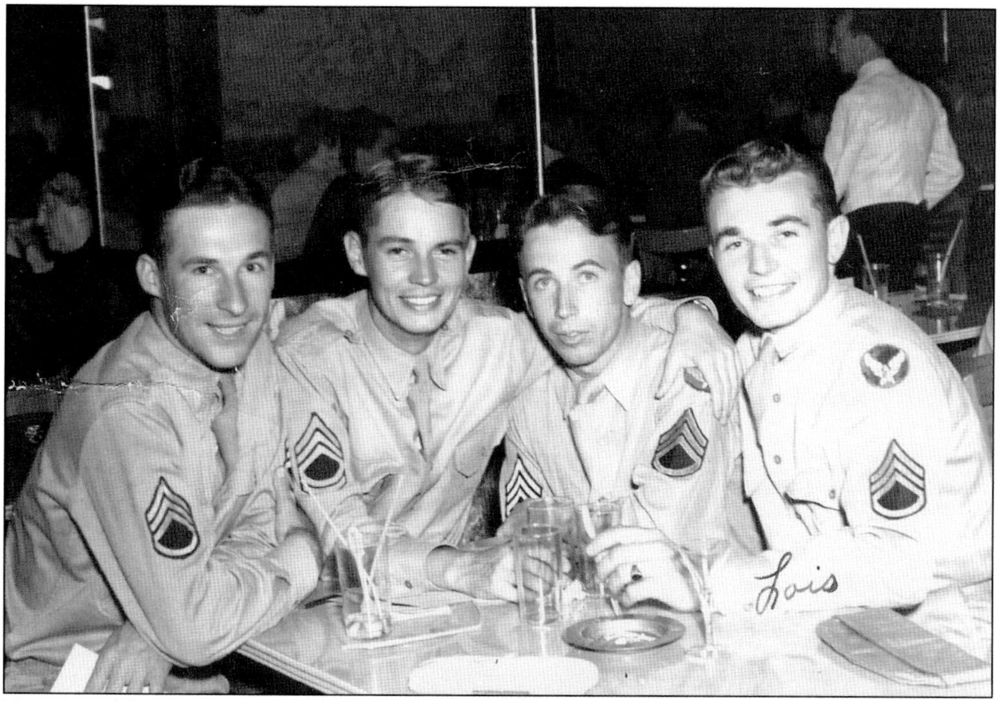

New friendships were made while the soldiers were a long way from home. Allen Titus (above, right) is enjoying some time off with fellow pilots. They were based in England and fought on the European front. In the photograph to the right, Charles Stress poses in full jump gear at an airport in England.

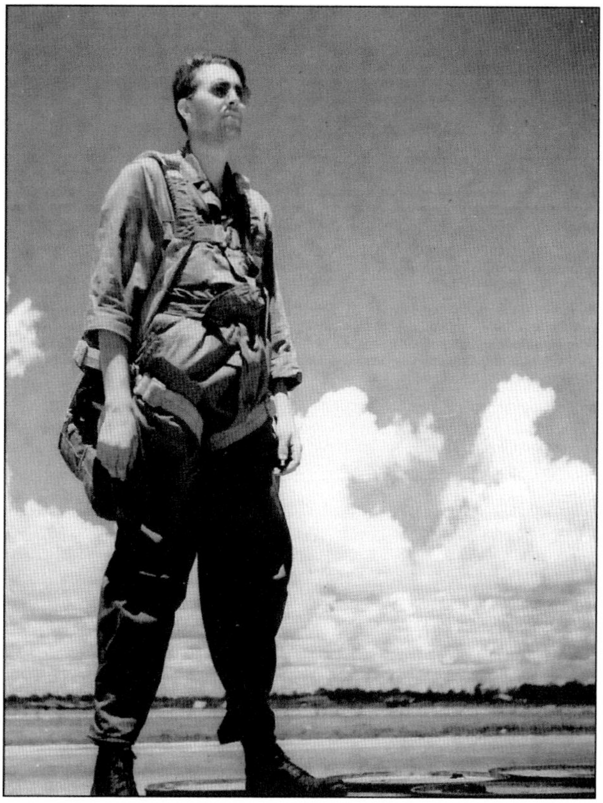

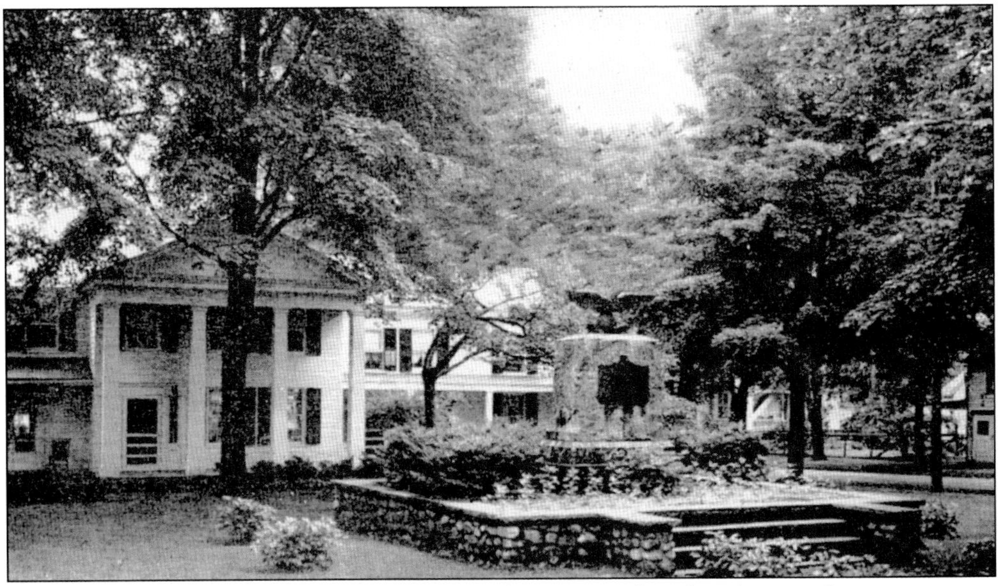

The citizens who were sacrificed in war have been remembered with special monuments in Milford. In the courtyard just north of the Tom Quick Inn on Broad Street is a fitting memorial to the soldiers lost in the world wars. Below, the Daughters of the Union unveil the Civil War monument placed on the Milford Courthouse. (Courtesy of the Pike County Historical Society.)

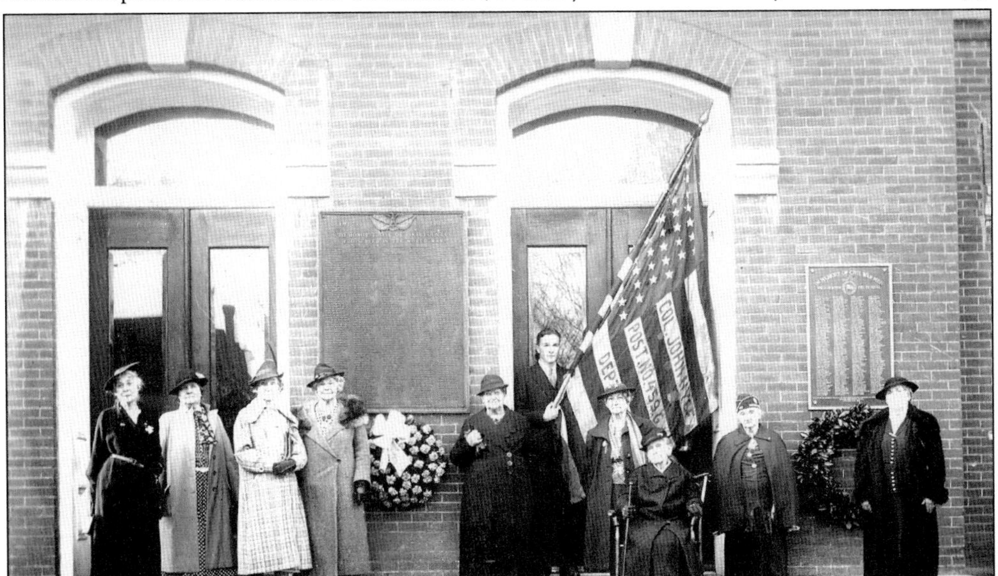

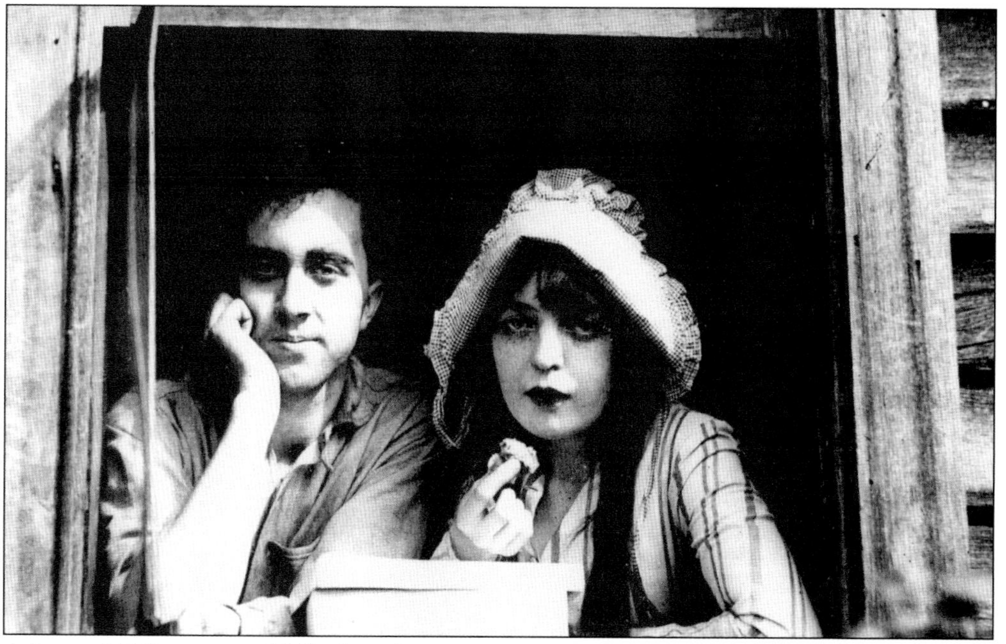

A bevy of VIPs came to Milford to shoot movies using the unique scenery of the area. Local citizens were often cast as extras. Resident Frank Crissman, seen above, was an extra in *The Informer,* and the actress is a member of the Biograph Players. Below, Mary Pickford and Walter Miller are caught in a dramatic moment while shooting a scene of *The Informer* on the cliffs overlooking the Minisink Valley. D. W. Griffith directed the film in 1912. (Courtesy of the Pike County Historical Society.)

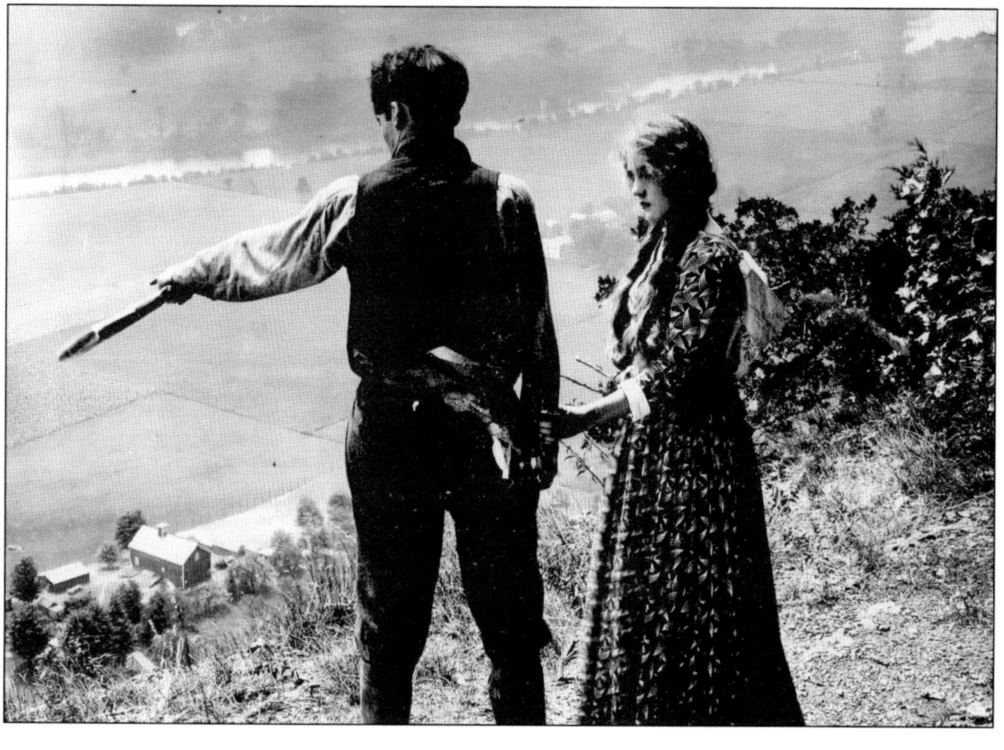

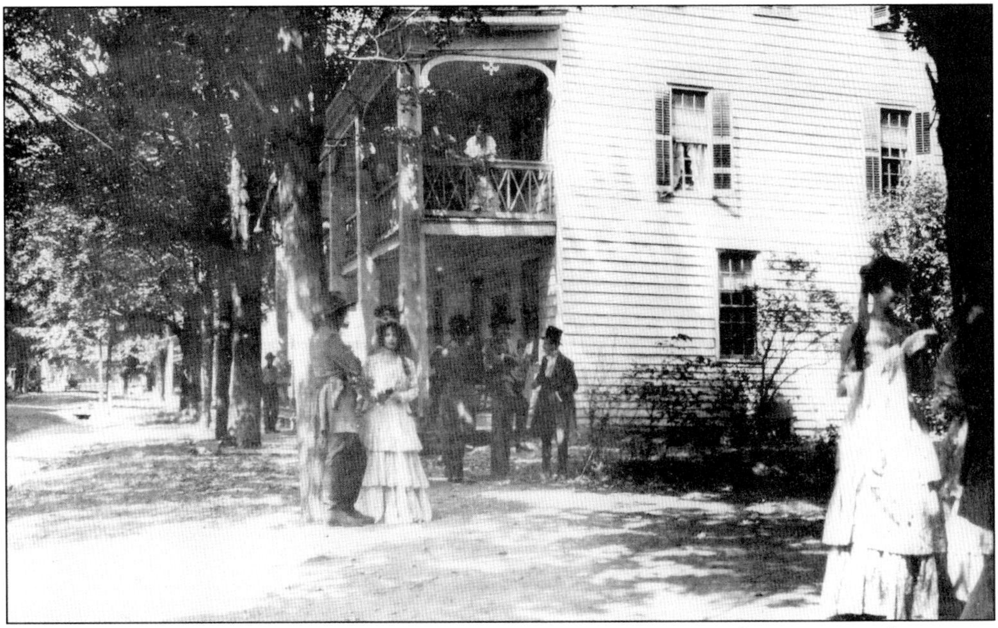

The Sawkill House and the streets of Milford provided a perfect setting for an 1800s village scene in *The Informer*. Below, actor Francis X. Bushman enjoys a moment with the local children. The children are, from left to right, Lillian Piergiorgi, Thorton Ryder, Mabel Ryder, and Edna Van Tassell. (Courtesy of the Pike County Historical Society.)

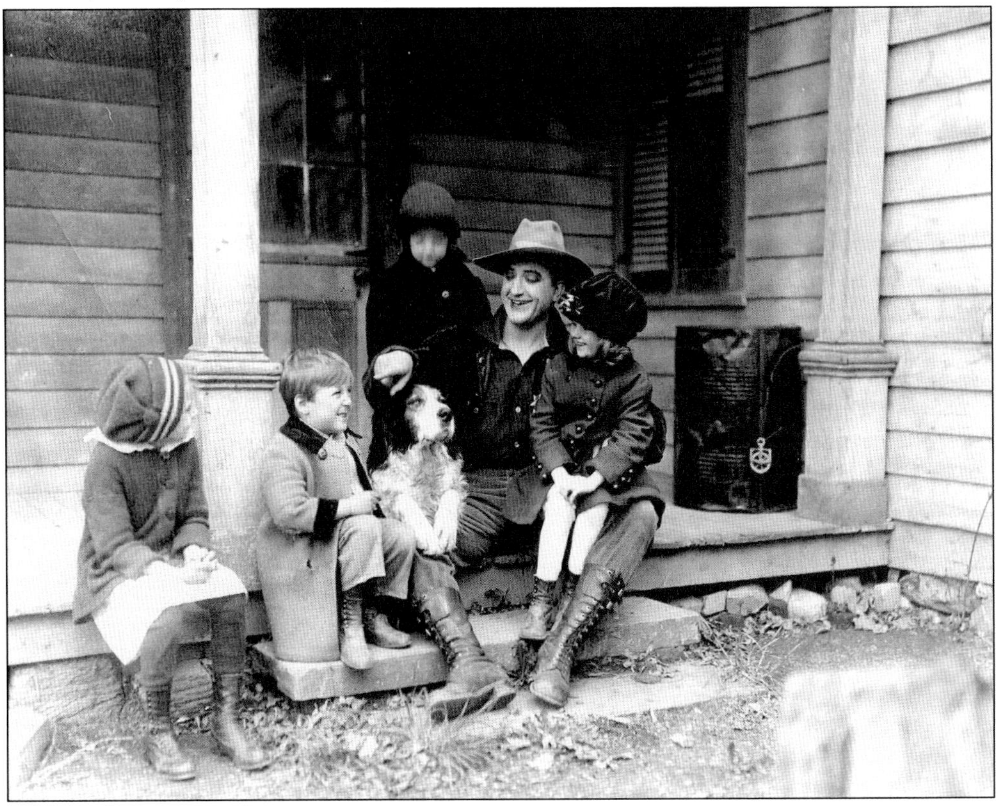

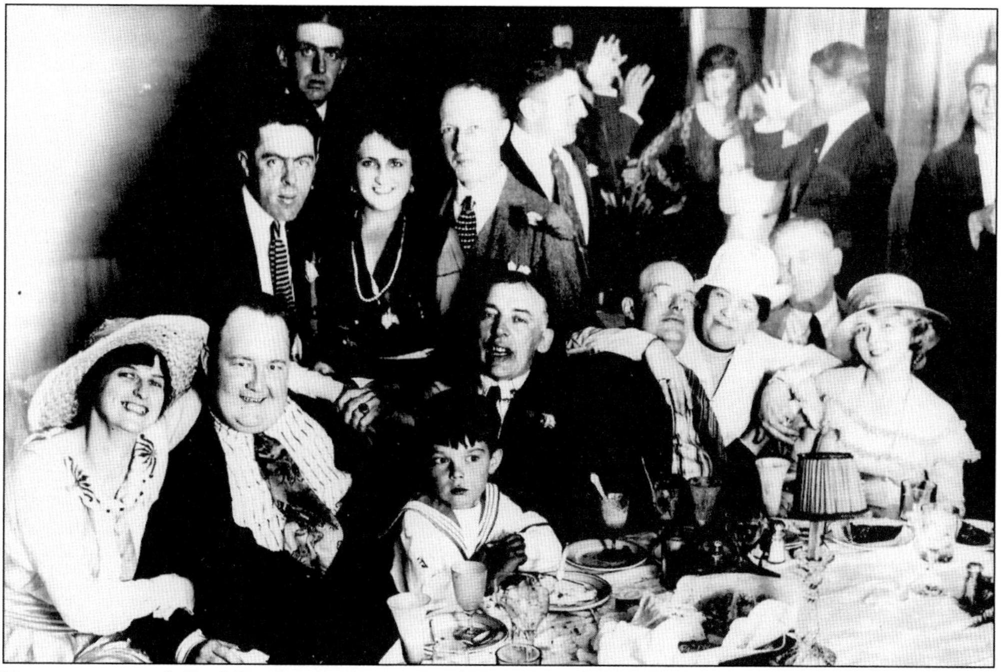

Evenings were full of fun for the actors as they enjoyed a good meal in town. Milford resident William Van Tassell (below, behind the wheel) was hired to chauffeur the actors while they were in town. (Courtesy of the Pike County Historical Society.)

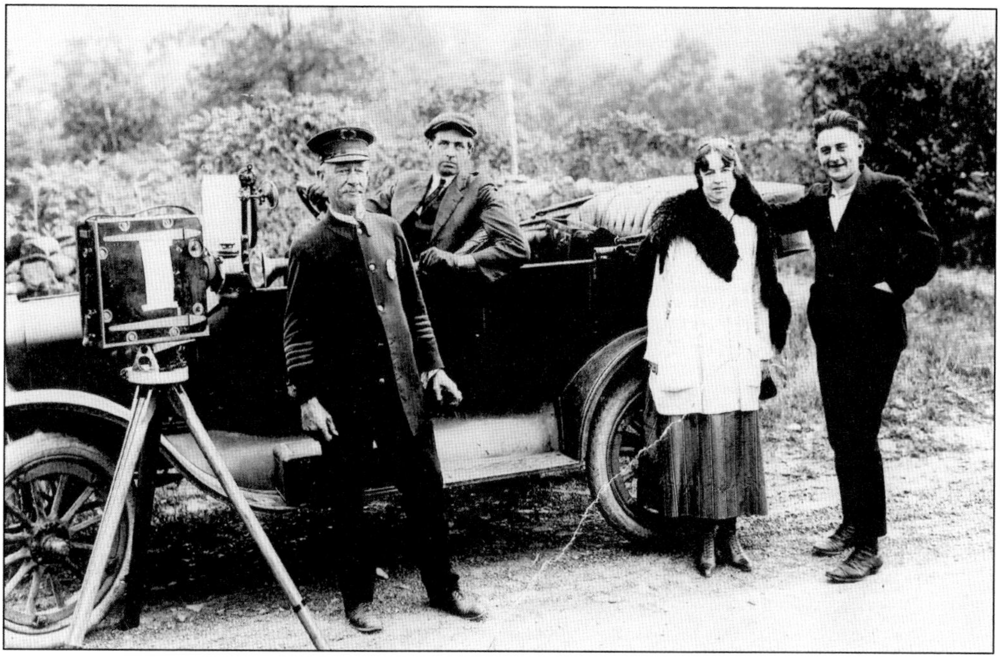

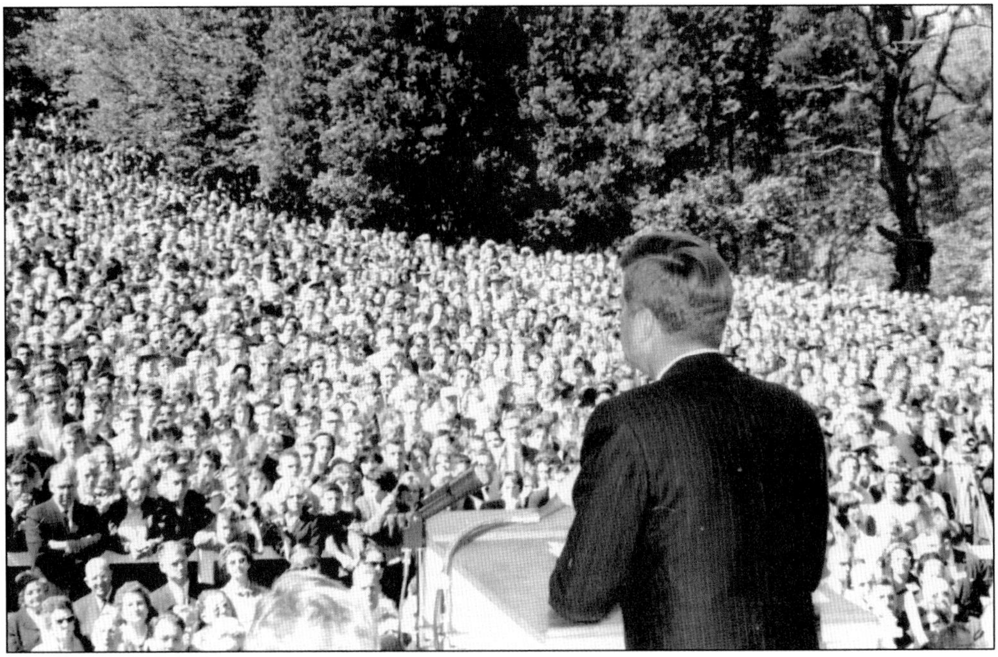

An exciting event in Milford was when Pres. John F. Kennedy visited to recognize Gray Towers as the birthplace of the U.S. Forestry Service and to dedicate the Pinchot Institute for Conservation Studies in honor of Gov. Gifford Pinchot. Folks came from far and wide to see their beloved president and to take part in the memorable event. The president's visit was in 1962, just two months before he was assassinated in Dallas. The whole town of Milford and the nation went into mourning when the tragic news came of his untimely death. (Courtesy of the Pike County Historical Society.)

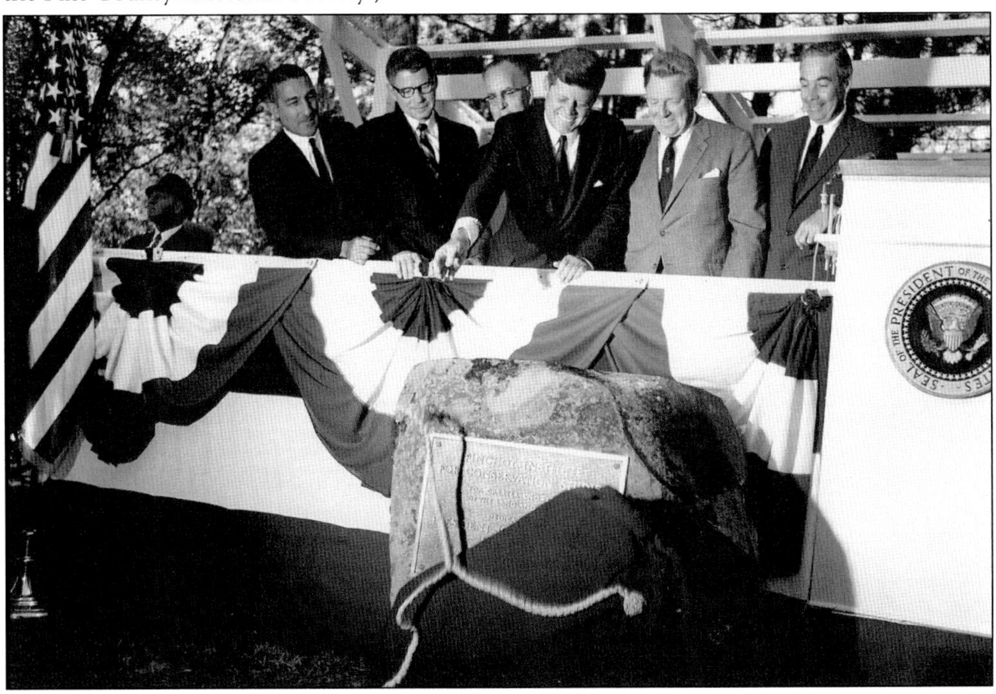

Seven

FROM LOGGING TO LODGING

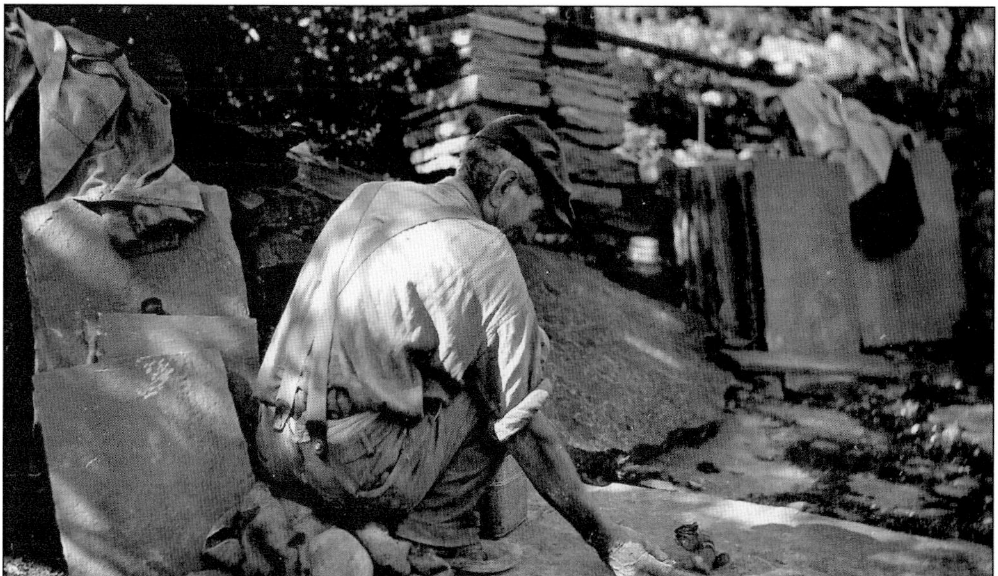

The Milford area provided a wide variety of ways to make a living. The natural resources brought the first settlers to the area with the rich fields, virgin forests, and bluestone mines. The area's beauty made it a perfect site for vacationers. This stonecutter extends a little friendship to a native of the woods. The father of the area's bluestone industry was John Fletcher Kilgour, who in his heyday employed over 600 people and controlled 12,000 acres of land with 23 quarries. Several buildings in Milford used bluestone in their construction, including Gray Towers, Forest Hall, the Ben Anthony house (at Sixth and Harford), and the Dr. Harvey Klaer house (on East Ann Street). (Courtesy of Diane Banach.)

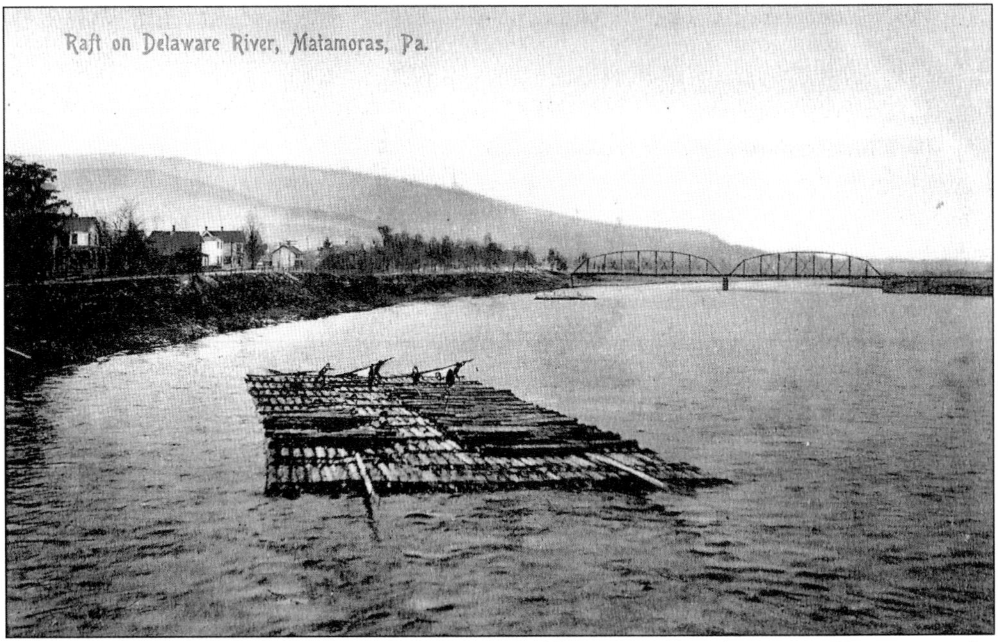

Rafting and lumbering were dangerous and profitable occupations for over 150 years on the Delaware beginning in 1764. The forests on both sides of the river were cut, and the logs were strapped together to float down the Delaware to Philadelphia. Great trees stood in the virgin forests when lumbering began, and bare hills were all that remained when it was done. Only the most inaccessible trees or trees protected by the landowners were spared. One of the last giant pine trees known to the lumbermen of the "Lackawack" was cut by Charles Kimble and run down the river to Philadelphia. It was 11 feet in diameter at its base. (Courtesy of Diane Banach.)

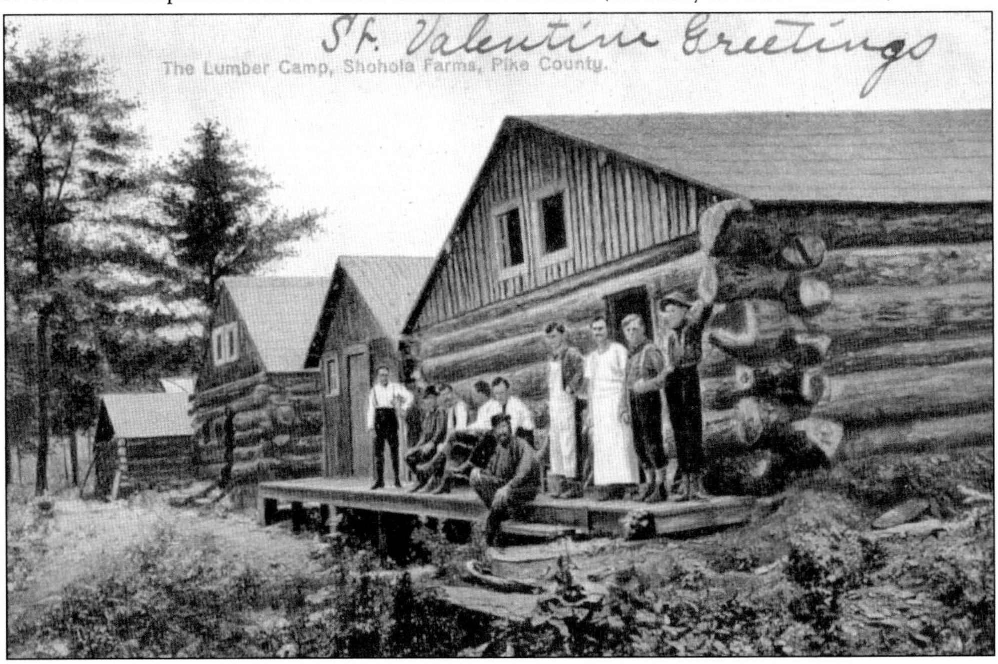

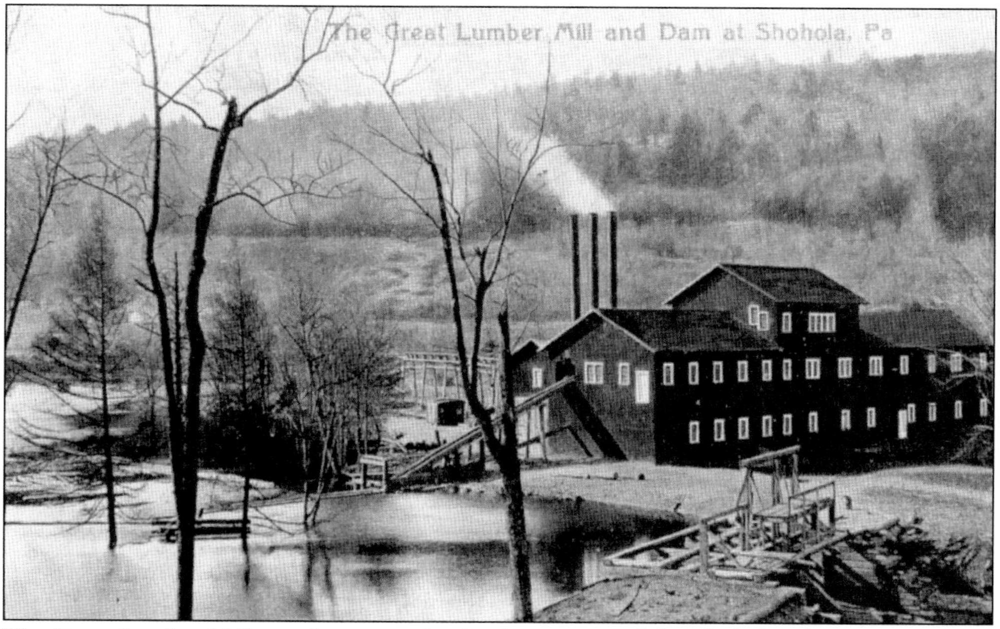

The Great Lumber Mill was the reason for the destruction of the Shohola Glen's reputation as a beautiful area to visit. The resulting destruction of the landscape and forests by the lumbering operations reduced the area to barren hills. Tanneries also played a large role in the deforestation. The poor-quality trees, particularly the pines, were suitable for extracting tannic acid used to tan hides. Mills used waterpower to process the grains from the harvests, cut lumber, and power equipment. (Courtesy of Diane Banach.)

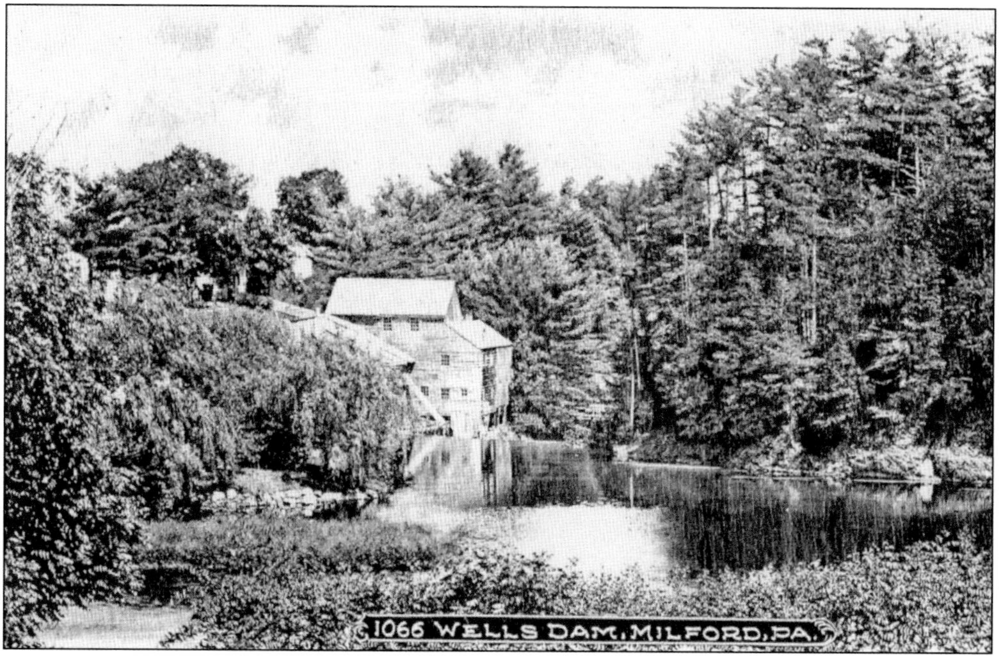

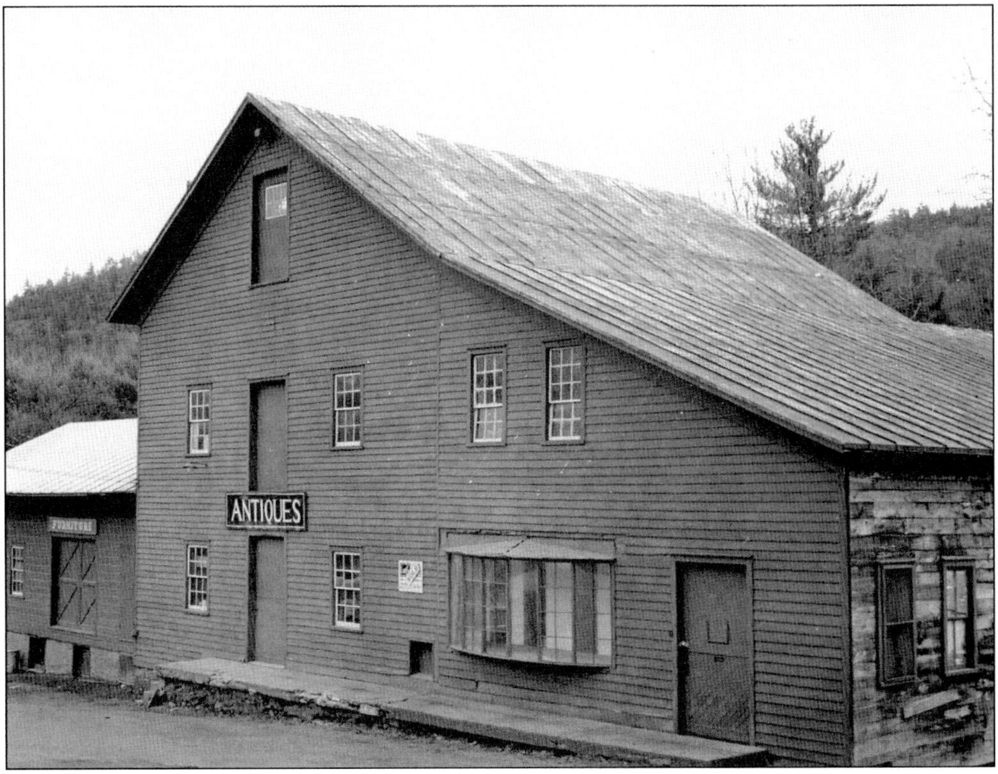

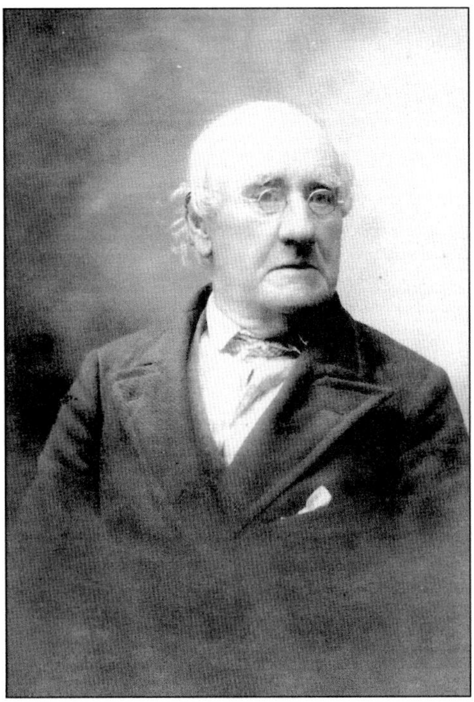

Gordon Mill, in Milford, is now known as the Upper Mill and is filled with specialty shops and a restaurant. Jervis Gordon settled in Milford in 1868 and purchased an old mill. In 1882, the mill was destroyed by fire. Jervis rebuilt the mill and operated it until it was sold in 1904 and renamed Rowe's Mill. It was then sold to the Saints and then became known as the Upper Mill. Robert Hartman and Leonard Freeman converted the mill into a retail complex that has experienced great success in attracting customers to the historic building. Visitors can still observe the mill wheel turning under waterpower and take a tour of the mill's inner workings, guided by information stations that tell the history of the mill and how each mechanism worked. Jervis Gordon (left) became a prosperous miller and established himself as a successful businessman of Milford. (Above, courtesy of the Pike County Historical Society; left, courtesy of the Gordon family.)

Jervis Gordon married Eliza Gish. They had seven children. After the death of Eliza, Jervis married Catherine (Van Etten) Rosenkrantz, and they had one daughter. (Courtesy of the Gordon family.)

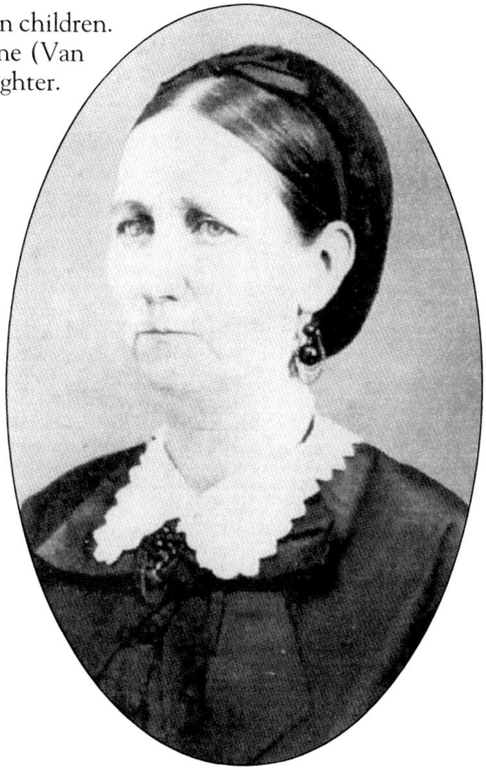

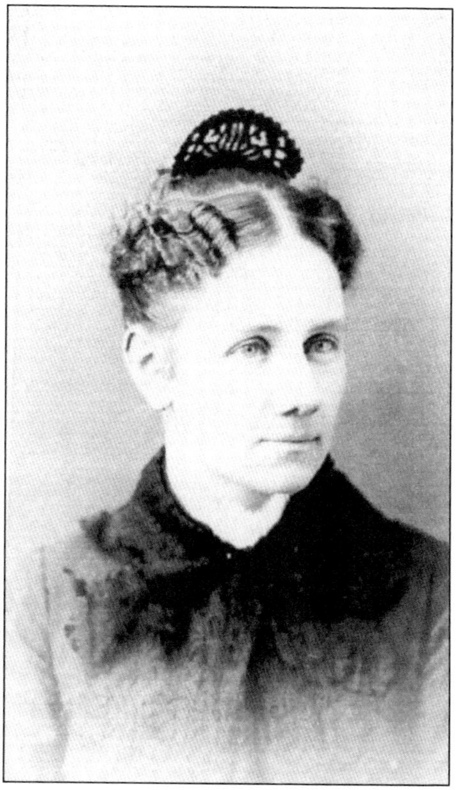

Jervis Gordon's daughter Emma, a deaf mute, married Oscar Merrill, also a deaf mute, and they had one child, Gertrude. The descendants of Gertrude have soul-searching correspondence between Jervis and the father of Oscar Merrill. The letters addressed the question as to whether it would be responsible of them to sanction the marriage. Happily, they both concurred that the marriage would be blessed. A doll that belonged to Jervis's daughter Annie Gordon McCraney is on display at the Pike County Historical Society. (Courtesy of the Gordon family.)

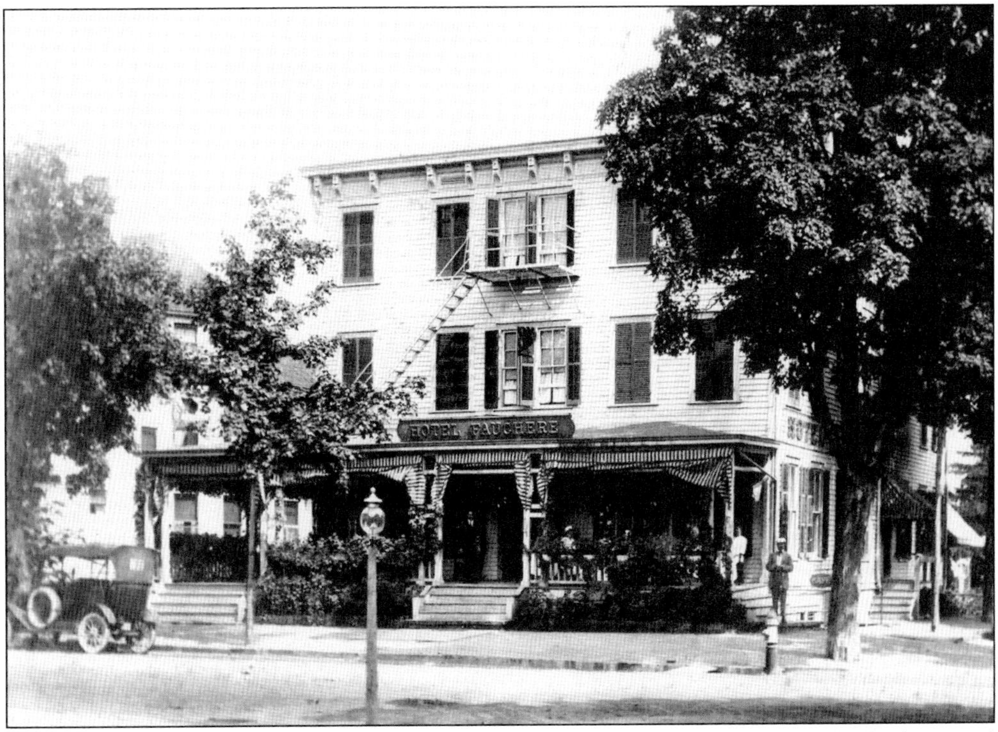

Louis Fauchere, a former chef at Delmonico's Restaurant in New York City, built the Hotel Fauchere in the 1880s on Broad Street. His reputation attracted such distinguished guests as Ogden Nash, the Rockefellers, and Sarah Bernhardt. Below is the hardware store known as Klein's, owned by Julis Klein. (Courtesy of the Pike County Historical Society.)

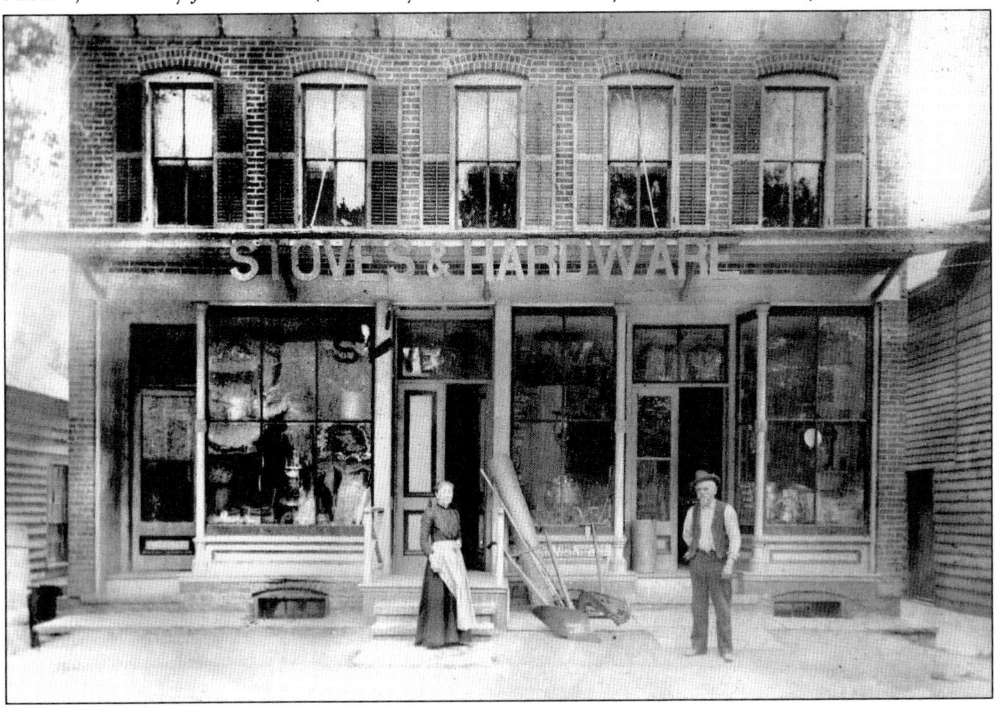

In 1880, Louis Fauchere built the beautiful hotel that bears his name. The cuisine was renowned far and wide, with the particularly tender Delmonico steaks being the favorite entree of the house. Before his arrival in America, Fauchere had increased his knowledge of fine cuisine in some of the finest hotels in Switzerland. Upon his arrival in New York City in 1851, he found work at Delmonico's. He shared his wonderful dishes with the visitors to the Fauchere until two years before his death, at which time his daughter took over the business.

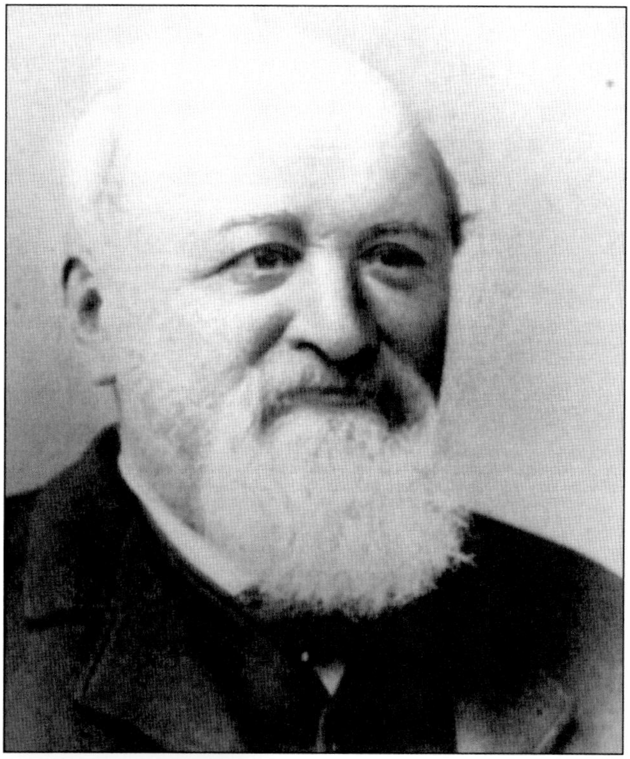

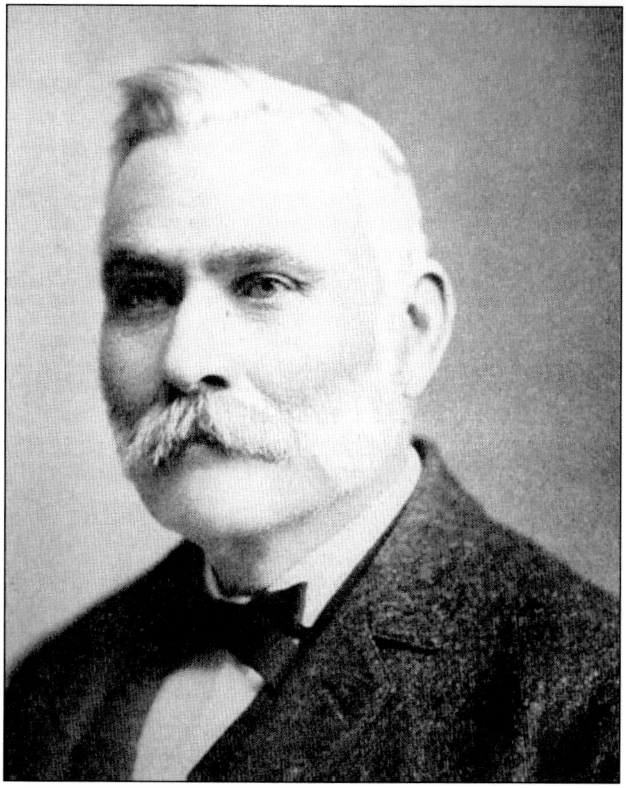

Hon. William Mitchell, a successful Milford merchant, represented the success of a true entrepreneur. He came to America in 1860 at the age of 19 with his sister and soon found his way to Milford. He clerked for C. C. D. Pinchot & Sons for over six years, and by 1868, he was in partnership in a mercantile business with J. B. Newman. In 1881, he and his brother built and established the largest general store in Milford. Many of William Mitchell's descendants still call Milford their home.

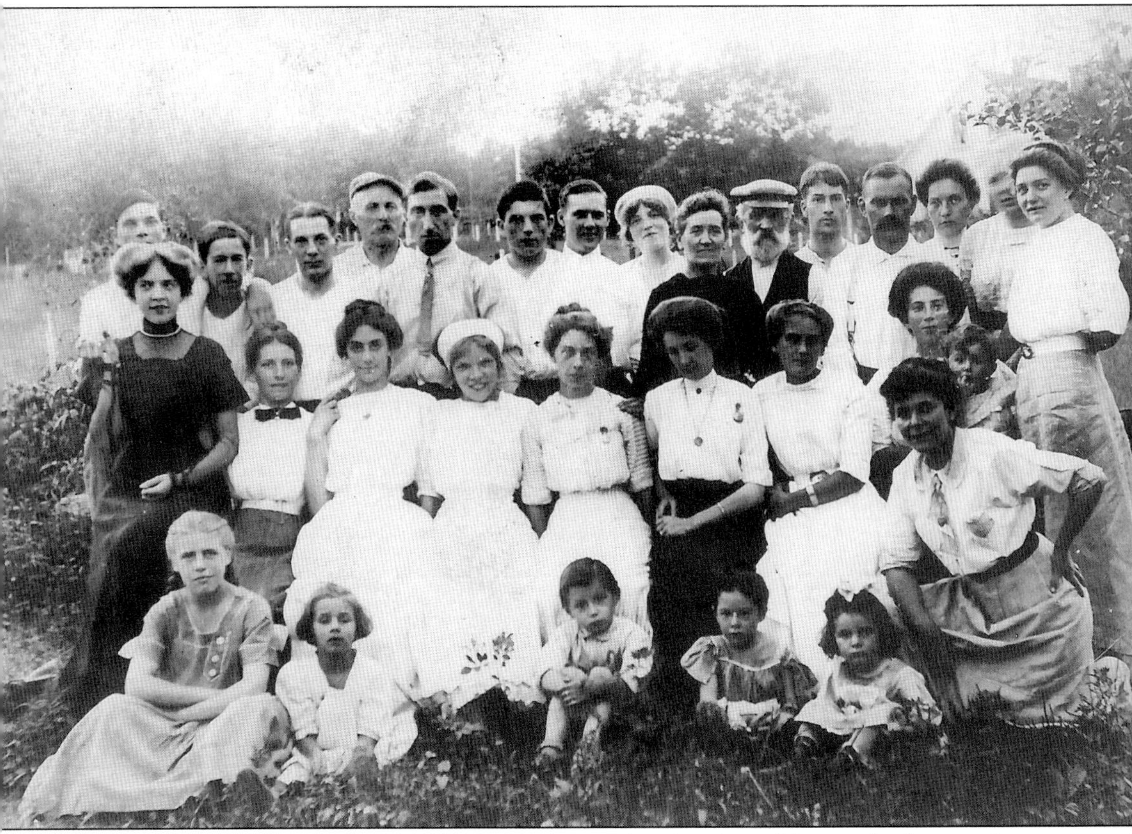

Summer visitors to the boardinghouses were very loyal and would come back year after year. Young couples who met "in the mountains" would marry and would later bring back their children for vacations. All ages were welcome, but many boarders were young eligible workers from the cities who came to escape the heat. They enjoyed continuous Octoberfest-like activities in the country boardinghouses and the pleasure of lovely, vibrant company. Many a permanent relationship began during these festive summer days. The young woman on the left appears to be in mourning attire but seems to be too young to be a widow.

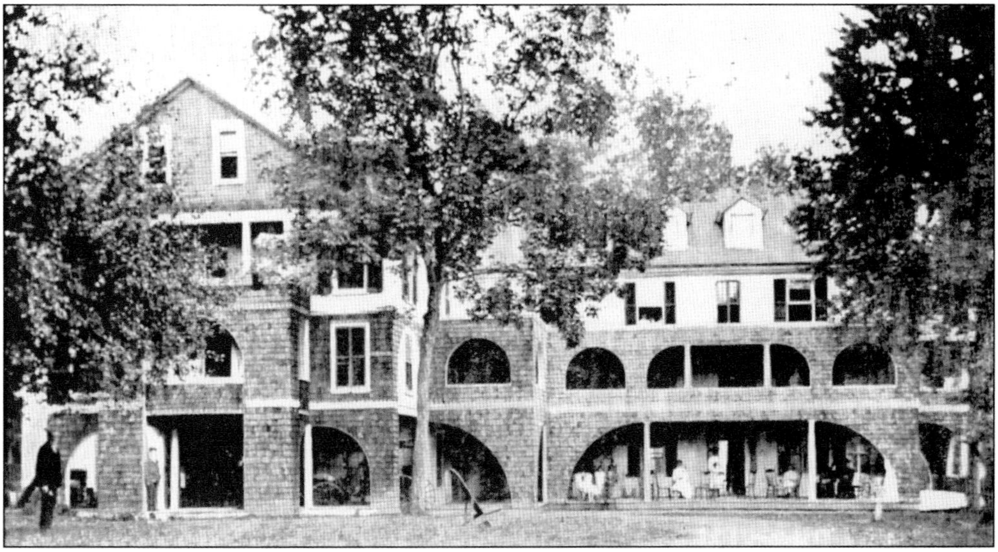

Pictured are two examples of the many boardinghouses and inns that served the visitors to Milford. The Homestead, built by Abram Brown in the late 1800s and destroyed by fire in 1975, could accommodate 100 guests in the late 1800s at a rate of $2.50 per day. The Maple Cottage (below), operated by John J. Ryman, was a small and accommodating establishment. (Courtesy of Diane Banach.)

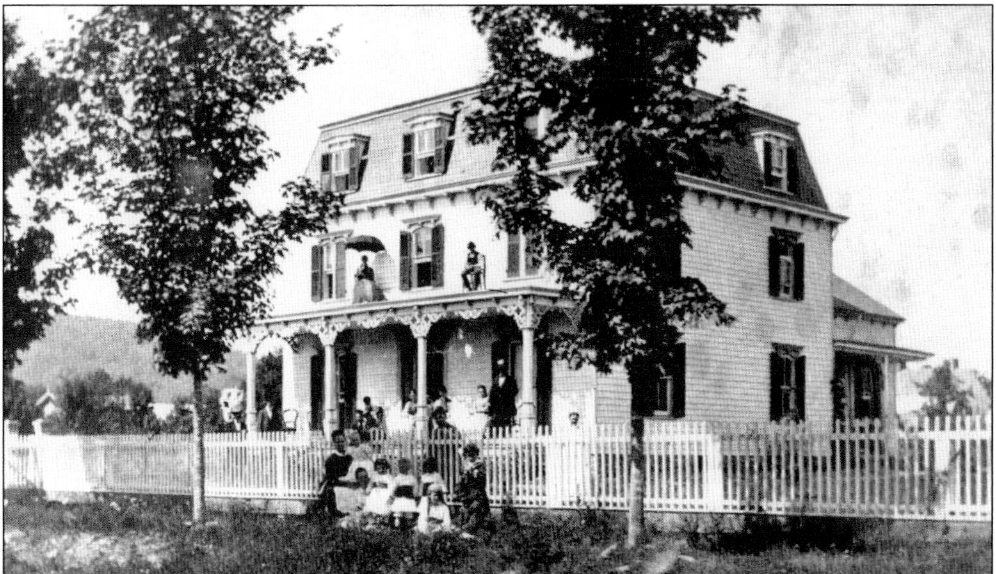

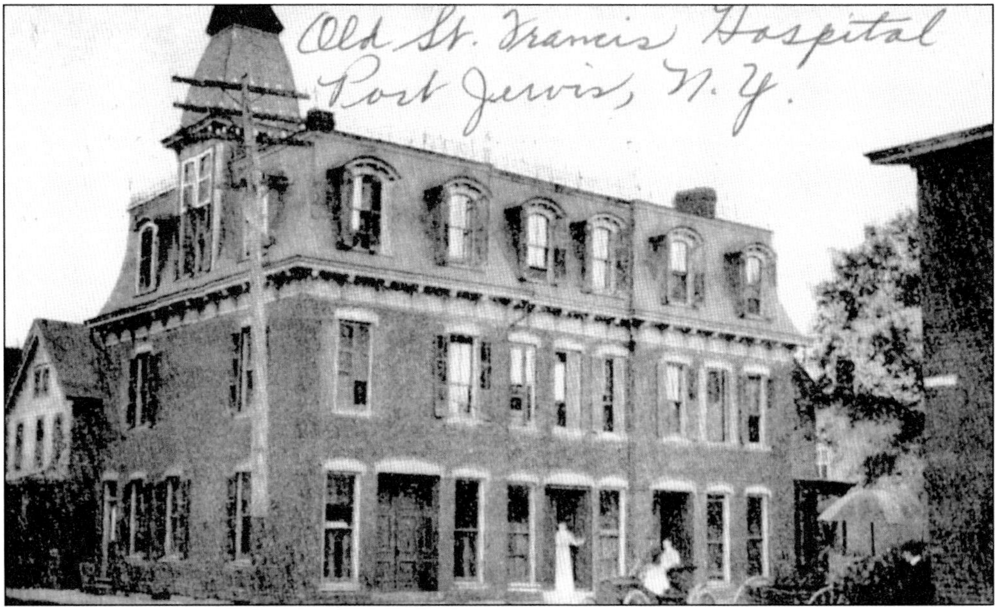

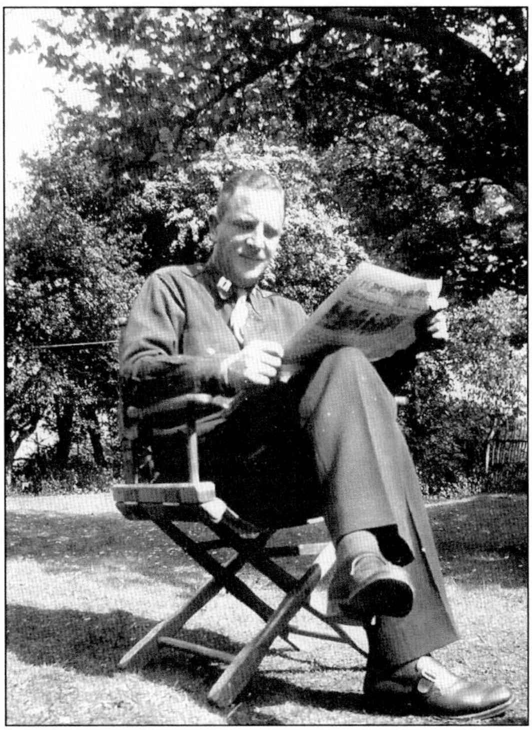

Access to healthcare has been a critical issue to the local residents. In the early 1800s, it was not unusual to go to the blacksmith to have a tooth extracted. Some found that a string tied to a grooved musket ball and then shot out of a musket was more effective at extracting an abscessed tooth. Many devoted physicians have served Milford through the years. The nearest hospitals were in Port Jervis, about eight miles from Milford. The hospital that has survived throughout the years is St. Francis, now known as Mercy Hospital. The above photograph shows the original building before the hospital relocated to its present site. In the photograph to the left, Dr. Harvey Klaer, who delivered many of the young residents from the 1940s to the 1960s, is relaxing in England in 1944. (Courtesy of Diane Banach and the Pike County Historical Society.)

Some of the tragedies of yesteryear were the diseases that plagued our forefathers. Consumption, or tuberculosis, was a tragic affliction that some survived, but most succumbed to its ravishing effects. Margaret Tumm (right) died of tuberculosis at the age of 18. Her family memorialized her in this special frame made with flecks of mother-of-pearl and glitter.

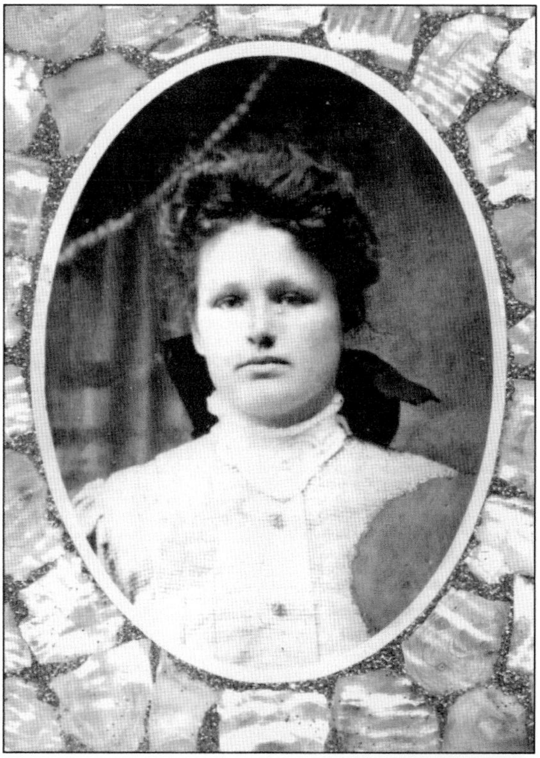

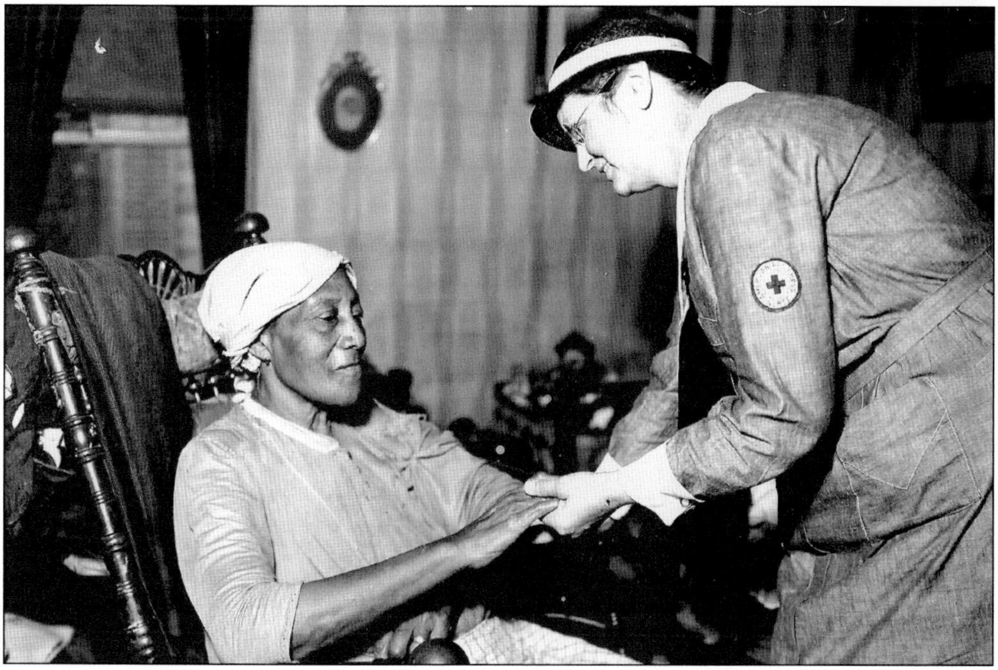

The limited availability of medical facilities and providers meant that visiting nurses were an important component of the healthcare system. Here, Bertha Tumm Stretz poses for a publicity photograph for the American Red Cross. She grew up in Greeley and lived her later days in a house in Matamoras, where she could be close to her family in Milford and Port Jervis.

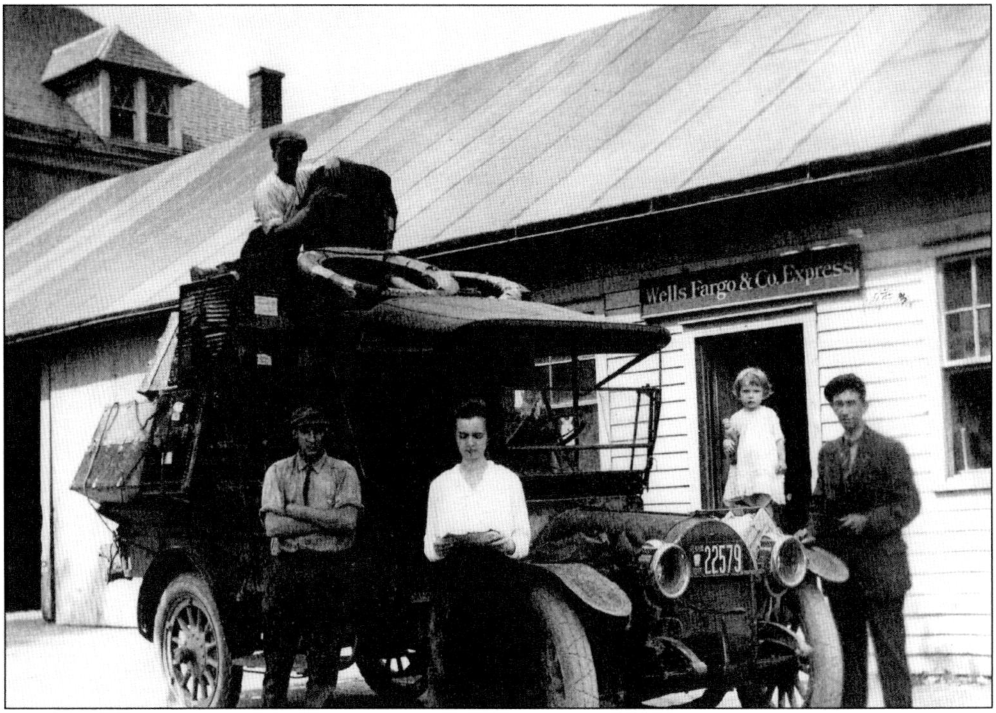

The Wells Fargo Express Station, located on Catharine Street where the firehouse is today, was the center for mail deliveries. On the far right of the c. 1918 photograph above is Charles A. Foster Sr. On the left is William Hinkel. The child is Doris Kellogg. Norman B. Hotalen, pictured below, delivered delicious pies and pastries to area businesses. (Above, courtesy of the Pike County Historical Society; below, courtesy of Frances Hotalen.)

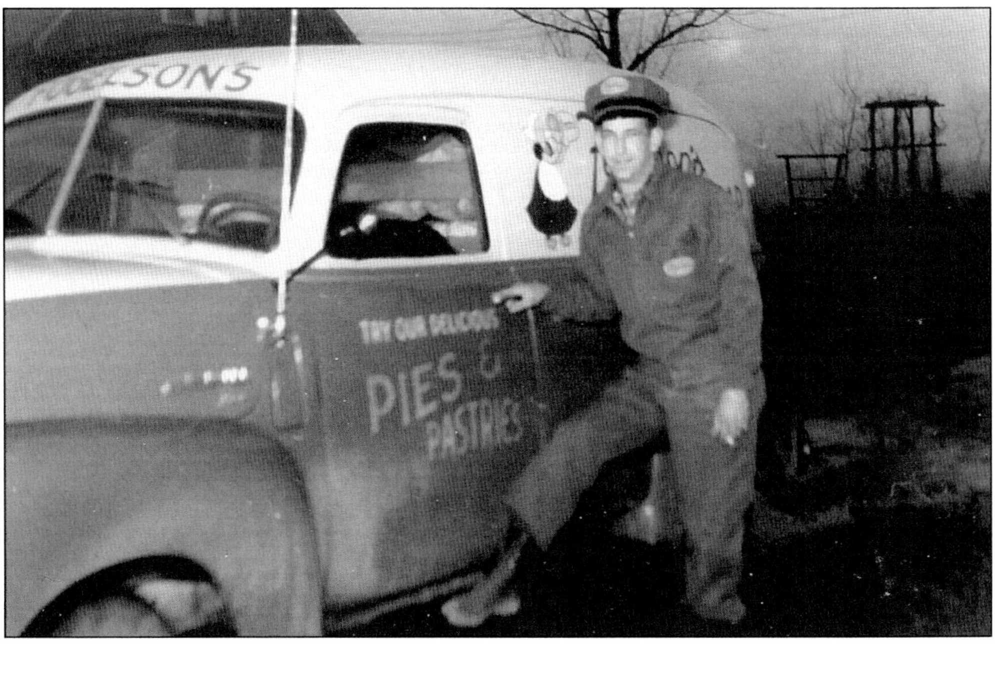

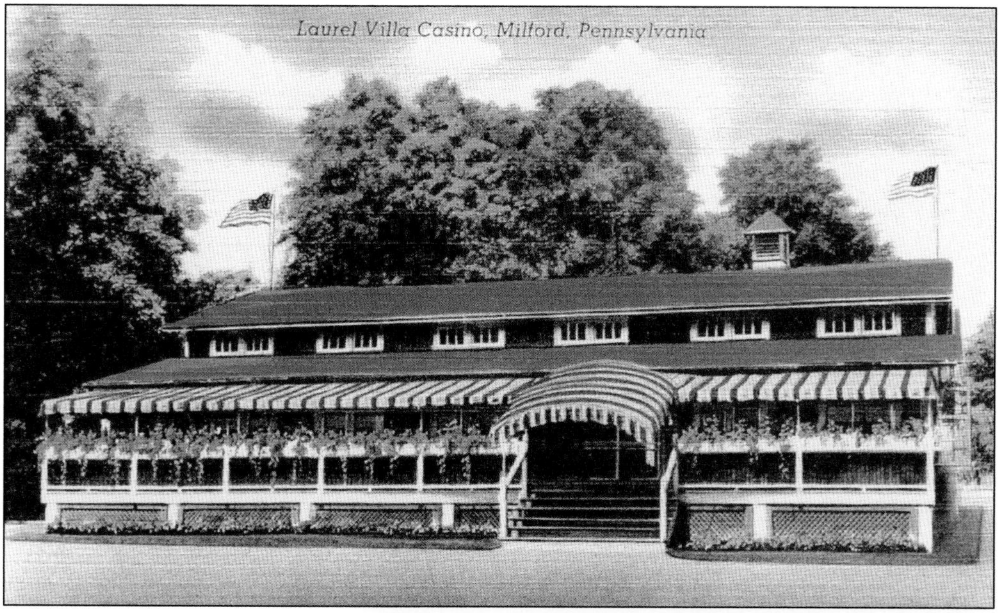

The Laurel Villa Casino was a popular gathering place in Milford. The author learned how to do the alley cat at the Saturday night dances in this building in the 1970s. Many a happy bride and groom held their wedding reception in the dance hall. Today, this building, one of five in the original complex, is a furniture store on Harford Street. The Laurel Villa Lodge, a popular bed-and-breakfast, is still in operation behind this building. Built in 1876, it has been operated by several generations of the Muhlhauser family. (Courtesy of the Pike County Historical Society.)

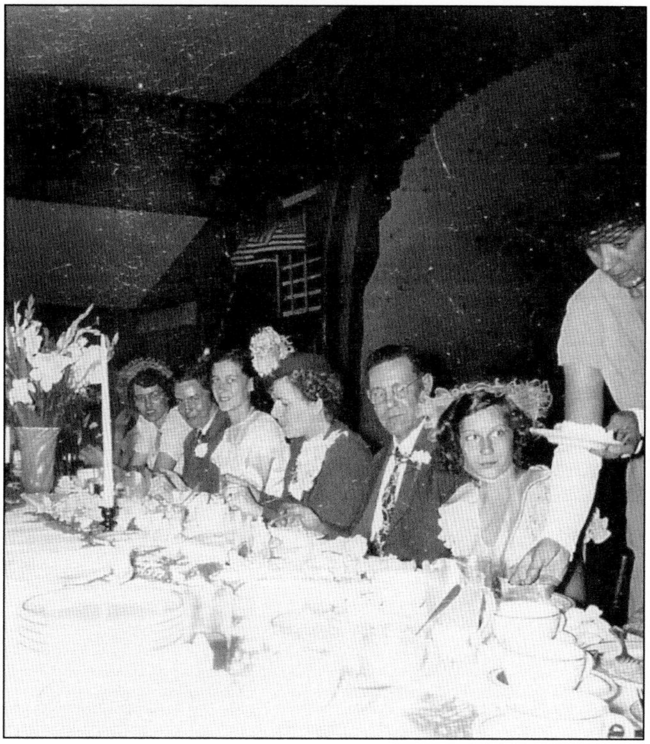

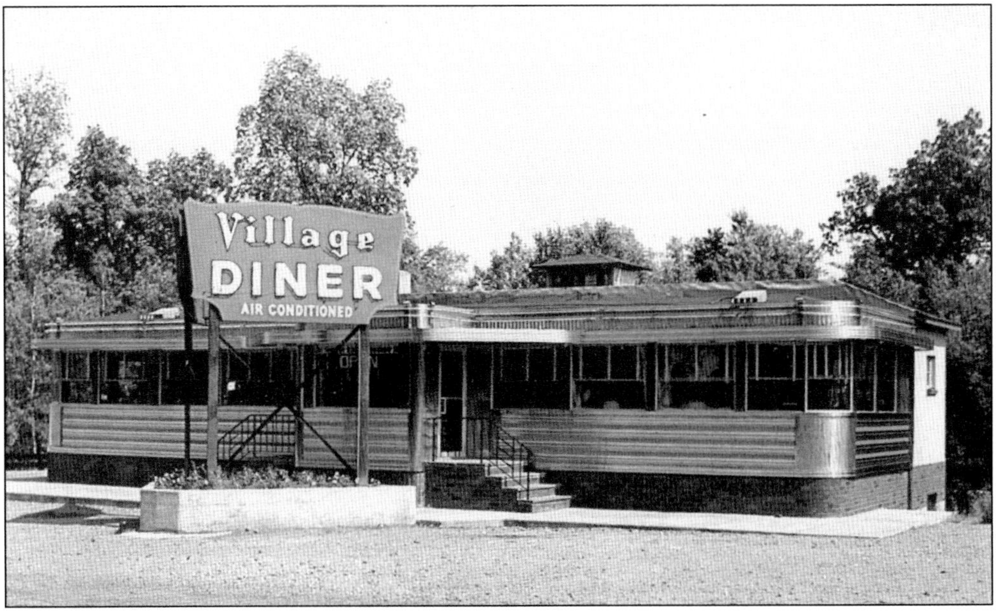

The Village Diner has been a fixture for many years on Route 6 on the way to Port Jervis. Its family-style cuisine filled the bellies of the locals and travelers through the latter half of the 20th century. The Milford Diner, operated by Graham Muselwhite, has served lawyers, business professionals, churchgoers, teachers, students, and visitors for over six decades. (Courtesy of Diane Banach.)

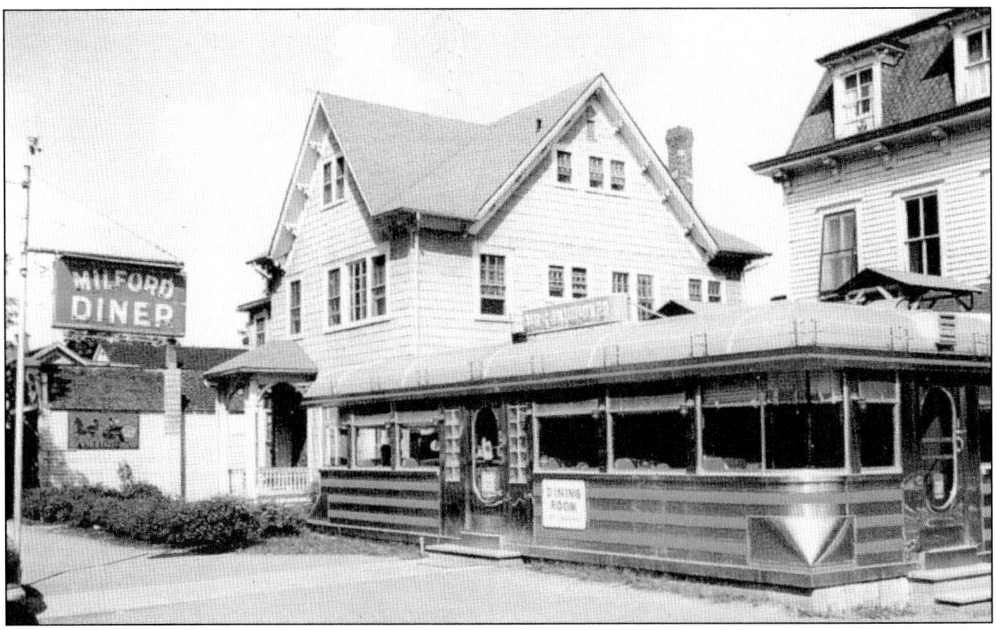

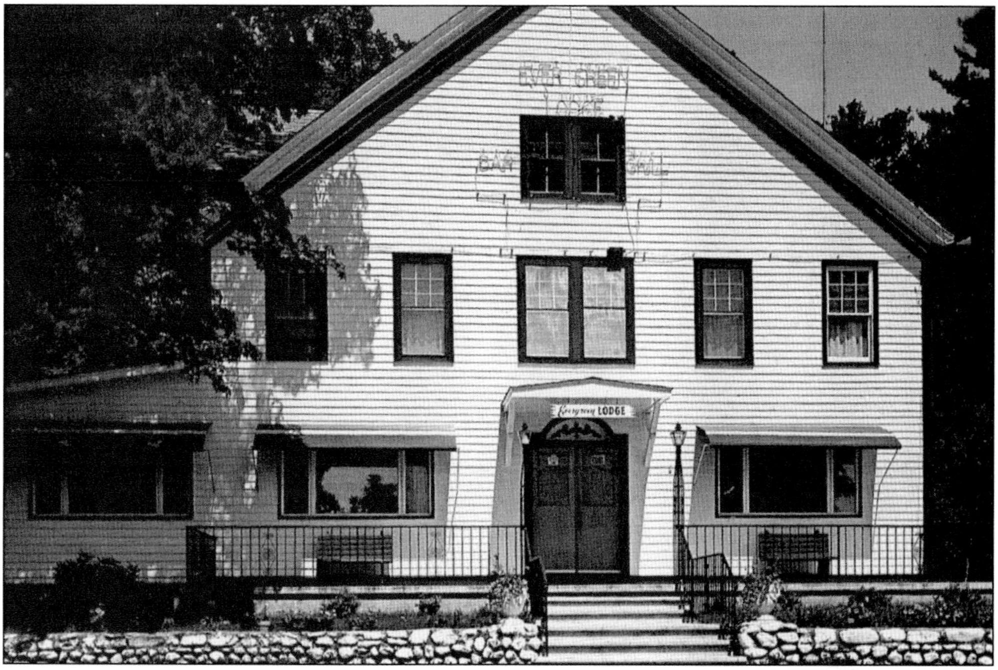

Another favorite restaurant during the 1950s and 1960s was the Evergreen. Many delicious Italian dinners were served on the tables in front of the picture windows, looking out toward the Delaware and Route 6. The building was demolished when Interstate 84 was constructed. The new Evergreen, built on Route 6, operated until the 1990s. It is currently a day-care center. (Courtesy of Diane Banach.)

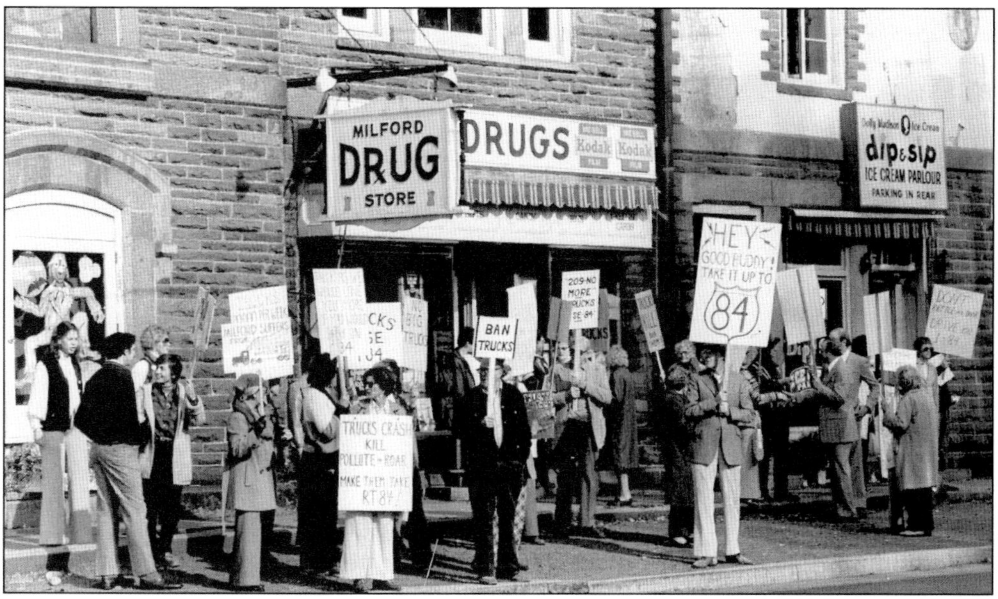

Milford residents found themselves in the position of protesting when trucks began taking a shortcut through the quiet town on Route 209. Here, citizens protest in front of Forest Hall. Their efforts were successful, and the town returned to its familiar peaceful atmosphere. (Courtesy of the Pike County Historical Society.)

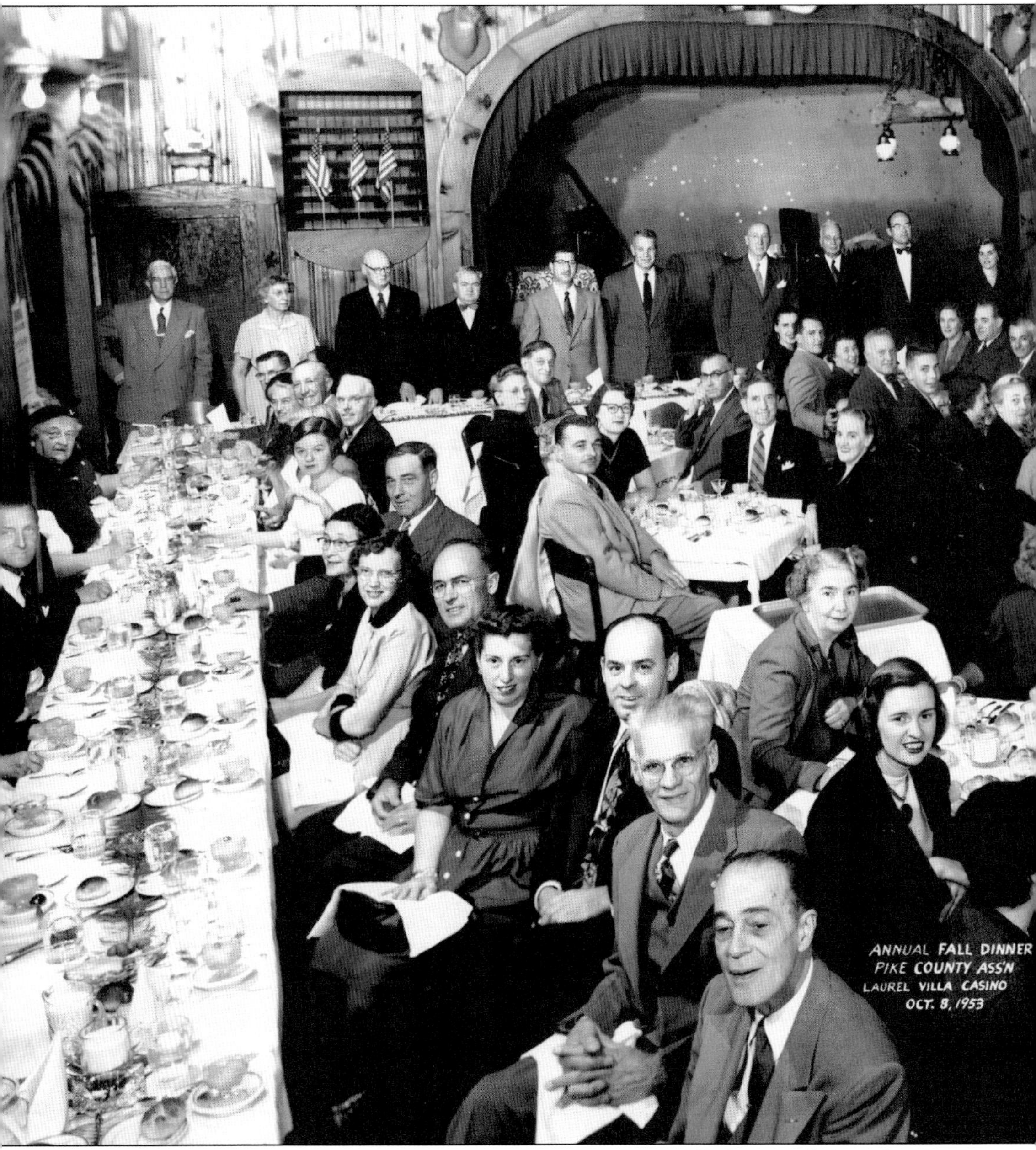

Held at the Laurel Villa Casino on October 8, 1953, the fall dinner of the Pike County Association was a major business event. James A. Daniel of Newton represents most of the local

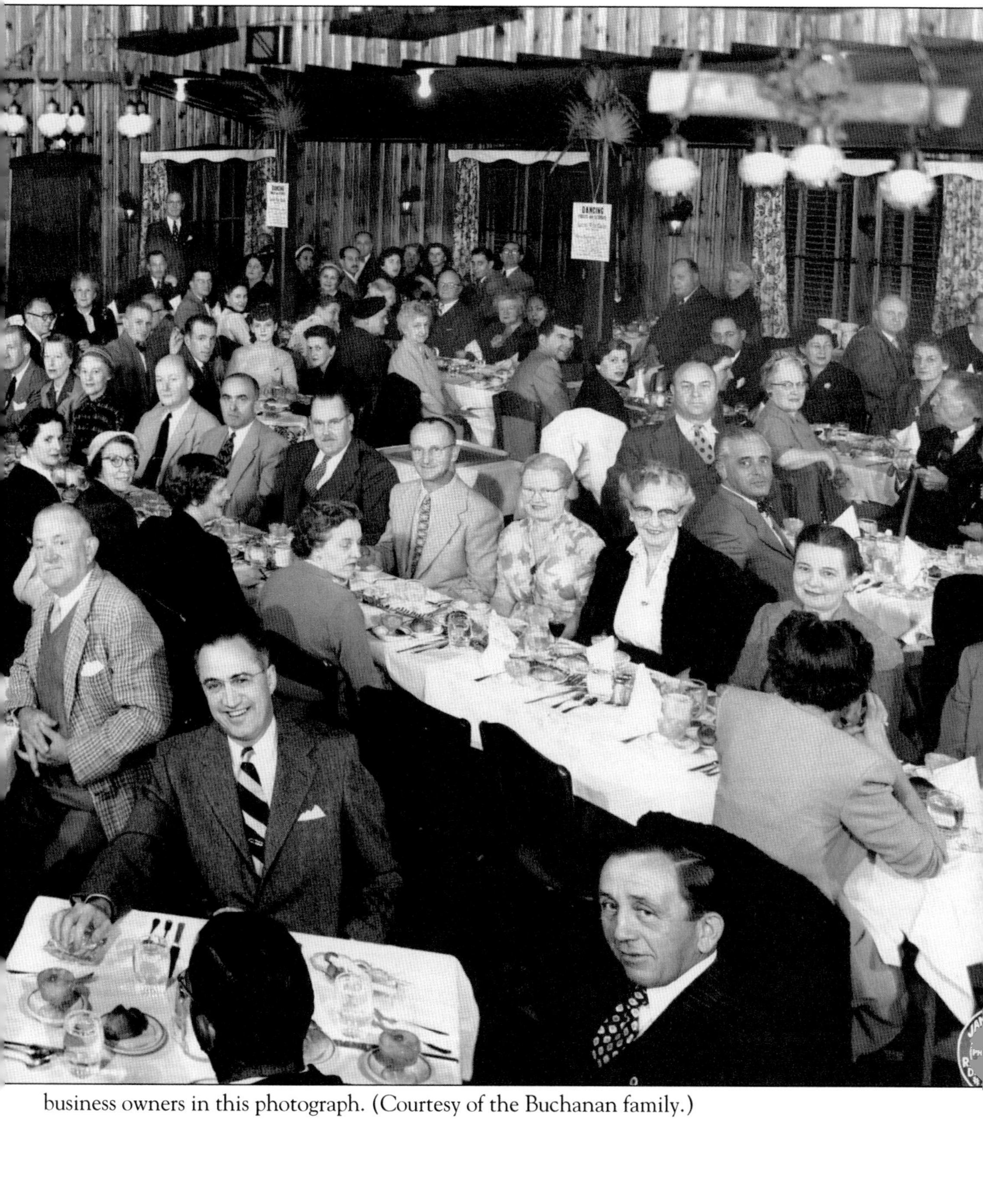

business owners in this photograph. (Courtesy of the Buchanan family.)

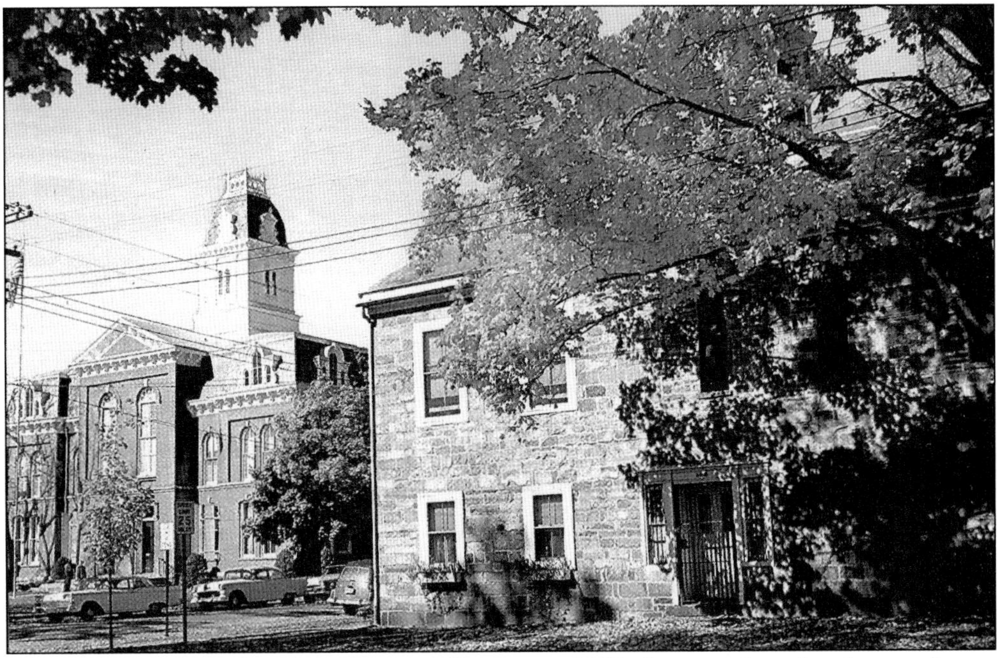

It cannot be forgotten that a large portion of business in Milford was conducted in the courthouse. Milford is the seat of Pike County, and the courthouse is the center of legal proceedings, deed recordings, tax collecting, and maintenance of vital records for the county. The jail (above, right), built in 1814, is the second-oldest courthouse in Pennsylvania. It was used as such until the current courthouse was built in 1874. (Courtesy of the Pike County Historical Society.)

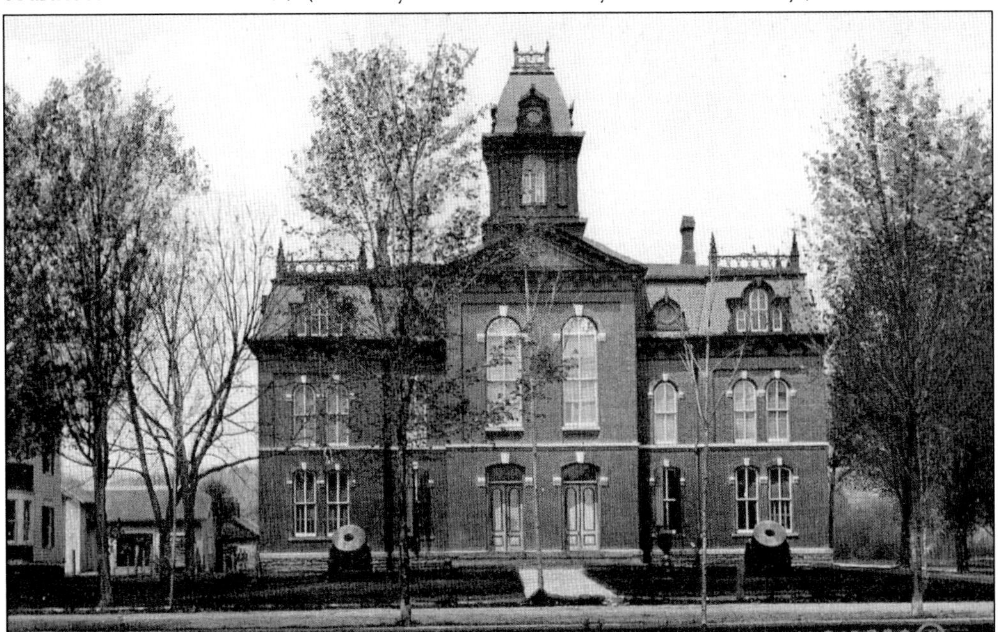

Eight

Things to See and Do

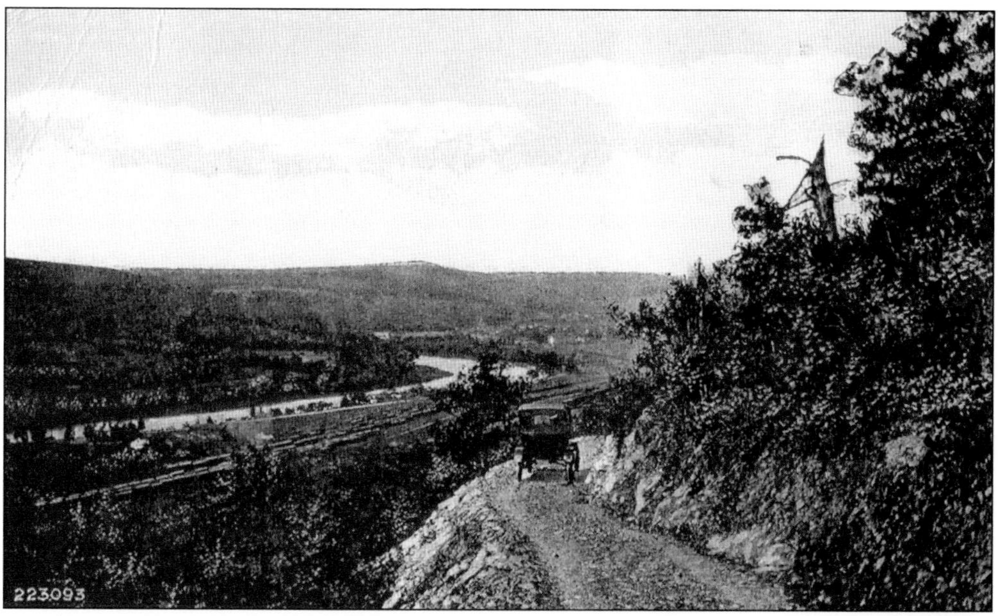

People came to visit or live in the Minisink Valley for many different reasons, but a compelling feature that attracted them was the varied landscape and beautiful scenery. Some came for peace and tranquility. Others came for excitement and thrills. The Hawks Nest, pictured here, was certainly a thrilling ride in the early days of the automobile. Hopefully, one's vehicle had very good brakes. (Courtesy of Diane Banach.)

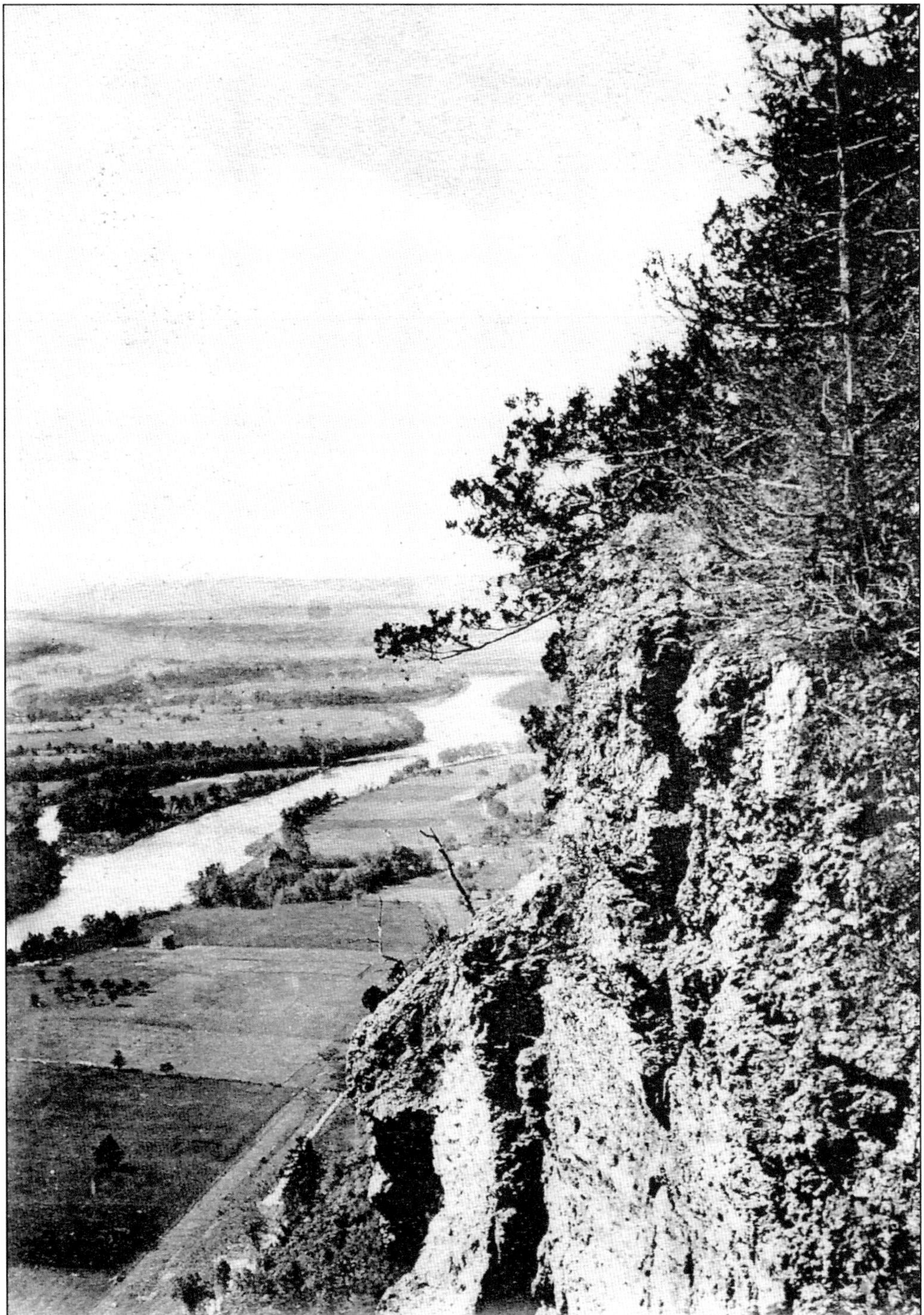

Another thrill was to stand on the edge of the cliffs and look down. Looking south toward the Delaware Water Gap, people were treated to a panoramic view filled with scenes of the Delaware River and the Minisink Valley. (Courtesy of Diane Banach.)

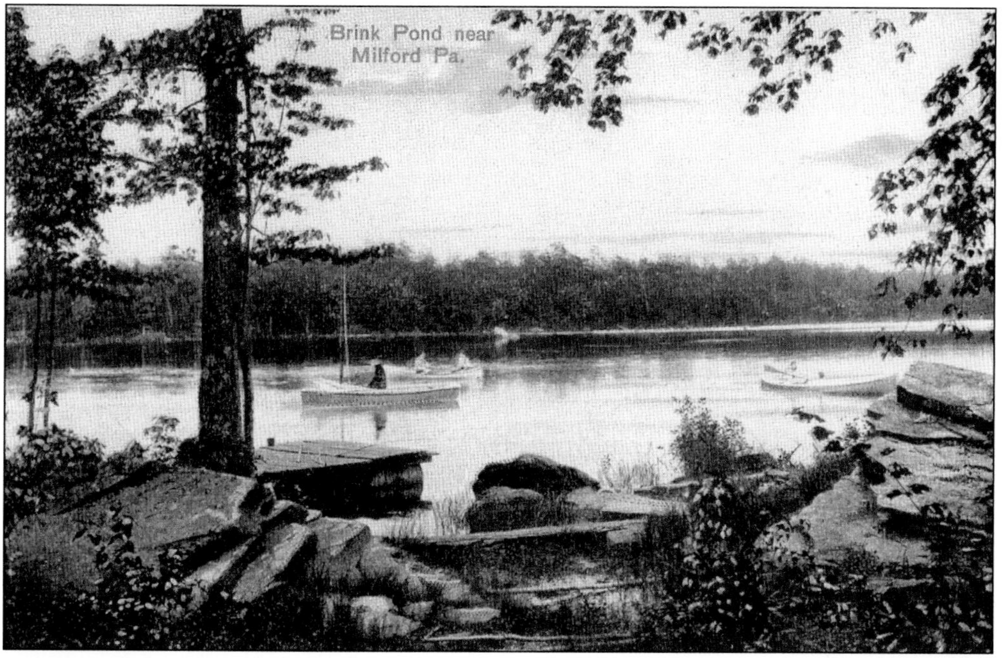

For those who would rather relax, a day's sojourn on the beautiful lakes and river offered a day full of revitalizing rest. (Courtesy of Diane Banach.)

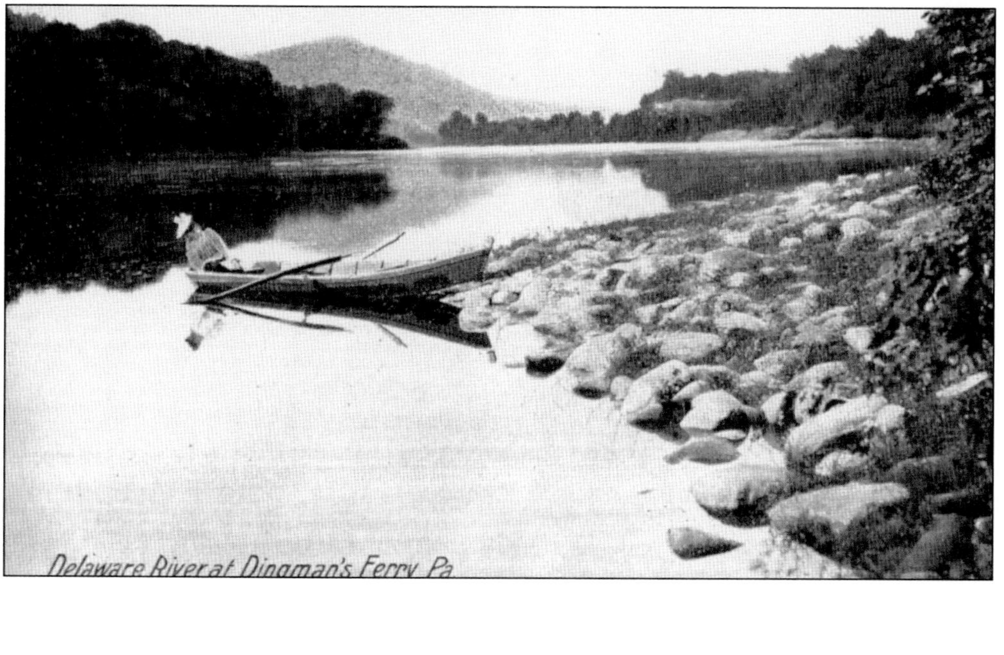

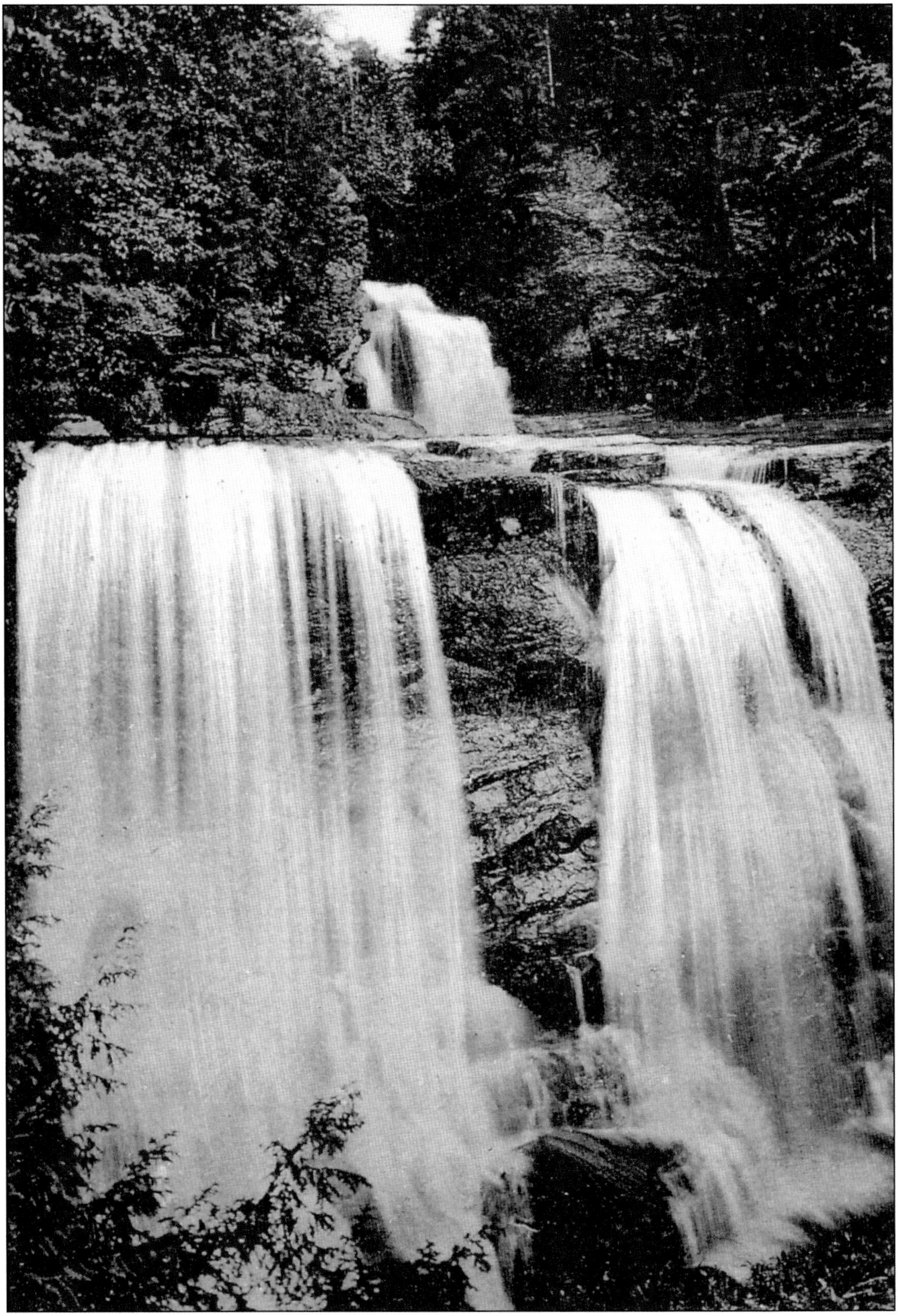

No visitor to the area would miss a hike to see some of the local waterfalls. Most visitors tried to capture the majesty of the cascading water in sketches, photographs, and paintings. The Sawkill Falls, located on the Pinchot estate, is one of the most beautiful waterfalls in the area.

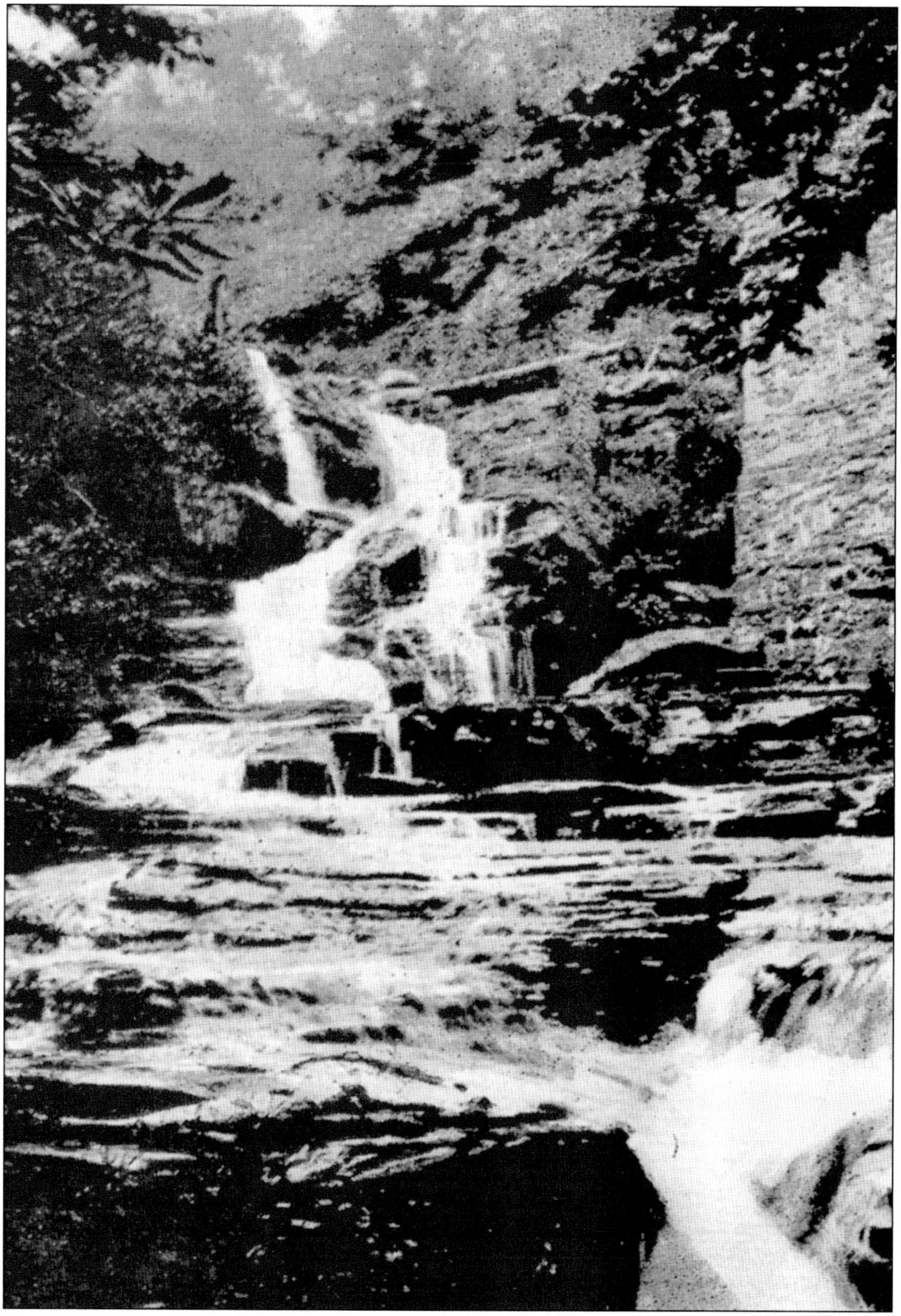

Waterfalls were enjoyed for their beauty, but they were also used to generate the power for the local mills. This is an example of such at Mill Rift. The remnants of the mill can be seen on the right. (Courtesy of Diane Banach.)

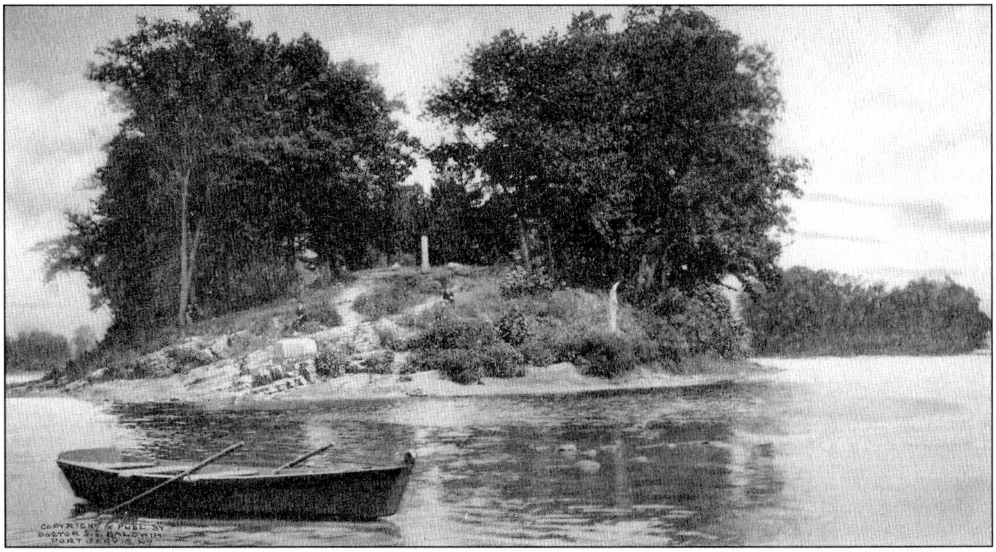

Many visitors and locals make a point of boating to the Tristate Rock in the Delaware, where New York, Pennsylvania, and New Jersey meet. Others hike to the tall ridges above the Delaware to catch the feeling of being a bird looking down on the small world below. (Courtesy of Diane Banach.)

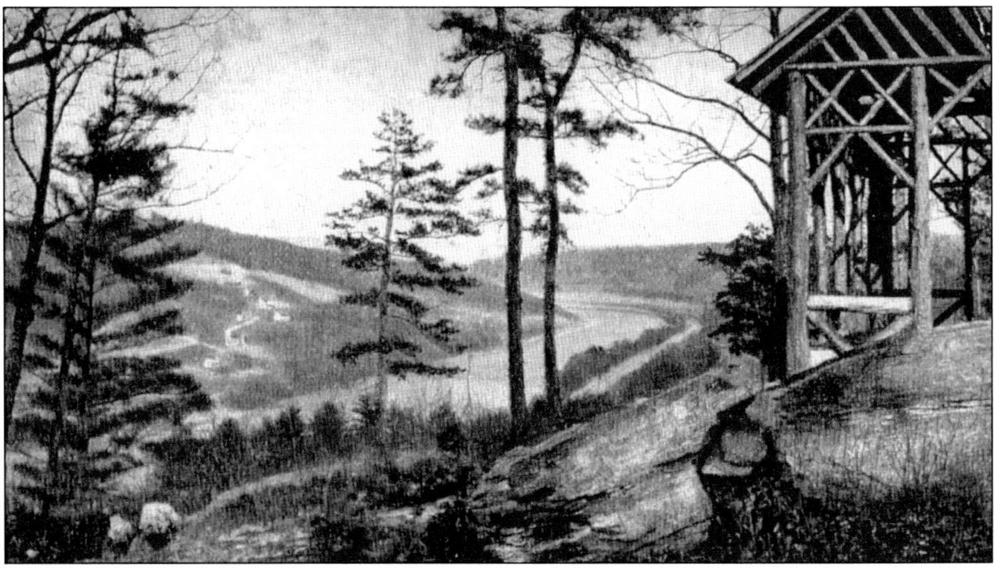

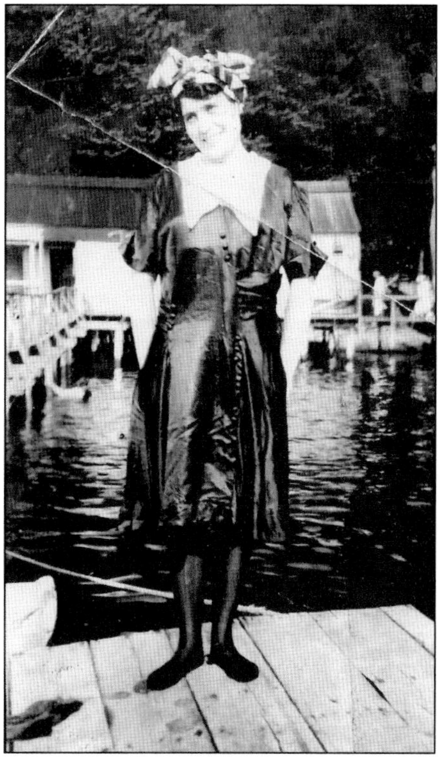

Escaping the heat of summer was the goal, and nothing less than a stylish bathing outfit would do. Maybelle Titus (right) visited the Milford area for years from New York City and eventually settled in Dingman's Ferry to conduct a real estate and insurance business. Below, another visitor appears totally refreshed from her swim.

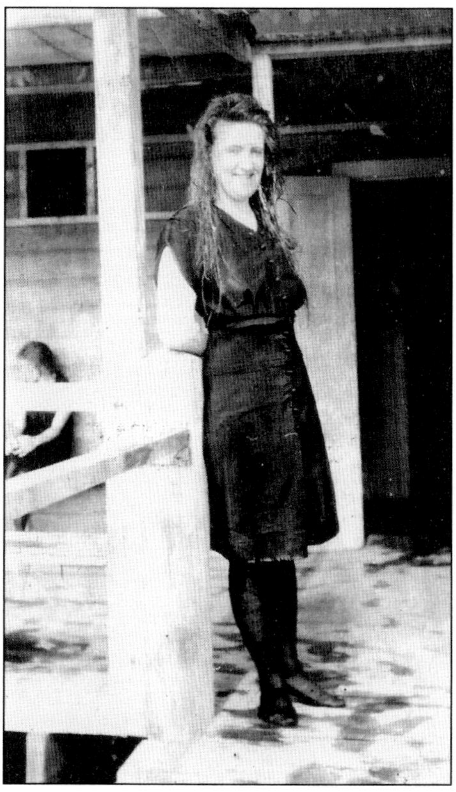

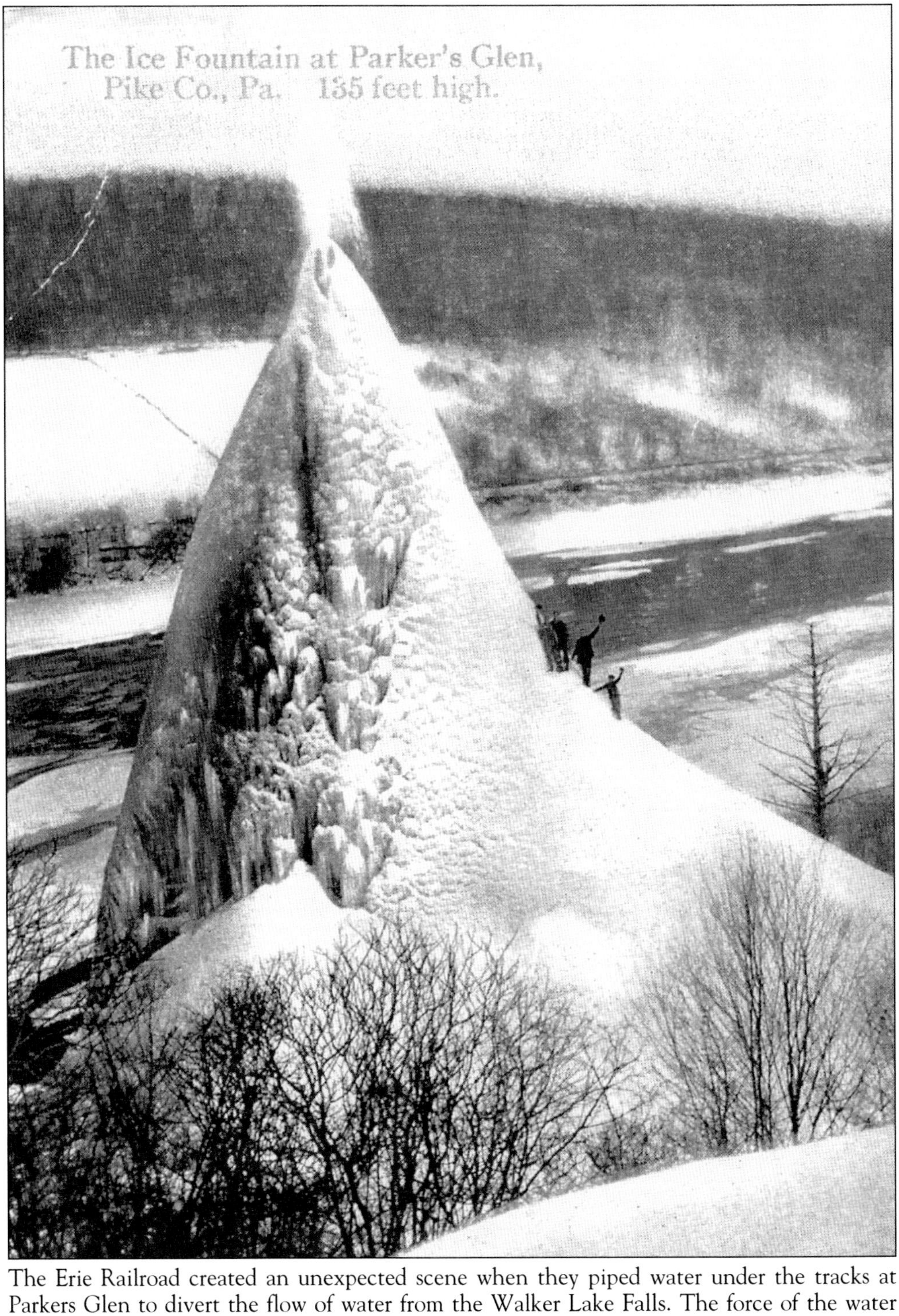

The Erie Railroad created an unexpected scene when they piped water under the tracks at Parkers Glen to divert the flow of water from the Walker Lake Falls. The force of the water flowing through the pipe created a beautiful fountain. Many visited to see the spectacle, especially in the winter months, when the fountain could freeze into a giant glacierlike peak. (Courtesy of Diane Banach.)

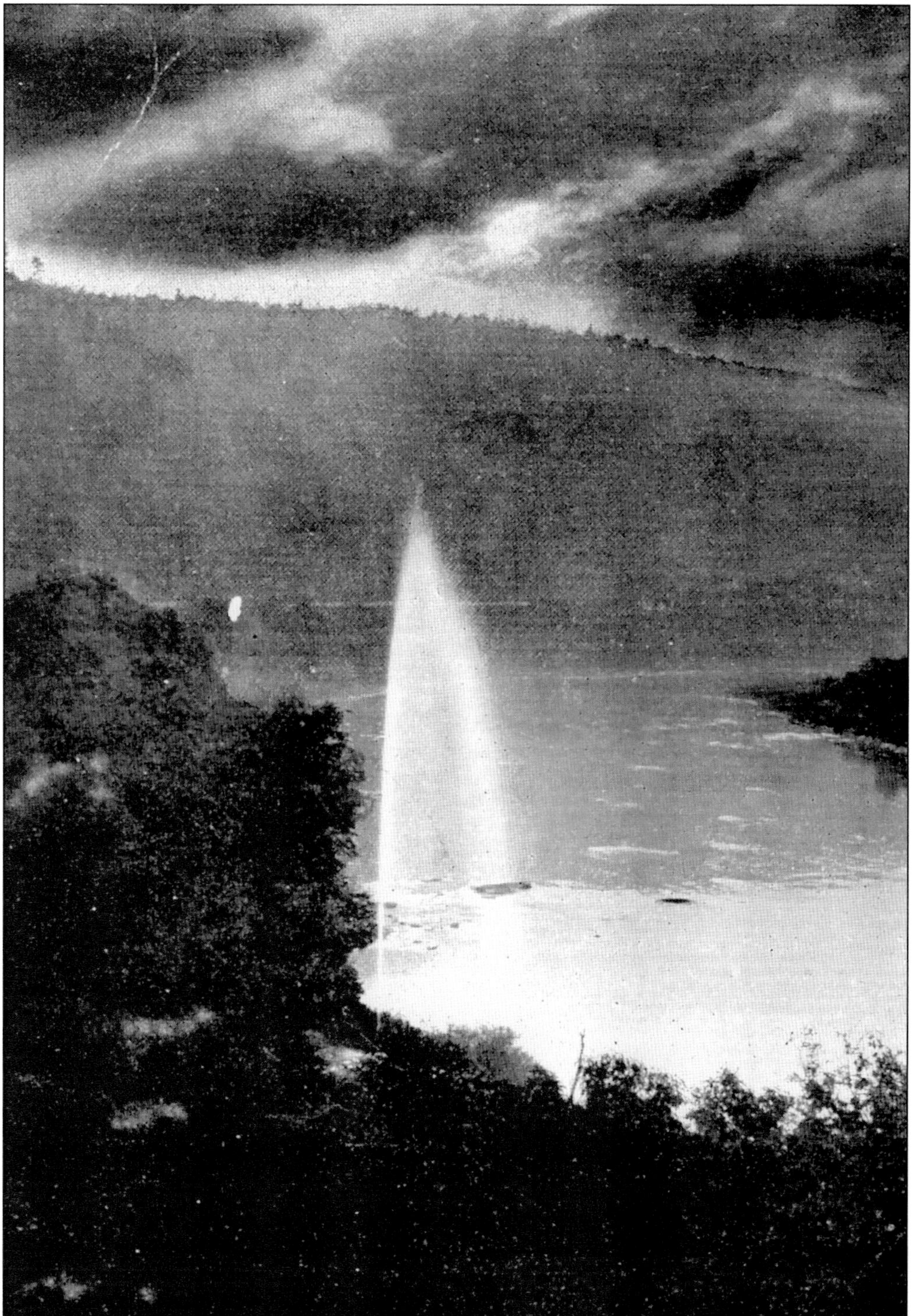

In all seasons, the Parkers Glen fountain was a beautiful sight, but one of the best views was on a moonlit night. The fountain was destroyed in 1955 during the flooding caused by Hurricane Diane. (Courtesy of Diane Banach.)

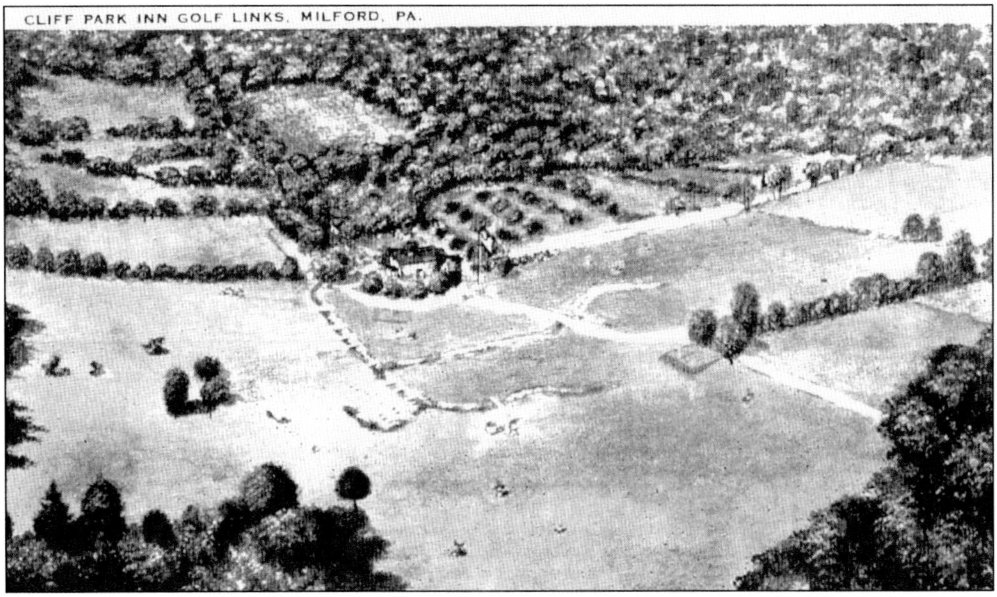

Recreational activities were in high demand during the summer season, and golf at Cliff Park was a common pastime. The beautiful Cliff Park Inn offered rooms, fine dining, horse-drawn carriage rides to the cliffs, and days full of golfing. The Buchanan family saw the value of developing a golf course and resort out of their family's farm in the 1800s. The family's history goes back to the early days of Milford, when George (Bowhannan) Buchanan removed from near Newburgh to Milford in 1800. At one time, he owned 30,000 acres and was credited with opening up Broad Street by "clearing out the brush." Some believe he hosted the first court proceedings for Pike County in his tavern in Milford. Below, the McDonalds enjoy a golf outing in August 1929. (Above, courtesy of Diane Banach.)

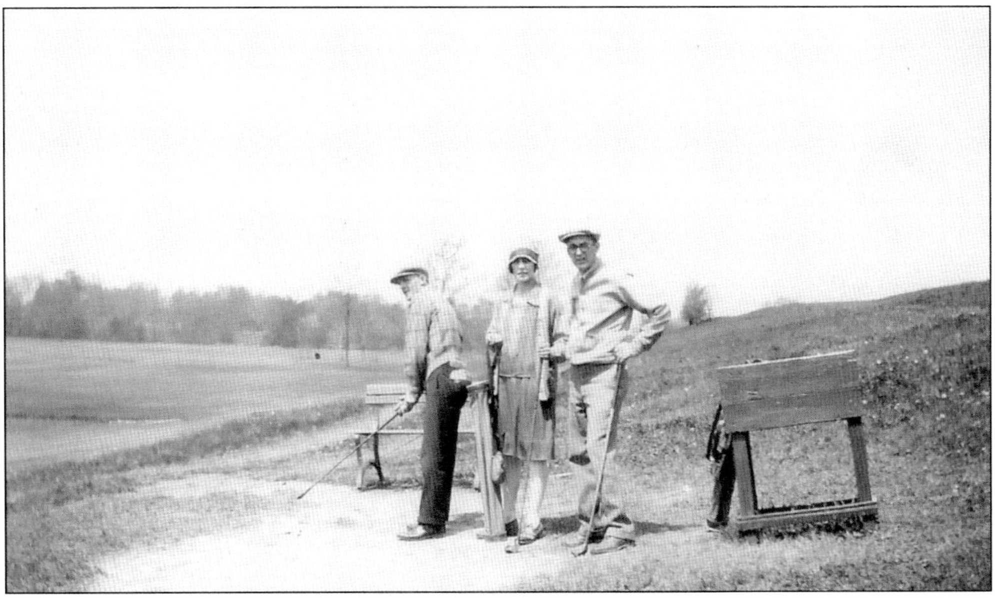

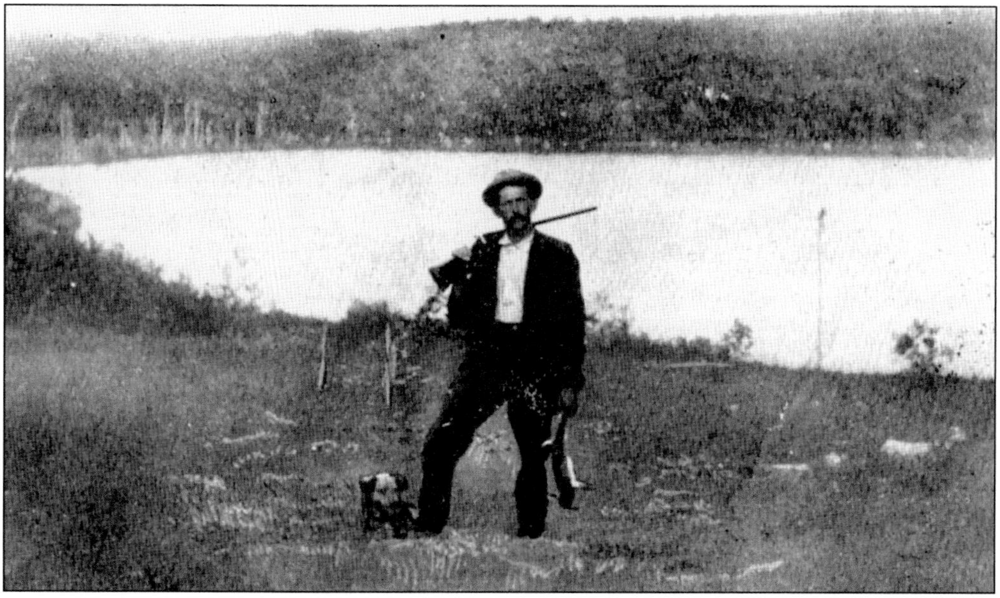

The woods, streams, and fields of the Minisink Valley always provided opportunities for great hunting and fishing. Some hunted and fished for much needed sustenance, while others were in it for the pleasure. In the early 1800s, one pioneer's summary of his year's hunting tells of the abundant wildlife found in the woods. He reported that he killed 175 deer, 5 bears, 3 wolves, many wild turkeys, and a panther. By the mid-1800s, most of the large creatures or the forest had disappeared from the woods. History books say that the elk, panthers, wolves, turkeys, and beavers were never found, and it was rare to see a bear or deer. Thankfully, licensed hunting and reintroduction programs have brought back all but the elk and wolves to the eastern woods. Below, Fred Titus emerges from the woods with his hunting partner. (Above, courtesy of Diane Banach.)

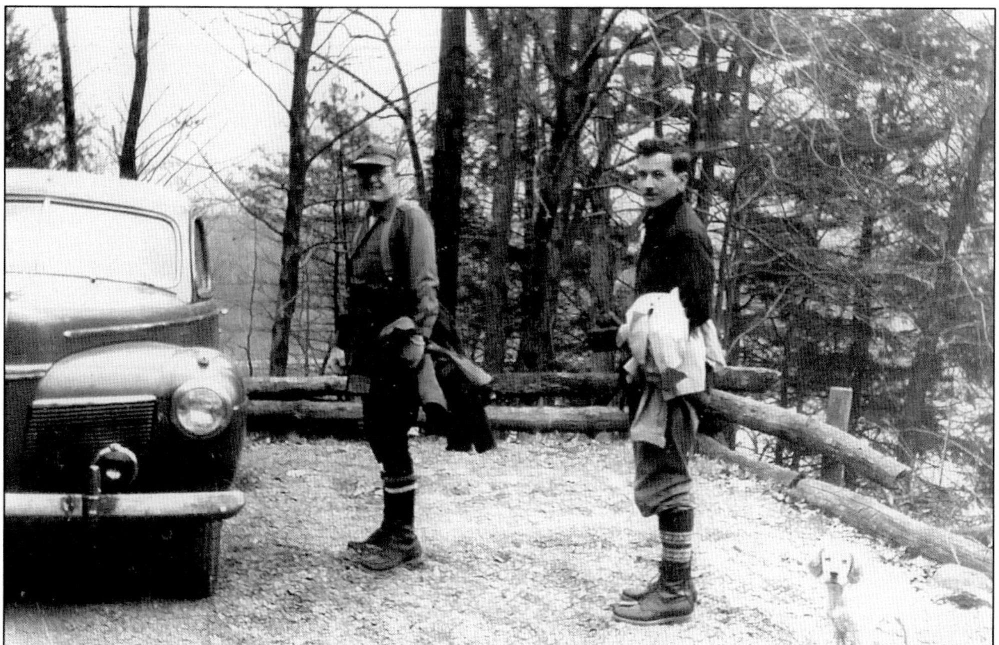

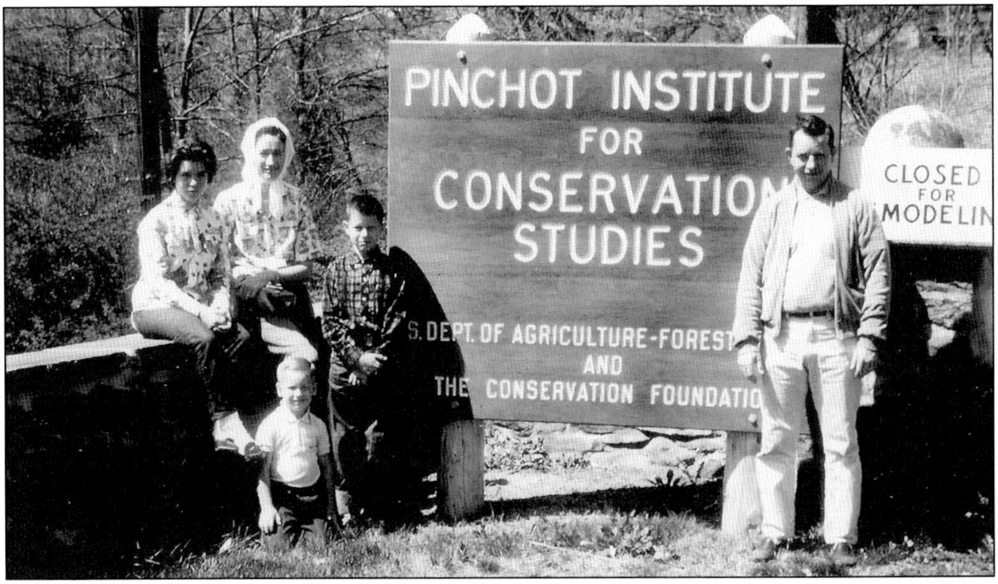

The great houses built in the Milford area gave reason enough to take a day touring. The private residence of Gifford Pinchot, Gray Towers, was opened to the public for tours in the 1960s, and many were drawn to its stately house and beautifully landscaped grounds. As seen above, the Stone family visited the grounds but missed the house tour because it was closed for remodeling. (Courtesy of Criss Crosby Stone.)

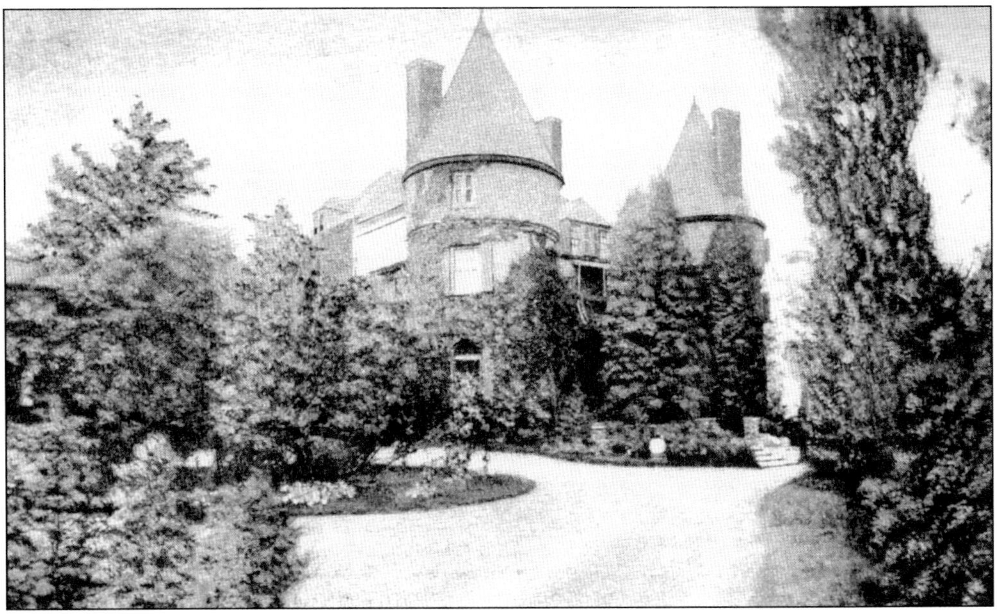

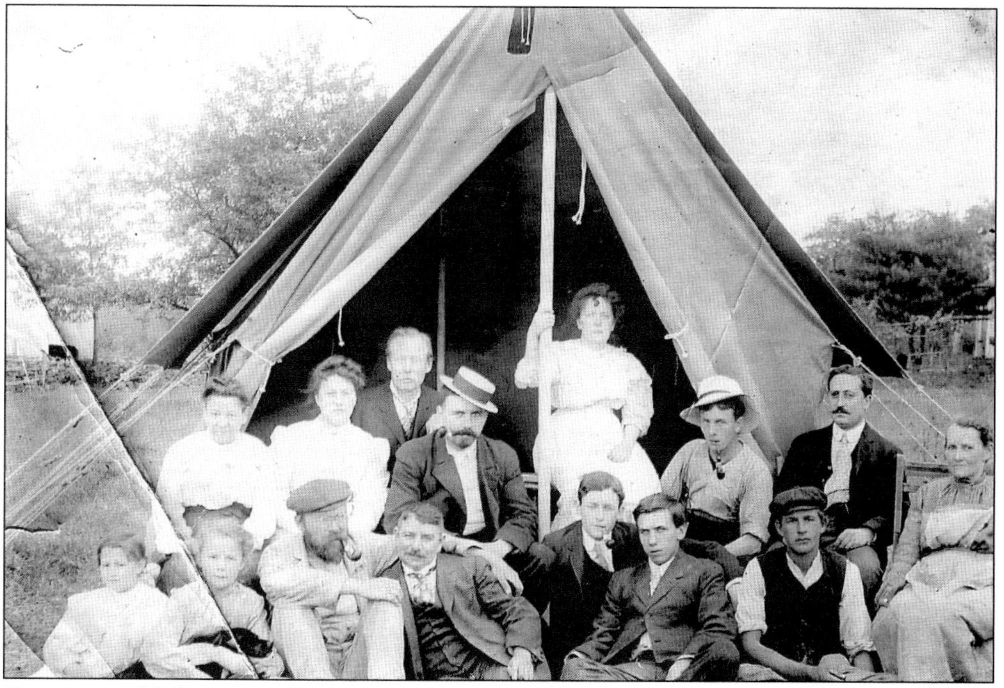

Camping and hiking were favorite pastimes enjoyed by everyone who knew the Milford area. Walks to the many waterfalls and beautiful glens were well worth the effort. Camping was always popular and brought the participants closer to nature and the great outdoors.

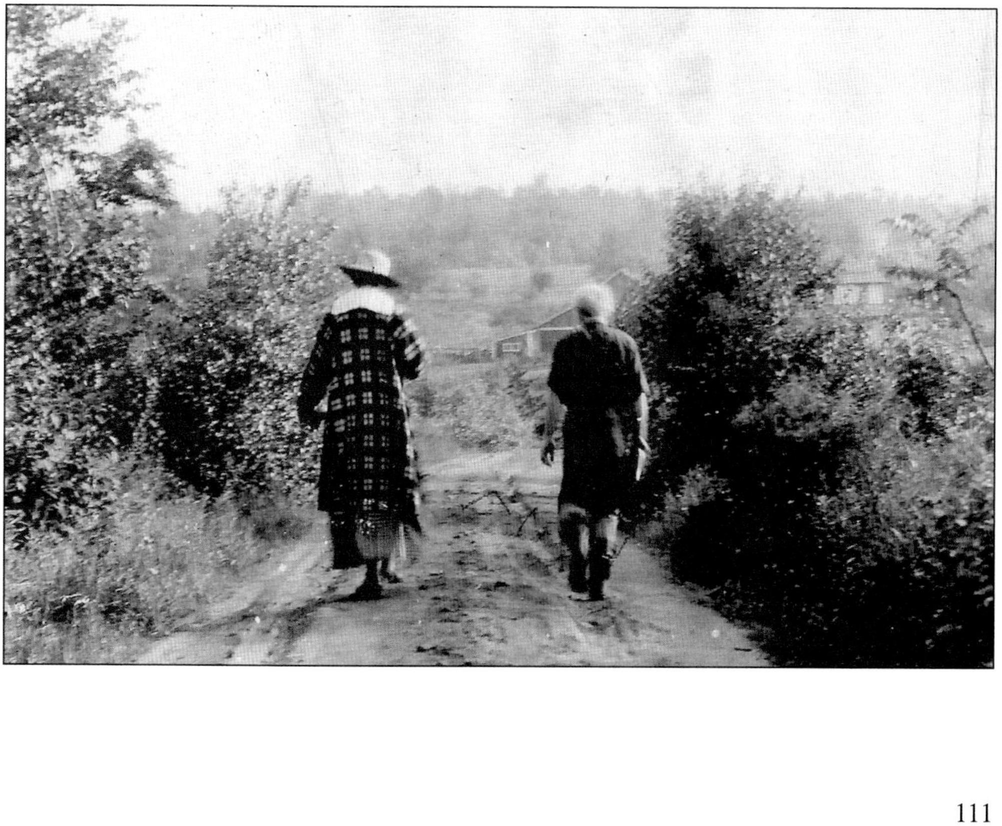

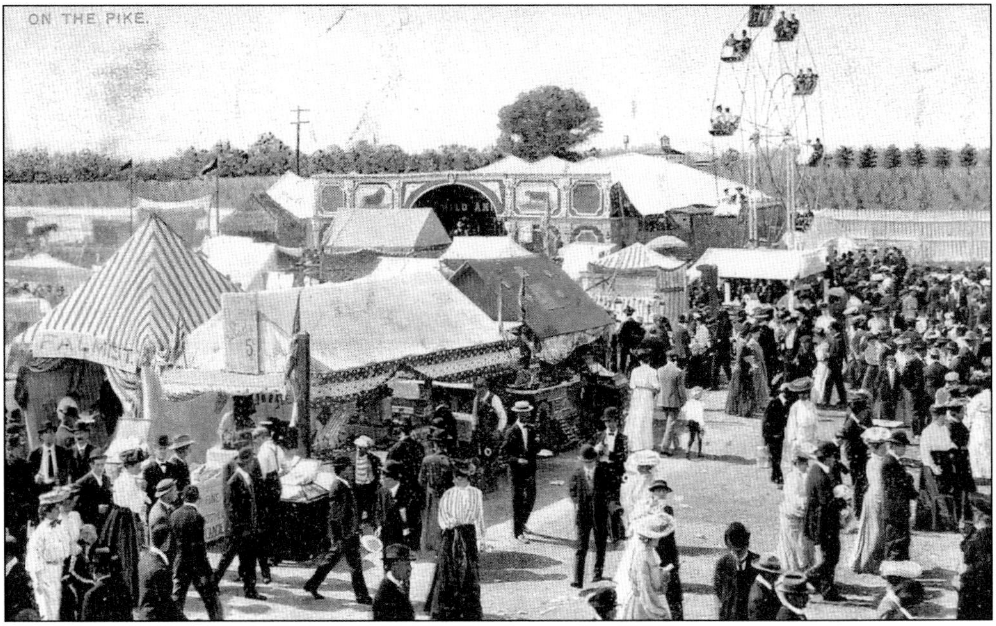

Everyone always looked forward to the carnivals and fairs held during the long summer months. It was a time to see neighbors and delight the children with new sights, sounds, and flavors. Milford had a small carnival that set up in the large lot next to the old Milford Inn in the 1950s and 1960s. The author remembers feeding peanuts to the elephants in the afternoons before the carnival started. Another activity for the local children was to go to the Catskill Game Farm and see the wild animals and enjoy the rides.

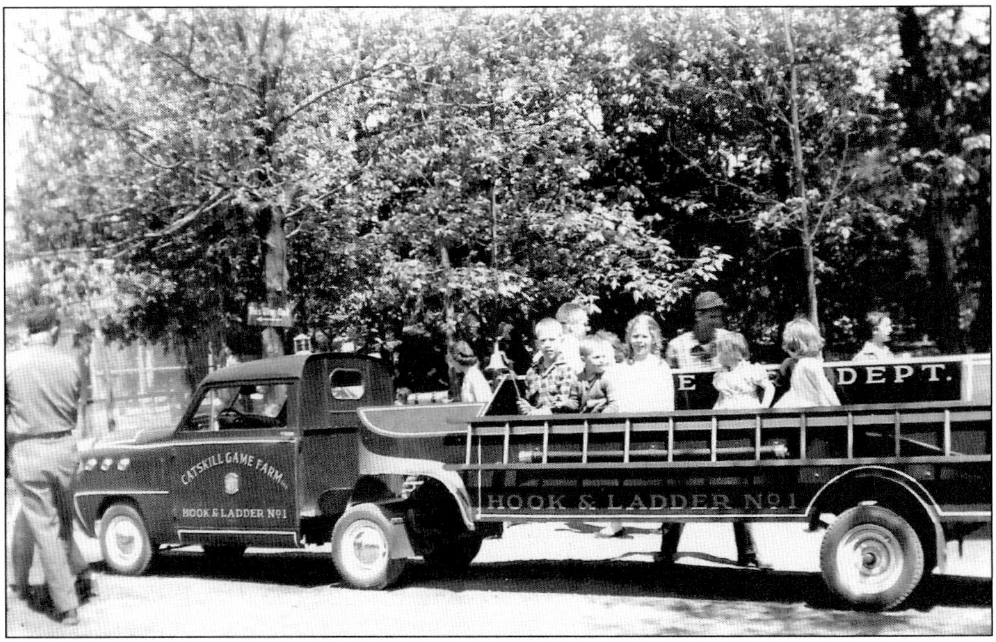

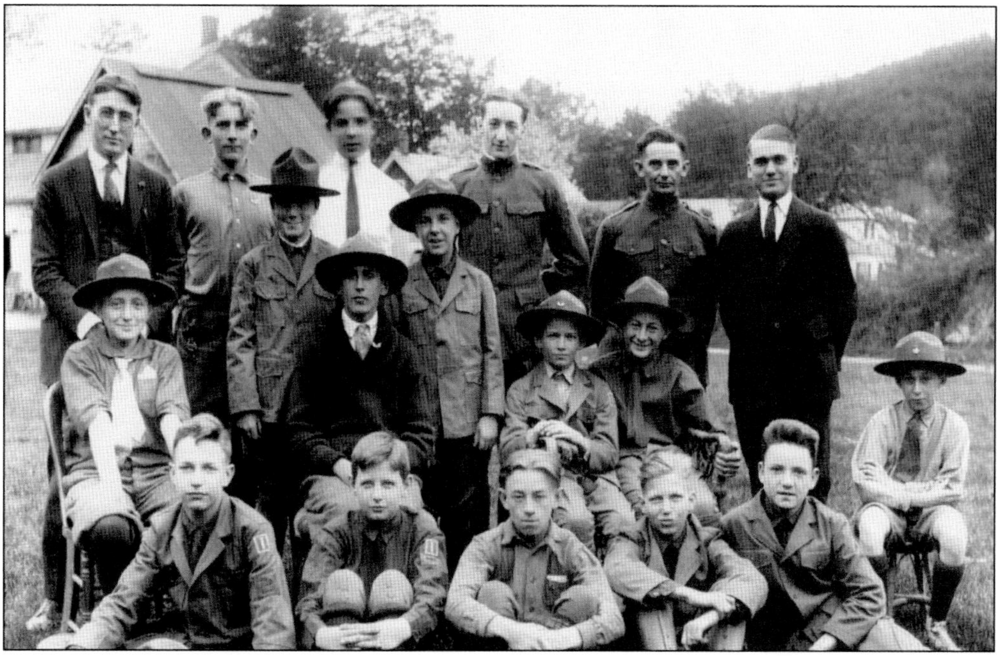

Organizations like the Boy Scouts were very popular for the boys to be educated in the ways of life and to be occupied with service, wilderness, and science projects. Below, teacher Frank Varney works with a group of boys on a woodworking project. The partial names for these boys are Casey, Lee, La Grande, Artie, Godfrey, Leo, and Ernie. (Courtesy of Criss Crosby Stone.)

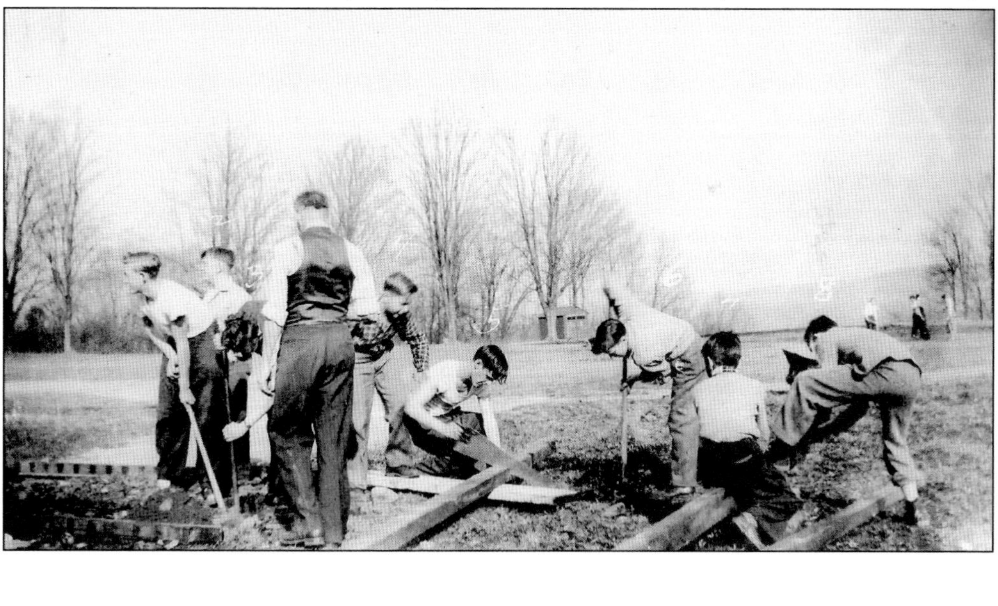

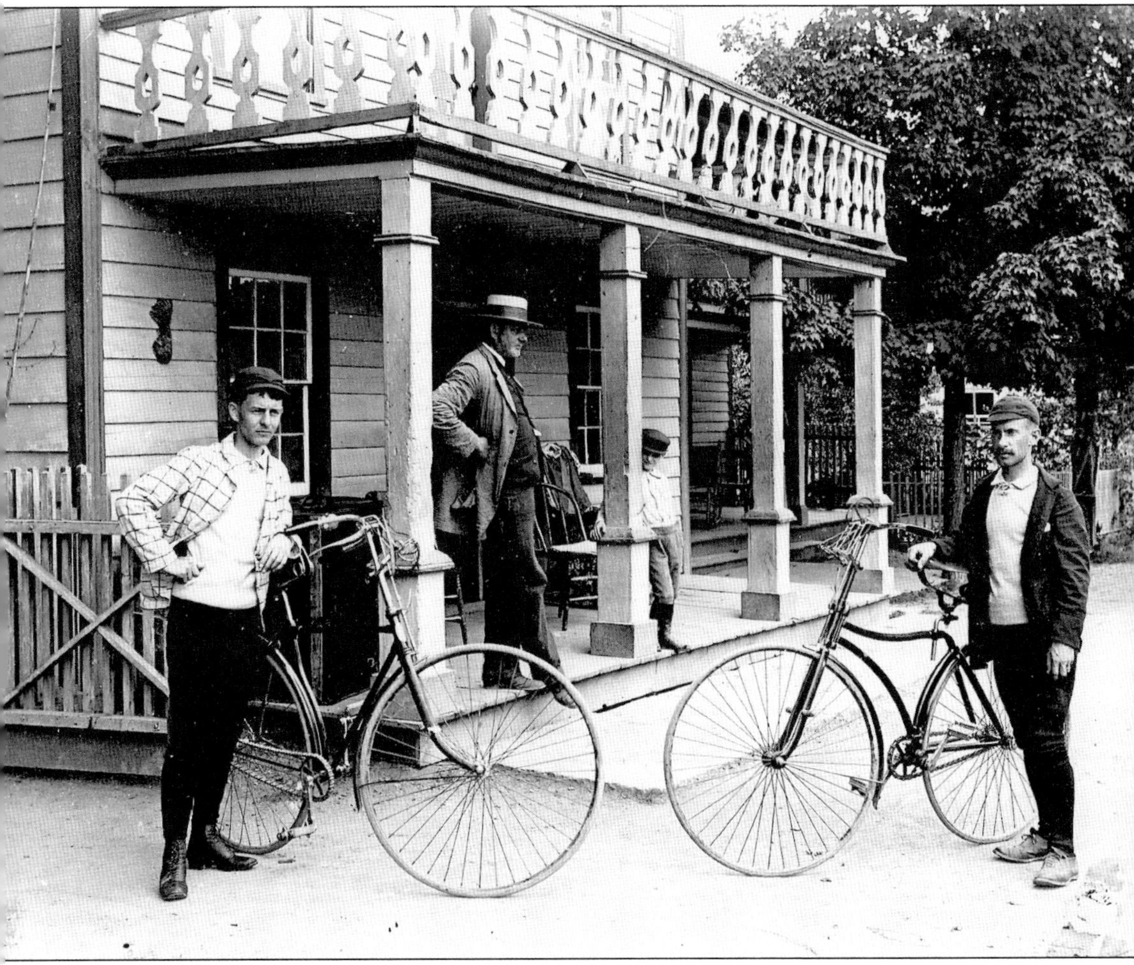

A popular pastime at the turn of the century that still prevails today is bicycling. Many young men joined bicycling clubs that went on extended trips of 40 to 60 miles per day and found it an inexpensive way to explore the countryside. Clubs competed against each other in races, and they were always looking for the next champion. Bicycles took the world by storm when they were introduced, and competitive bike racers were treated like celebrities. Women soon discovered the freedom offered by the bicycle and, much to the chagrin of some, adopted the bloomers to make it easier to clear the spokes and gears. A telling quote by Chipping in the movie *Goodbye Mr. Chips* shows his chagrin when he finds out the young lady he just met on the mountain is bicycling around Europe. He said, "I don't approve of all this rushing around on wheels. The other day a man passed me in a cloud of dust. He must have been doing at least 15 miles per hour. You know, human beings were never intended to go that speed." (Courtesy of the Pike County Historical Society.)

Nine

From Trails to Trains

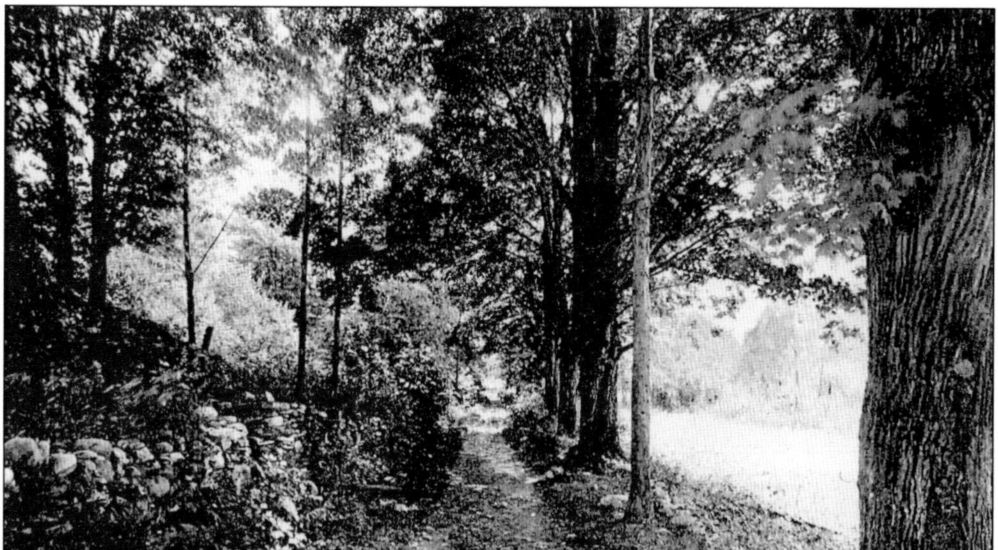

Early byways to and through Milford were nothing more than dirt paths through the woods. Most followed the ancient trails where Native Americans had found the most tried and true routes over thousands of years of use. Many of Pennsylvania's highways today followed these trails, such as Routes 6, 209, 191, and the Old Mine Road. Engineers found that they usually got in trouble with water hazards, sinkholes, natural obstacles, and snowdrifts when they diverted from these original trails. Records show that Broad Street through Milford was no more than a path until it was cleared of brush after 1800 by George Buchanan. (Courtesy of Diane Banach.)

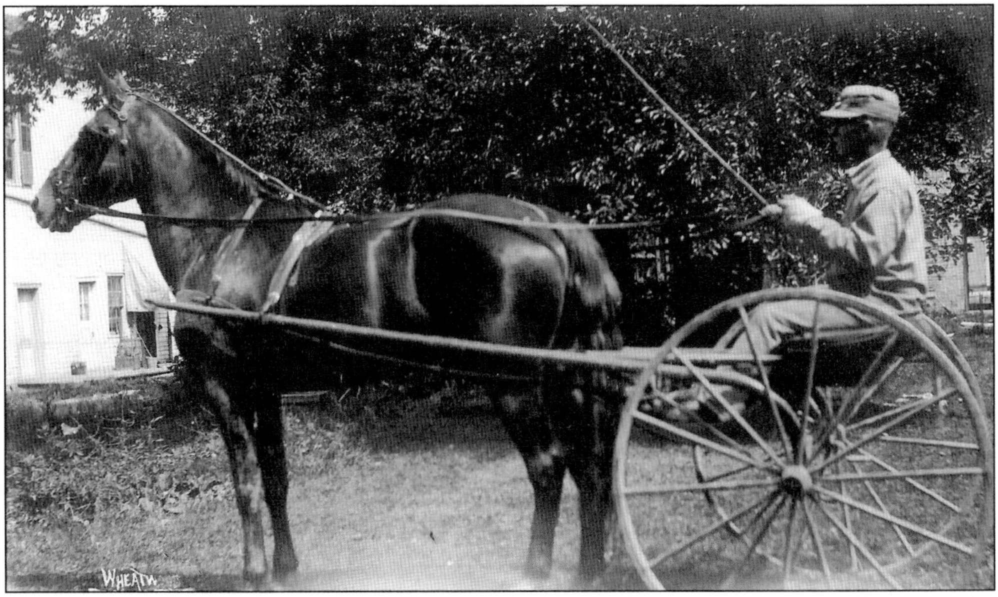

Horses were very important to the family and made farming and quick travel possible. In the early pioneer years, they were not as practical because of their need for open grazing with secure fencing, vulnerability to snake bites and wild predators, and injury and expense. A settler was more likely to walk or use water transport and an oxen or cow for the heavy farm work and transport. Cows were very important as a source of milk and food. Above, this horse and chase show a fine turnout. The driver would have preferred smooth roads because the chase bounced so much. Bridges across the Delaware were very rare until the mid- to late 1800s, and most crossings were done on the ferries. Ferries were so important that towns were named after their ferries, as is the case with Dingman's Ferry below. The site of Milford was originally named Wells Ferry because the Wells family ran a ferry between Milford and New Jersey. (Courtesy of Diane Banach.)

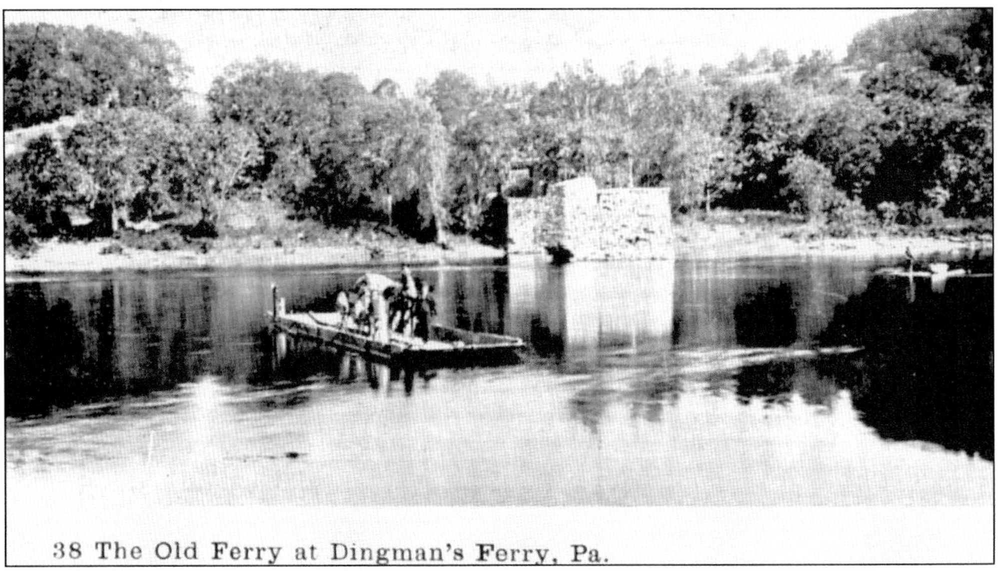

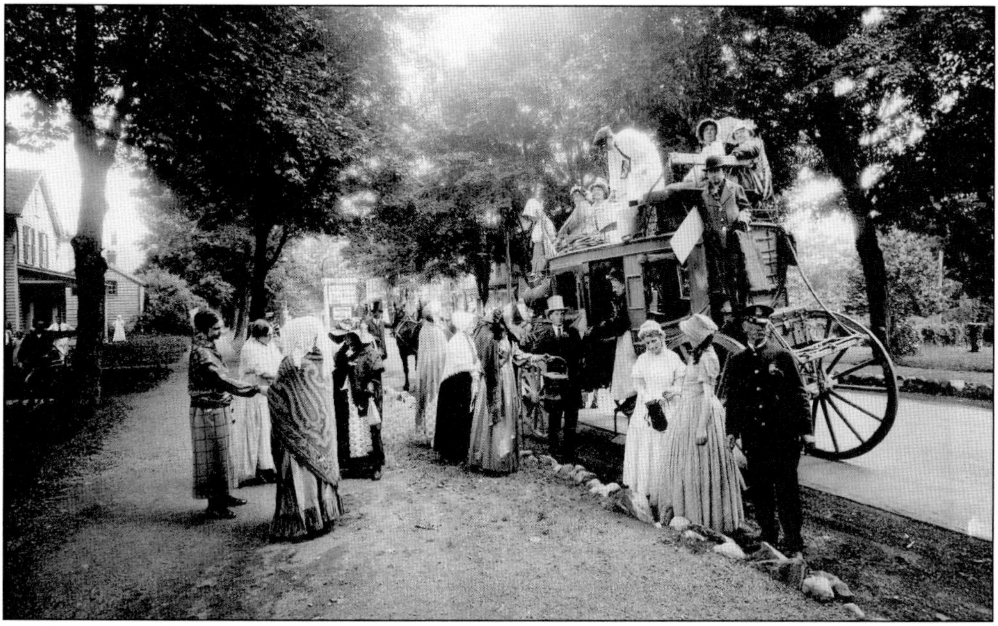

Travel by stagecoach became possible as the roads improved. Above, a reenactment in Milford shows how the Hiawatha stagecoach (now restored and on display at the Pike County Historical Society) would be fully utilized by travelers between Milford and Port Jervis. From 1840 to 1890, the Finley family owned the stagecoach line. A seasoned driver for Queen Victoria, Mr. Finley even drove the coach across the frozen Delaware when possible. A stagecoach line called the Owego Trail ran up the river on the Pennsylvania side all the way to Hancock, New York, a distance of over 60 miles. The steep precipices down to the river must have given many a passenger second thoughts about the value of faster travel. The palace car seen below transported passengers between Milford and Stroudsburg in the late 1800s. (Courtesy of the Pike County Historical Society.)

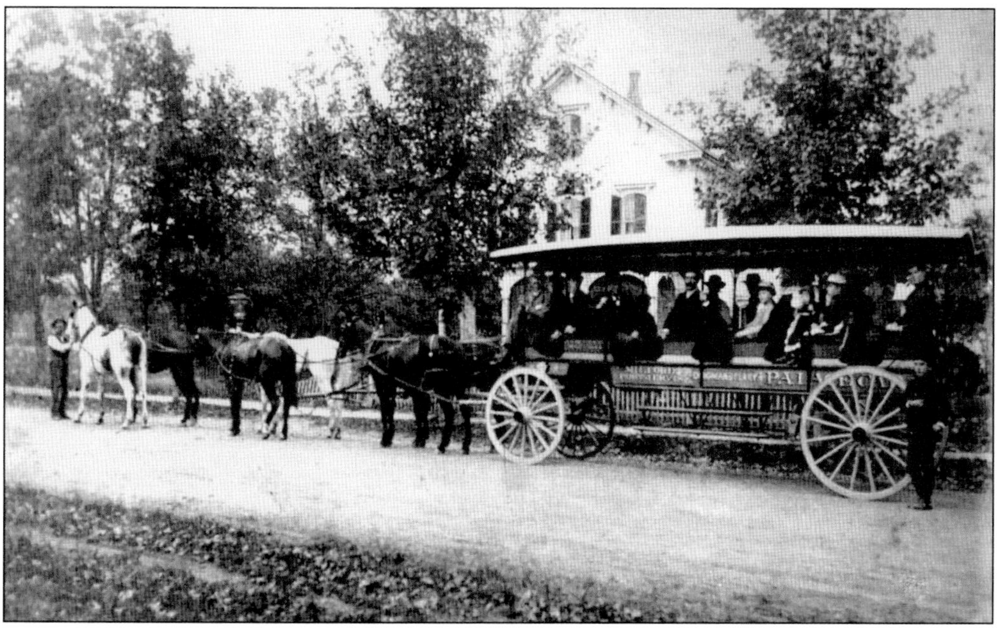

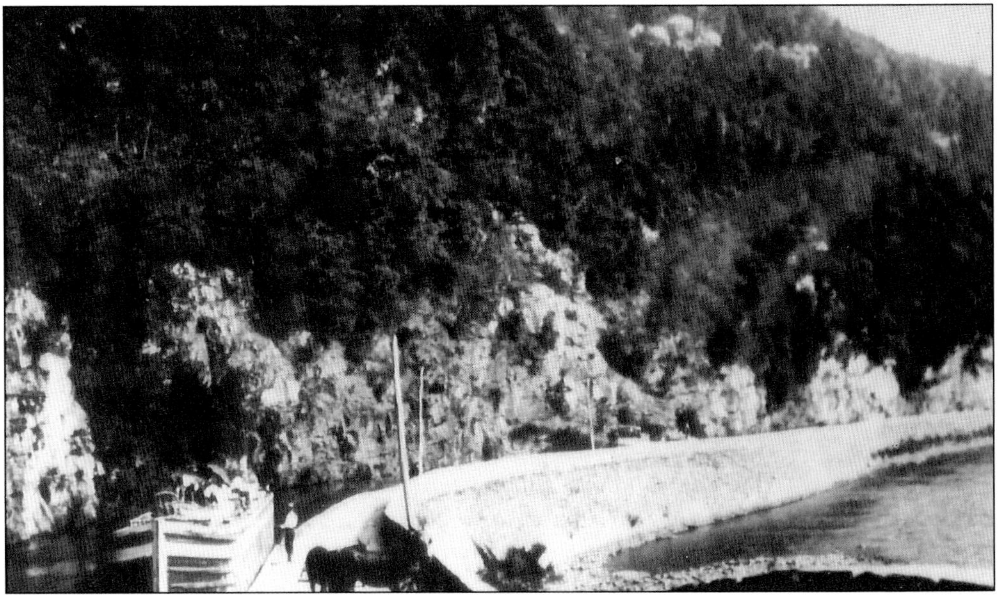

Getting large amounts of materials and goods to the city markets was very important to the local economy. Bluestone, cut lumber, produce, coal, hides, and other products were transported on the Delaware and Hudson Canal. The nearest access to the canal was on the New York side of the Delaware River. It was also a popular means of travel to and from Milford when there was a need to get to the city. The canal was not without its problems, and destructive flooding could render sections of the canal useless. (Courtesy of Diane Banach.)

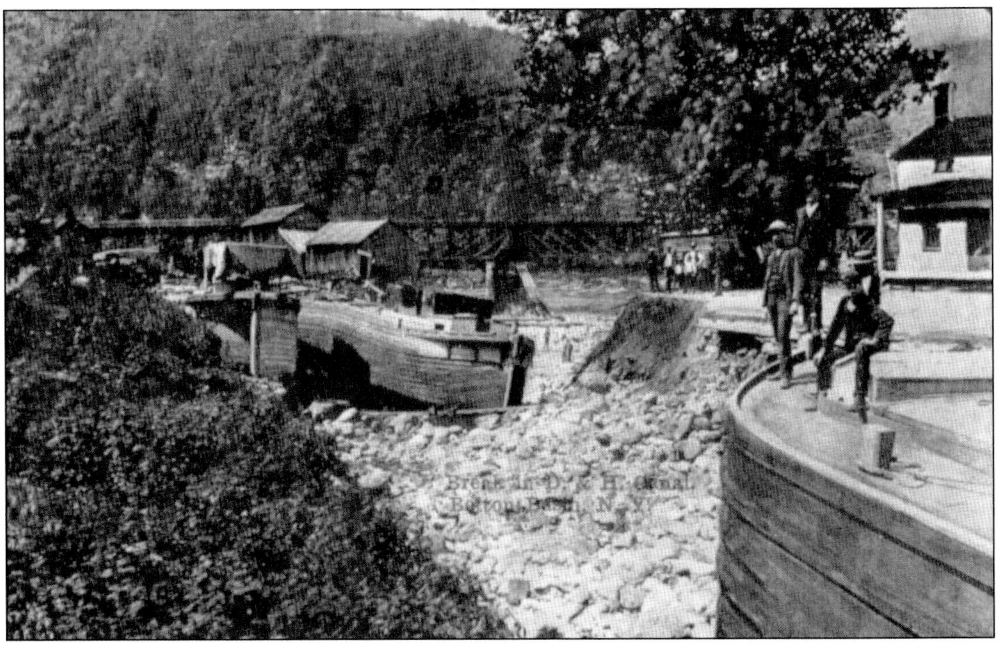

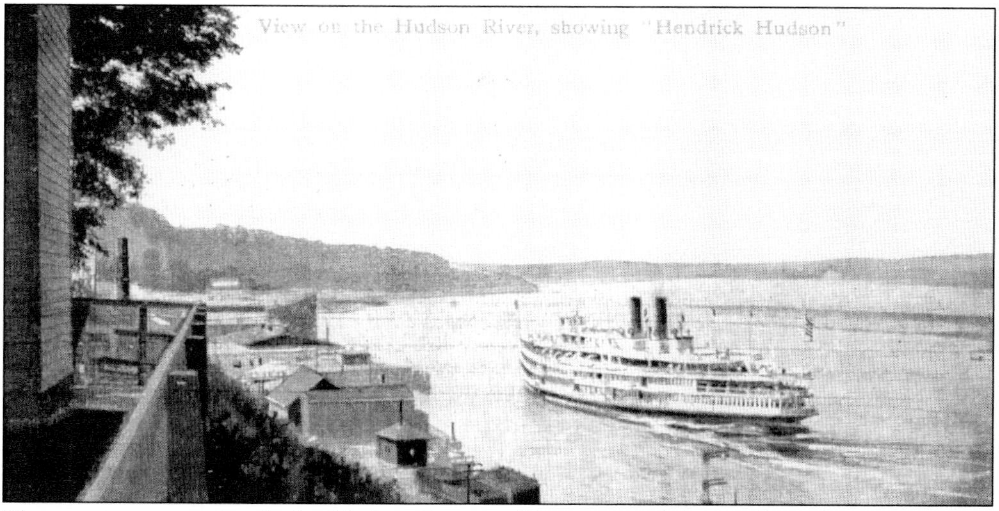

The canal connected with the Hudson River in Kingston, and the goods and passengers were transferred to steamers that completed the trip to the ports of New York City. (Courtesy of Diane Banach.)

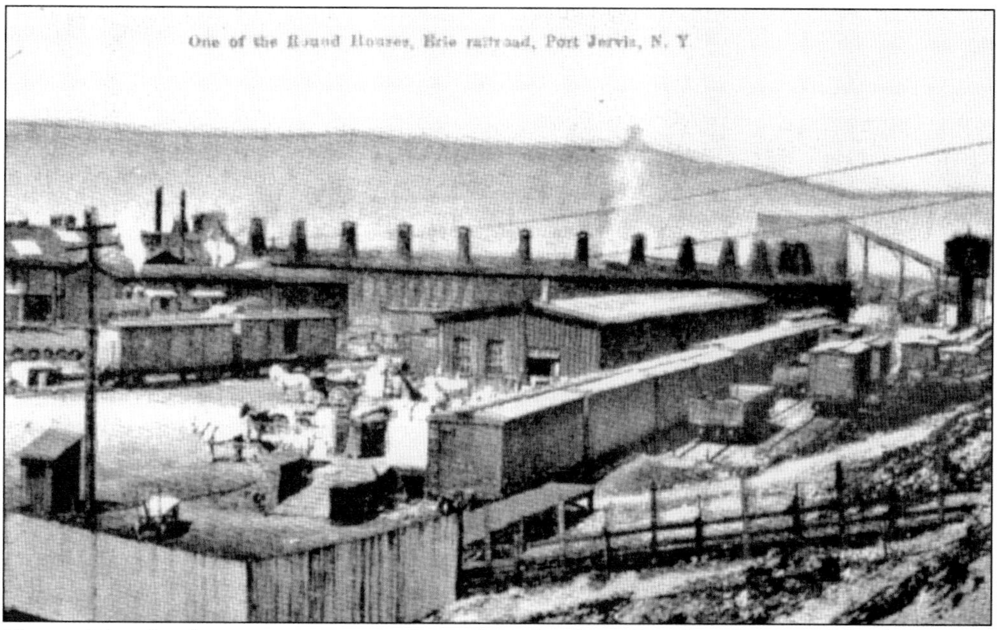

Competition for the transportation industry brought the railroad to the area. The decision to have the railroad built on the New York side of the Delaware River instead of through Milford completely changed the landscape of Port Jervis and was the defining moment that protected the character and architecture of Milford. Port Jervis became an important maintenance and switching center with a roundhouse for turning the trains. (Courtesy of Diane Banach.)

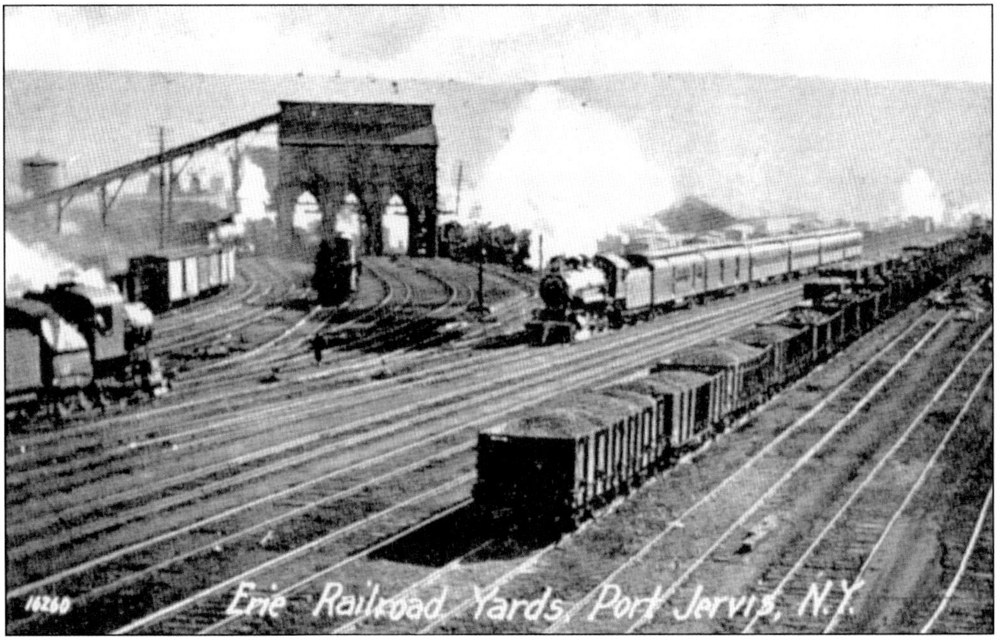

The rail system grew in Port Jervis as it became an important hub for the Erie Railroad. Travelers from both the New York and the Pennsylvania sides of the river caught the train at the Port Jervis station of the Erie Railroad. Modernization came to Port Jervis with the prosperity brought by the railroad business. Paved streets, high-rise buildings, and trolleys are a few examples seen in this picture. (Courtesy of Diane Banach.)

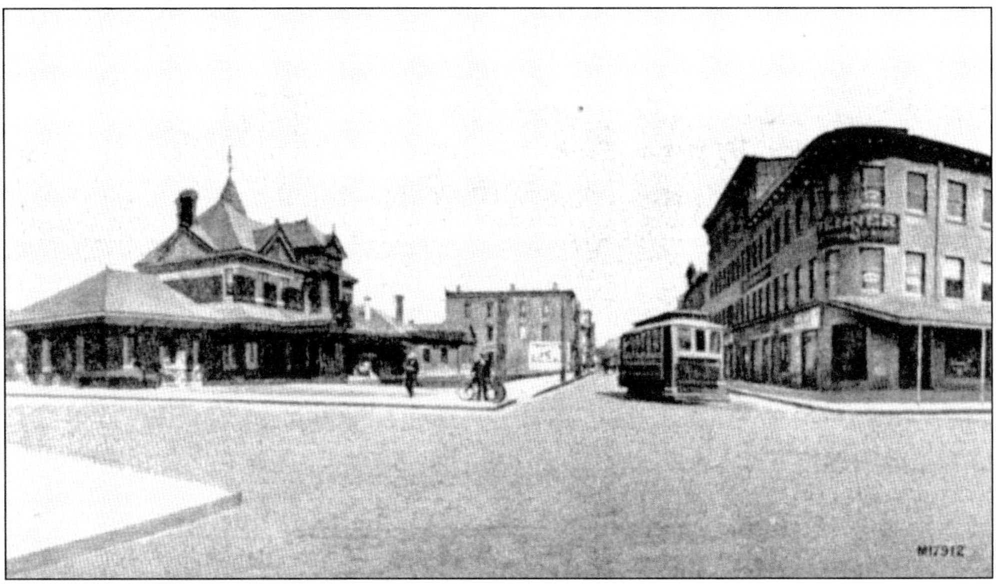

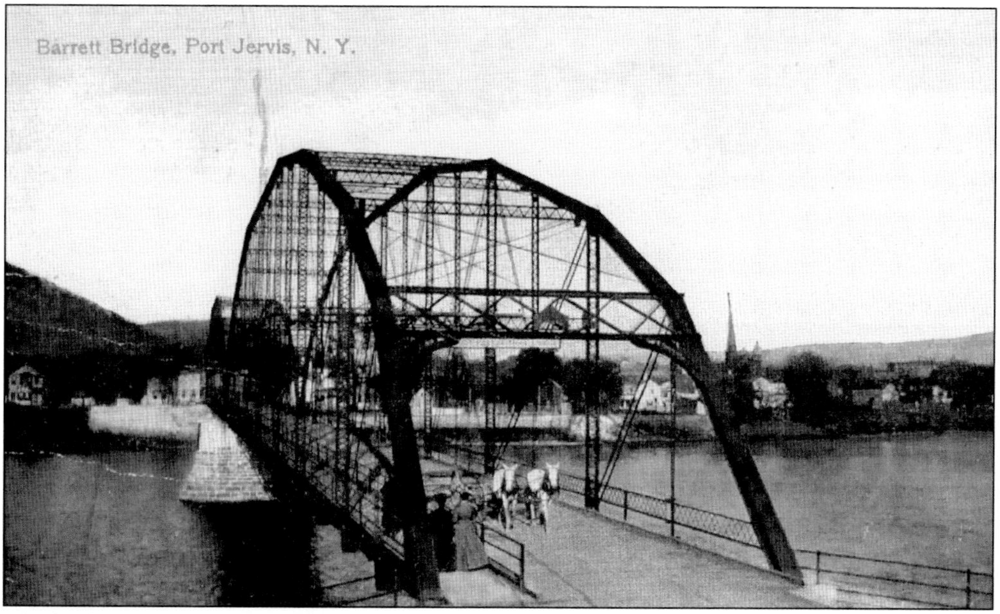

The bridge across the river from Port Jervis was a vital link to the Pennsylvania communities. Above, Joe Brooks, whose father was a doctor, is driving across the Barrett Bridge to Port Jervis. Whenever floods or ice jams destroyed the area's bridges, the local Pennsylvania residents and businesses were virtually cut off, and creative means had to be employed to cross the river. Even the ferries were pressed back into service, as was the case after the Pumpkin Flood, when the ferry at Dingman's was put back into service. At the turn of the century, bicycles became an important means of transportation and great sport. Below, Fred Titus Sr., a famous record-setting racer on the Spaulding Bike Racing Team of New York City, completes a trip from New York City to the mountains to visit his mother, Marietta Allen, a descendant of the Bulls of Orange County, on his first bicycle in the 1890s. Fred Titus Sr. was the husband of Maybelle Titus, who ran a real estate and insurance business in Dingman's Ferry. Their sons were Allen and Fred Titus. (Above, courtesy of Diane Banach.)

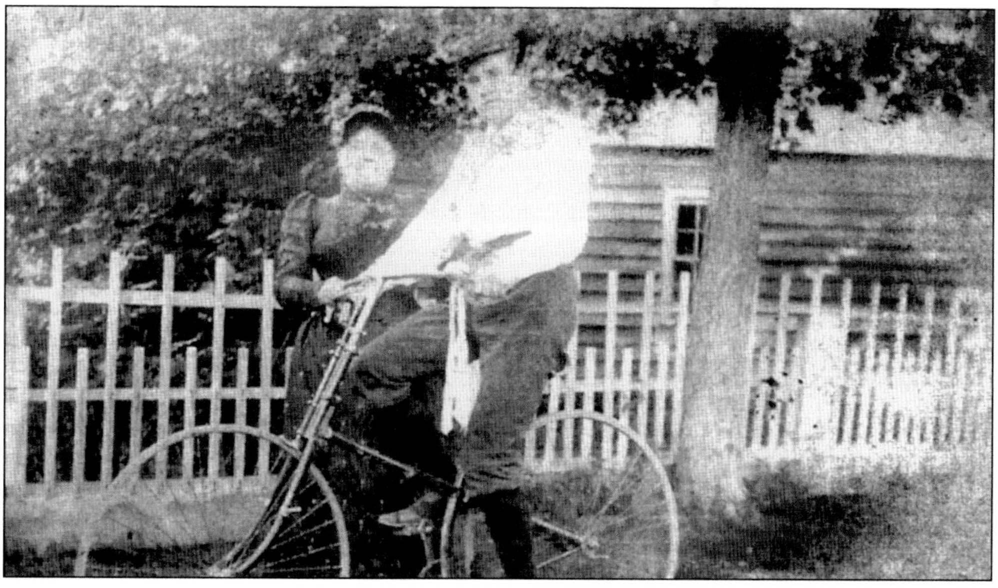

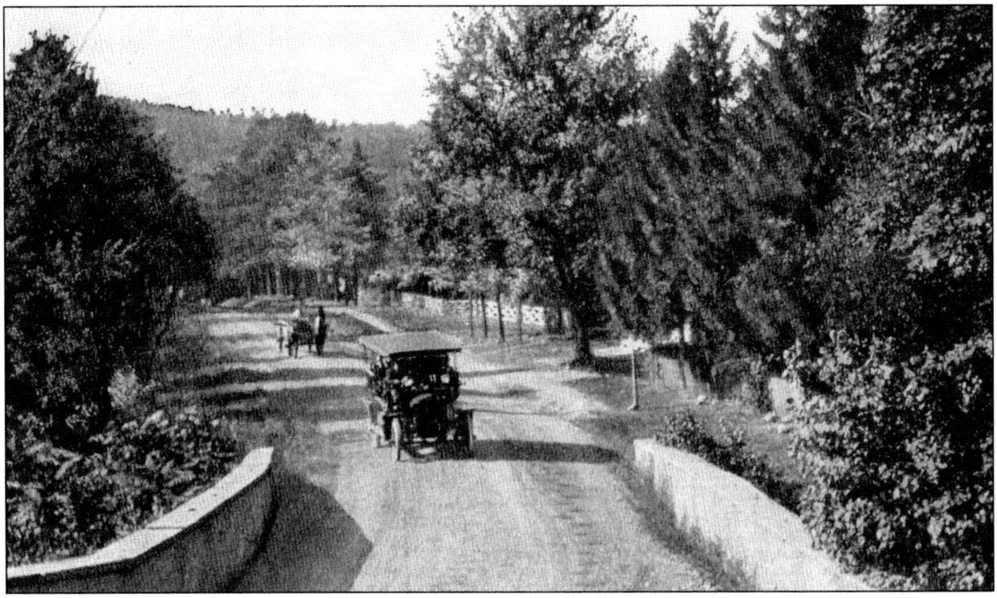

The automobile quickly replaced horse-drawn conveyances. Above, the auto stage is pictured leaving Milford for Port Jervis. Families quickly found that the automobile was a ticket to independence and fun. Postcards were often sent home reporting on trips and how many blown tires hampered the trip. Many local boardinghouses had to close because the automobile took their once faithful guests to new vacation destinations such as Niagara Falls and points west and south. Faster trains and the development of air travel made matters worse. The heyday of the boardinghouses was soon over. (Above, courtesy of Diane Banach.)

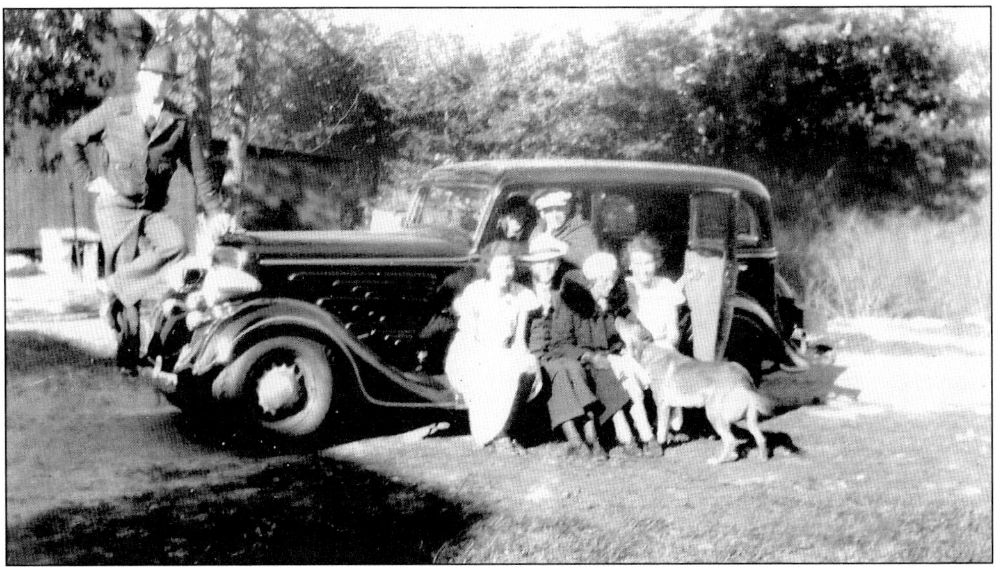

Ten

CHURCHES

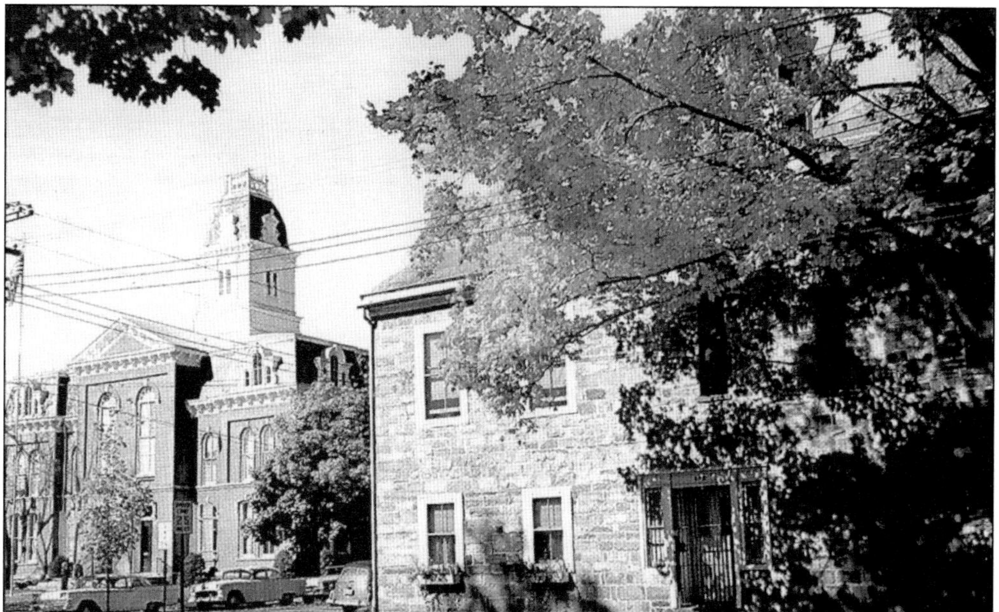

Church services in Milford were first held in 1823 in the old courthouse, built in 1814. The Milford Presbyterian congregation was officially recognized in February 1824. Moses Bross started a Sunday school with the assistance of James Wallace, Samuel Depuy, William Freel, Louisa Ross, Jane Depuy, and Caroline Wells. An official organization of the Presbyterian church with the election of elders and the appointment of a minister occurred on September 25, 1825, marking the birth of the first church in Milford. A Methodist congregation also held services in the original courthouse in 1845, when a legal matter regarding their title forced them to vacate their new church on Ann Street. (Information courtesy of the First Presbyterian Church.)

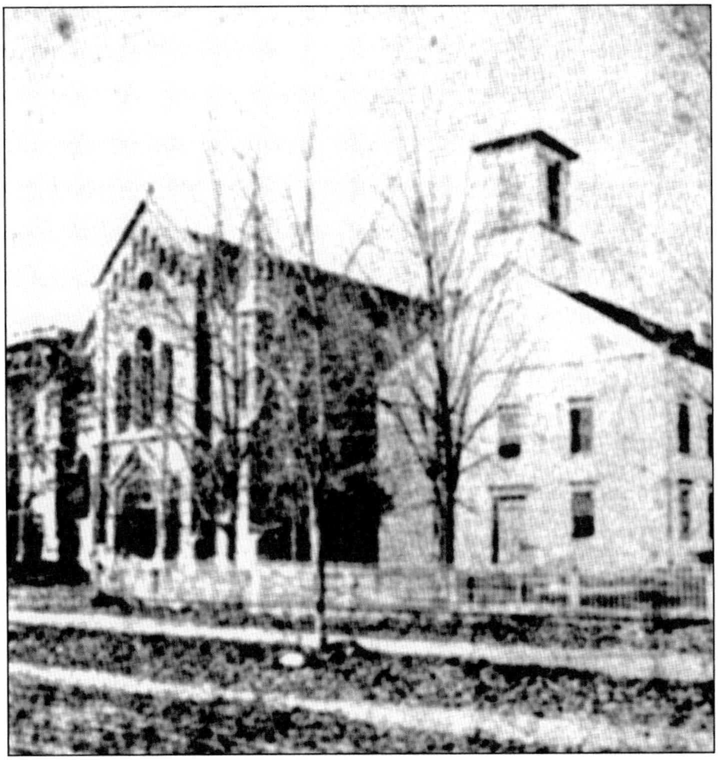

In 1875, the original Presbyterian church building was auctioned off to the highest bidder, and the new building assumed its role as the Presbyterians' worship center. The church has served countless citizens of Milford and visitors from the surrounding area. In 1878, the manse was built on the site of the original church. *Manse* is the Scottish word for the residence of a Presbyterian minister. As soon as the manse was paid off in 1882, the congregation raised funds to complete the tower on the church and retire the church's debt. (Courtesy of the Pike County Historical Society.)

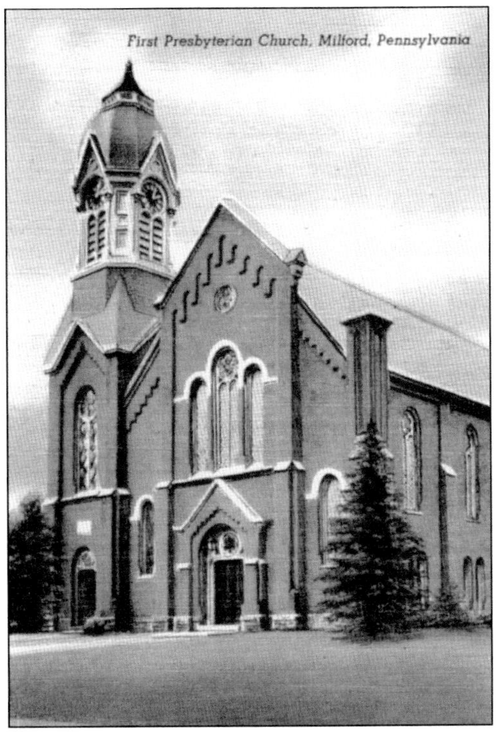

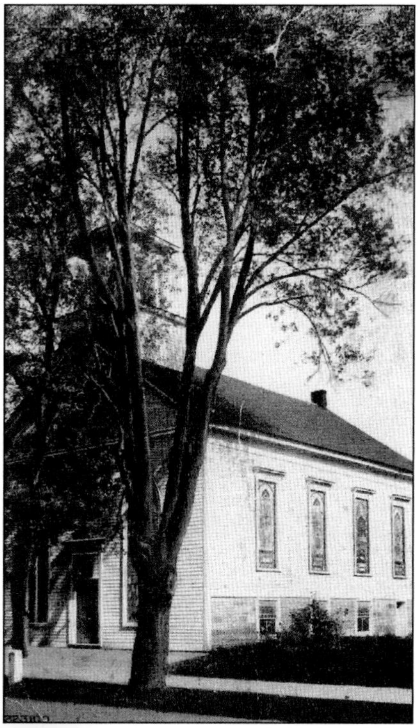

The second-oldest church in Milford is the Methodist church. It was established in 1827 (about a year after the Presbyterian church was founded), but its original location on the river proved to be too vulnerable to flooding, and the church was moved a parcel of donated land on Ann Street. A preacher's occupation was not always easy in the early days of a settlement where the sabbath was not honored and the consumption of alcohol was too often preferred over scripture. Some of the early preachers found stones thrown through their windows. Even at the turn of the century, the pastors still felt challenged because of the worldly influence of the visitors from New York City. Rev. Charles Scudder put it succinctly in a 1901 report: "Difficulty grows out of the unrest that has come because prevailing ideas in this place have been overturned in many minds by the social ideas transplanted by the city people." As seen below, Criss Crosby married George Stone in September 1948 in the Milford Methodist Church. (Courtesy of Criss Crosby Stone.)

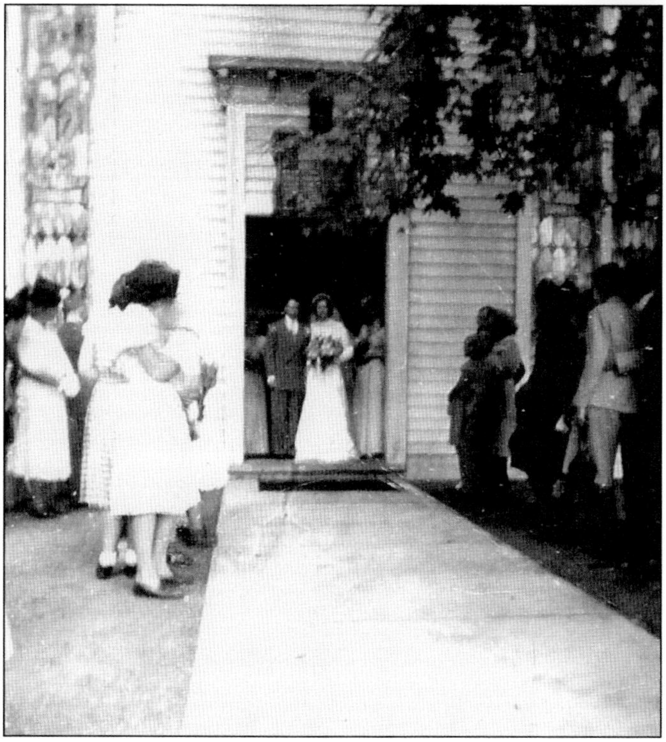

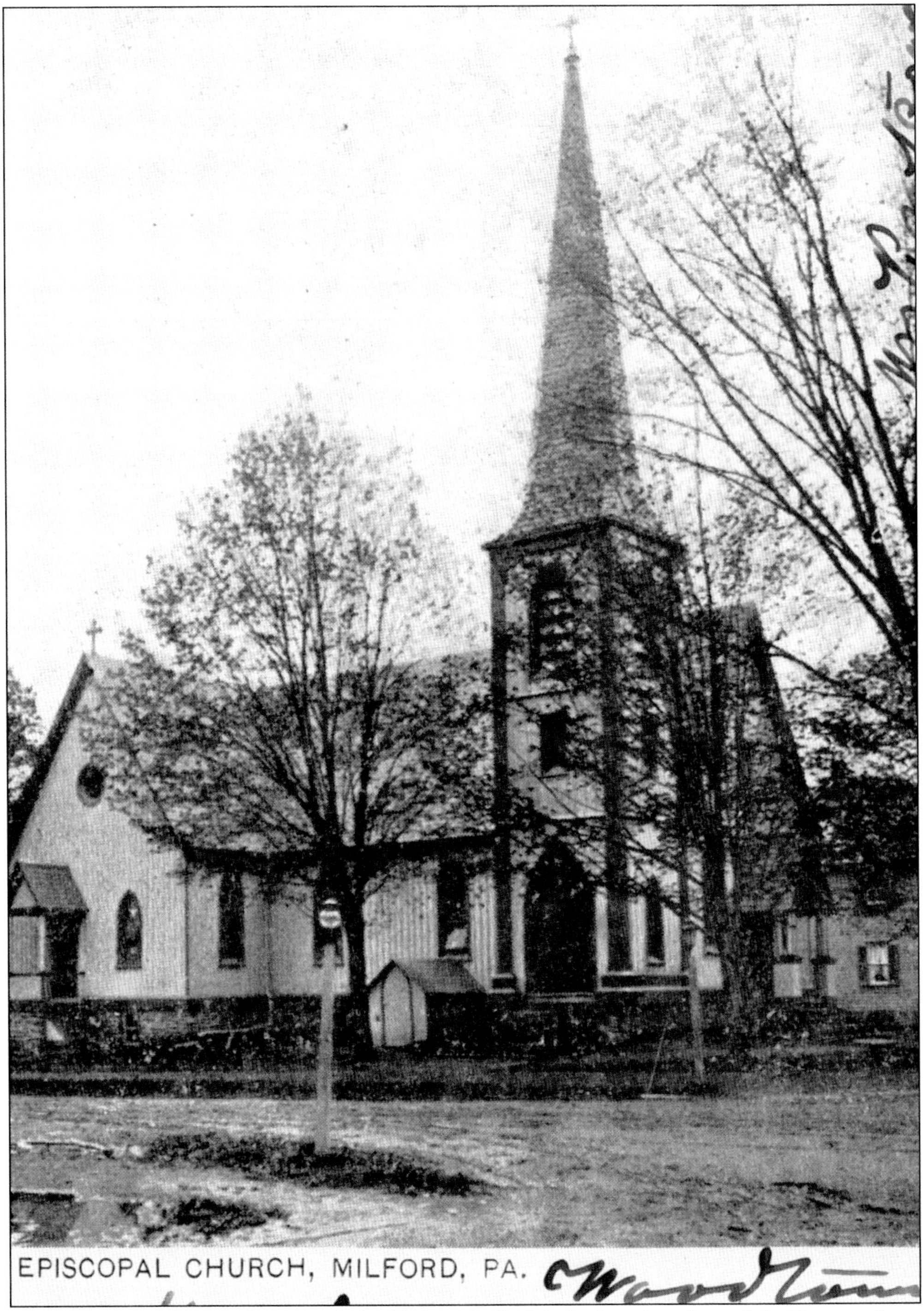

The Episcopal congregation shared a building with the Methodist church until the Episcopalians raised the funds to build their own structure. (Courtesy of Diane Banach.)

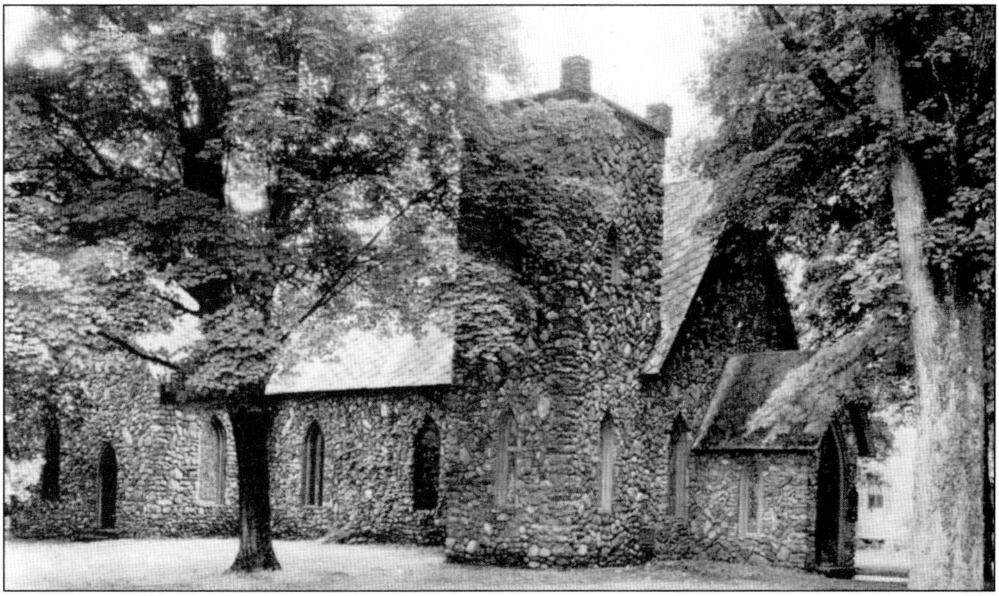

Another beautiful church in Milford is the Church of Good Shepherd. Its facade was originally painted, but it was later stoned over to result in a beautiful finish. Below, a class at the Methodist church school represents a good cross section of the families in Milford at the time of the photograph. (Above and below, courtesy of the Pike County Historical Society.)

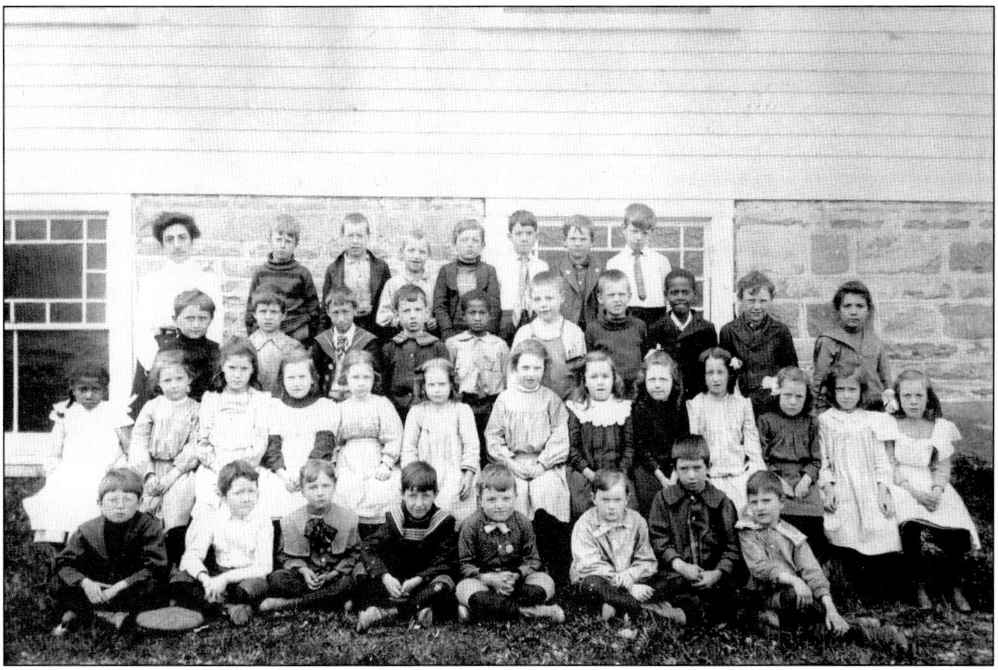

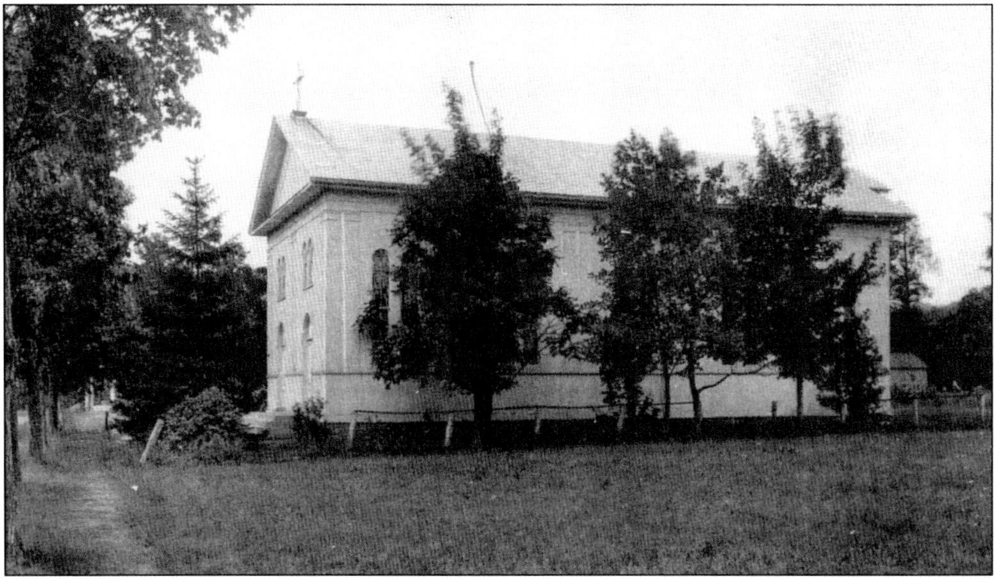

The Catholic church called St. Patrick's was established as part of the Scranton Diocese and quickly flourished. In the mid-1900s, it served as the site for kindergarten for many of the children of the town. Its congregation has grown through the years, and an addition was built to accommodate the larger attendance at services. (Courtesy of Diane Banach.)

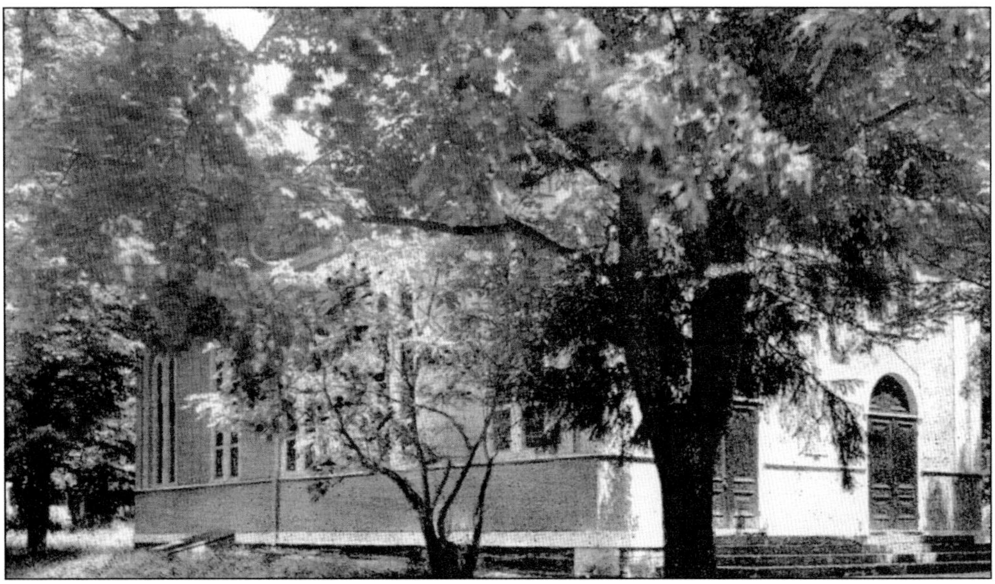

The commitment of the pastors and congregations in the early 1800s contributed to the success of the area churches. The congregations thrived, and the facilities benefited from their devotion. Today, Milford is graced by some of the most beautiful places of worship of any small town in Pennsylvania.